# PRAISE FOR TWO GENERALS

"*Two Generals* is a compelling portrait of two Canadian officers during the Second World War, with an extreme attention to detail in the dress, troop movements and battles, and especially their day-to-day lives . . . an endearing success."
**– NATIONAL POST**

"Chantler's pacing is unerring: rapidly sequenced panels conveying breathless action . . ."
**– MONTREAL GAZETTE**

"[*Two Generals* is a] stunning success in bringing home the real foot soldier's experience of those awful days."
**– TORONTO STAR**

"[A] profoundly moving account of ordinary men caught up in extraordinary, and often horrifying, circumstances."
**– STRAIGHT.COM**

"*Two Generals* is a beautifully illustrated graphic novel."
**– QUILL AND QUIRE**

"*Two Generals* is a beautifully crafted graphic novel. . . . Historical novices or casual readers could hardly ask for a better, more personal entry point to Canada's involvement in the Invasion of Normandy."
**– FAST FORWARD WEEKLY**

"Chantler is a talent not to be ignored."
**– THE ONION, "AV CLUB"**

# TWO GENERALS

## SCOTT CHANTLER

McCLELLAND & STEWART

Cloth edition published 2010
Emblem edition published 2011

Emblem is an imprint of McClelland & Stewart Ltd.
Emblem and colophon are registered trademarks of McClelland & Stewart Ltd.

**Library and Archives Canada Cataloguing in Publication**

Chantler, Scott
Two generals / Scott Chantler.

ISBN 978-0-7710-1959-3

1. Chantler, Law – Comic books, strips, etc. 2. Chrysler, Jack – Comic books, strips, etc. 3.
Canada. Canadian Army.
Highland Light Infantry of Canada – Officers – Biography – Comic books, strips, etc. 4.
Canada. Canadian Army – History – World War, 1939-1945 – Comic books, strips, etc. 5.
World War, 1939-1945 – Campaigns – France – Normandy – Comic books, strips, etc. 6.
Normandy (France) – History, Military – Comic books, strips, etc. I. Title.

D756.5.N6C43 2011    940.54'21421    C2011-902199-4

We acknowledge the financial support of the Government of Canada through the
Book Publishing Industry Development Program and that of the Government of Ontario
through the Ontario Media Development Corporation's Ontario Book Initiative.
We further acknowledge the support of the Canada Council for the Arts and the
Ontario Arts Council for our publishing program.

Published simultaneously in the United States of America by McClelland & Stewart Ltd.,
P.O. Box 1030, Plattsburgh, New York 12901

Library of Congress Control Number: 2011928274

Design: Jennifer Lum
Lettered using Blambot fonts
Printed and bound in China

McClelland & Stewart Ltd.
75 Sherbourne Street
Toronto, Ontario
M5A 2P9
www.mcclelland.com

1   2   3   4   5      15   14   13   12   11

*For Andrew, Miles, Ryan, Mason, and Bradley*

Can storied urn or animated bust
Back to its mansion call the fleeting breath?
Can Honour's voice provoke the silent dust,
Or Flatt'ry soothe the dull cold ear of Death?

Perhaps in this neglected spot is laid
Some heart once pregnant with celestial fire;
Hands, that the rod of empire might have sway'd,
Or wak'd to ecstasy the living lyre.

— THOMAS GRAY,
*Elegy Written in a Country Churchyard*

# PART ONE

## THE KNELL OF PARTING DAY

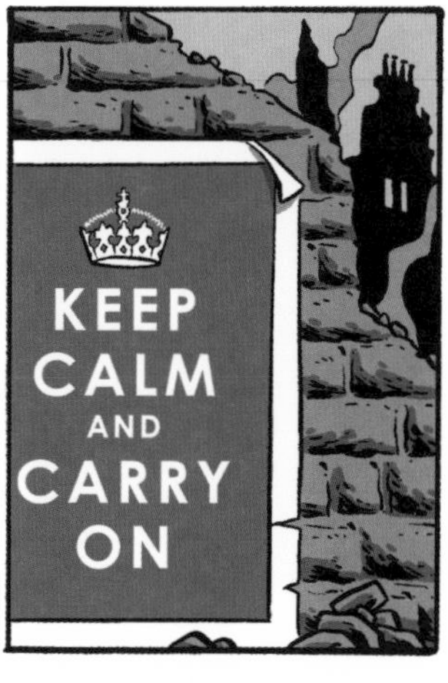
KEEP
CALM
AND
CARRY
ON

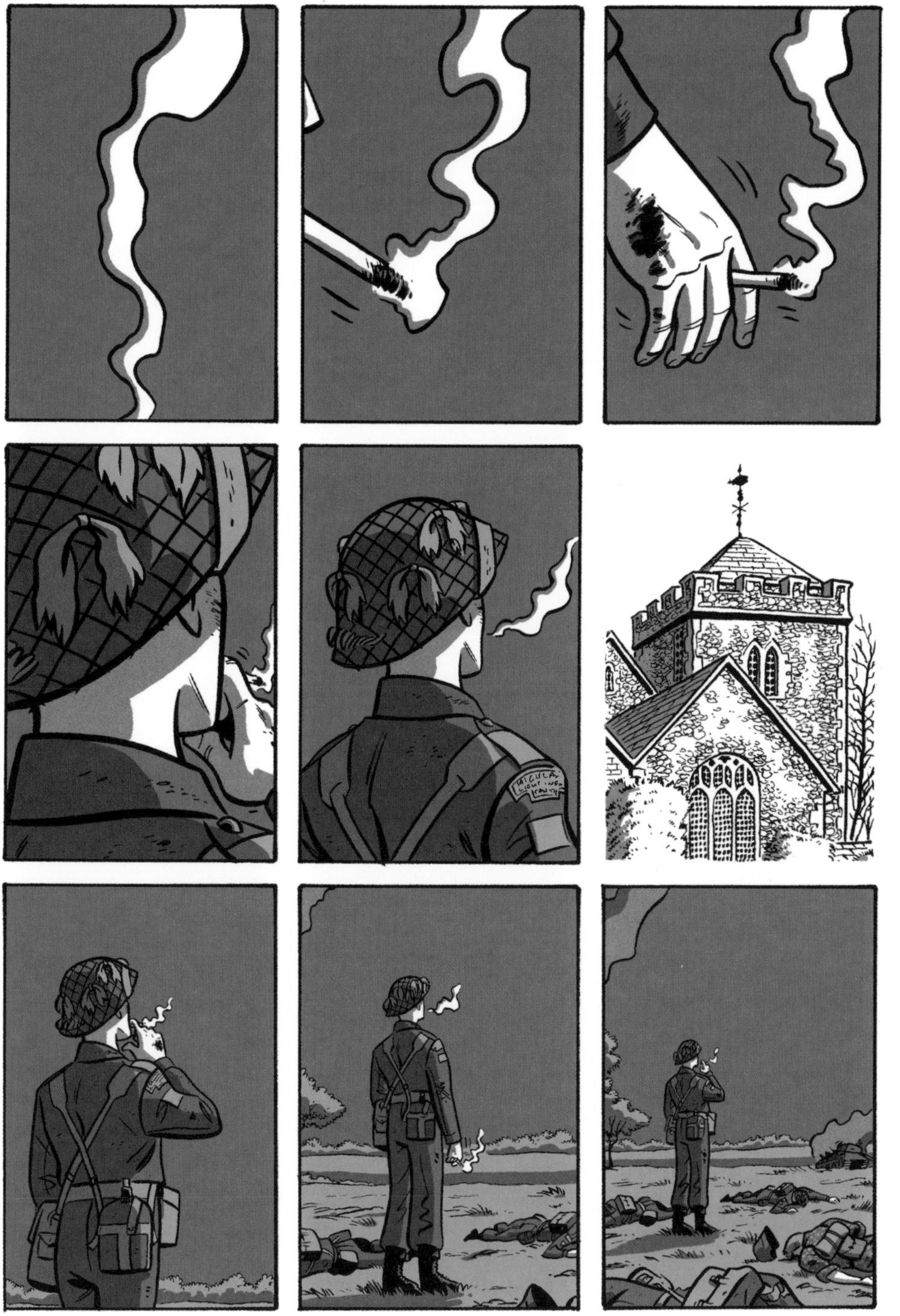

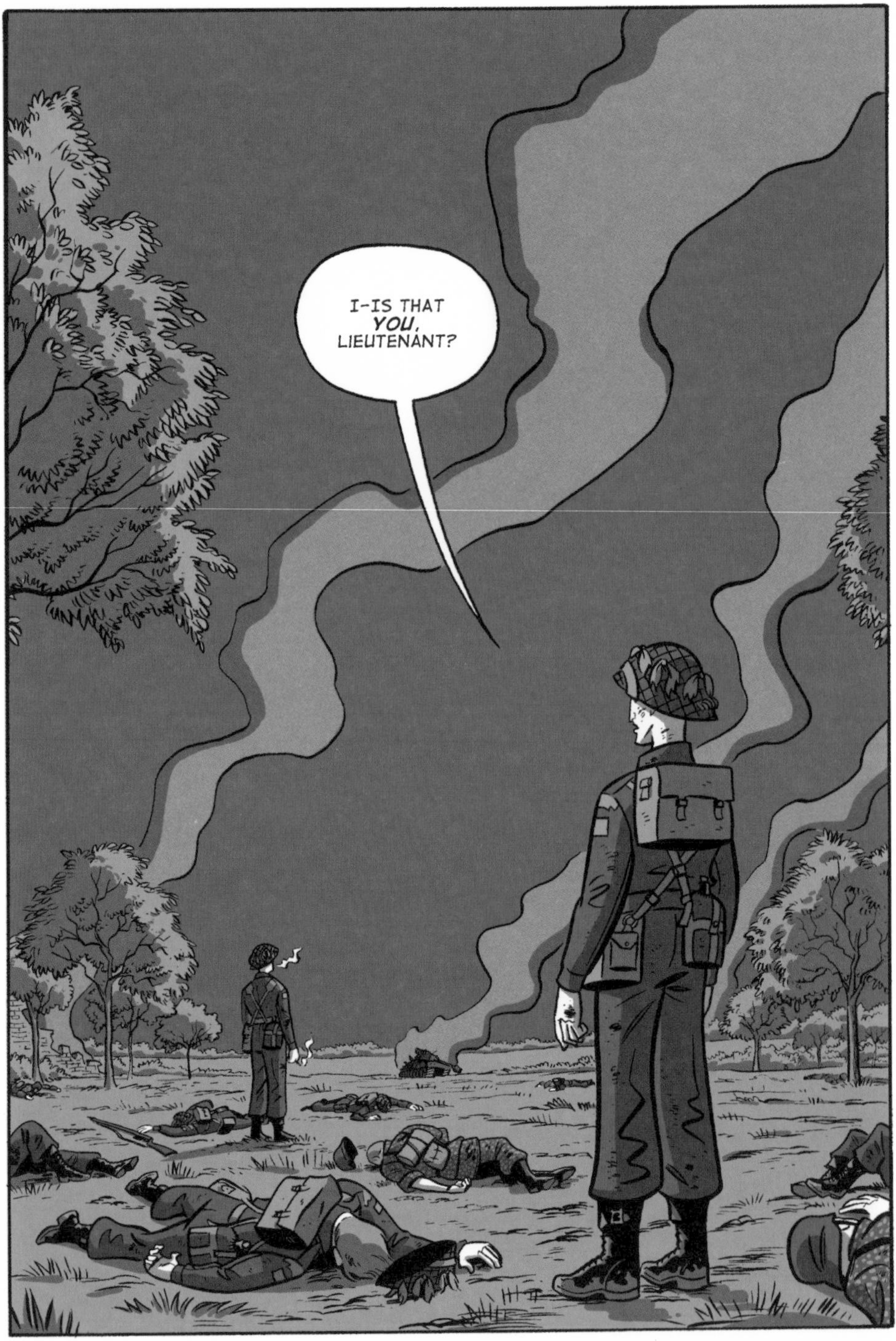
I-IS THAT *YOU*, LIEUTENANT?

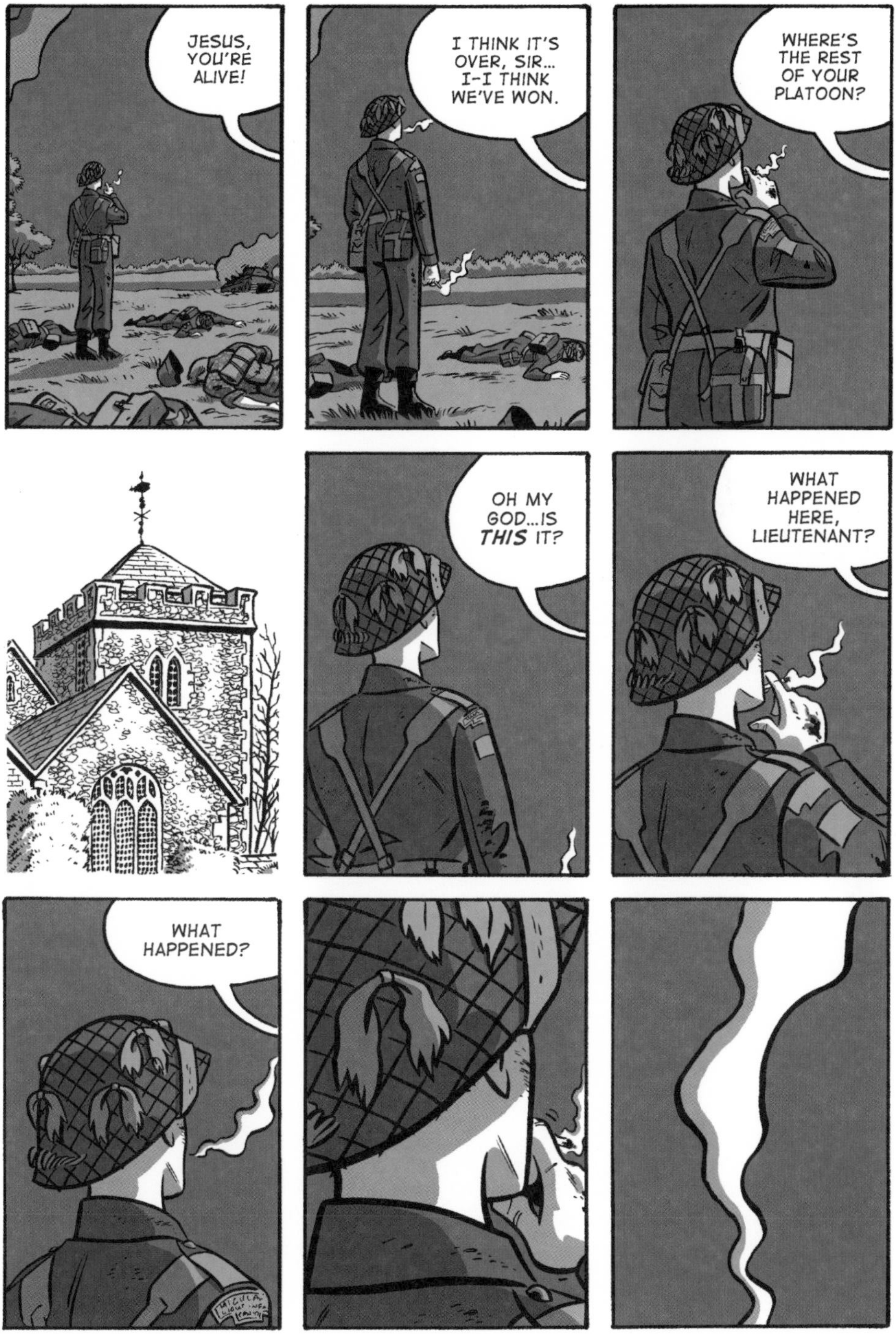
JESUS, YOU'RE ALIVE!
I THINK IT'S OVER, SIR... I-I THINK WE'VE WON.
WHERE'S THE REST OF YOUR PLATOON?
OH MY GOD...IS *THIS* IT?
WHAT HAPPENED HERE, LIEUTENANT?
WHAT HAPPENED?

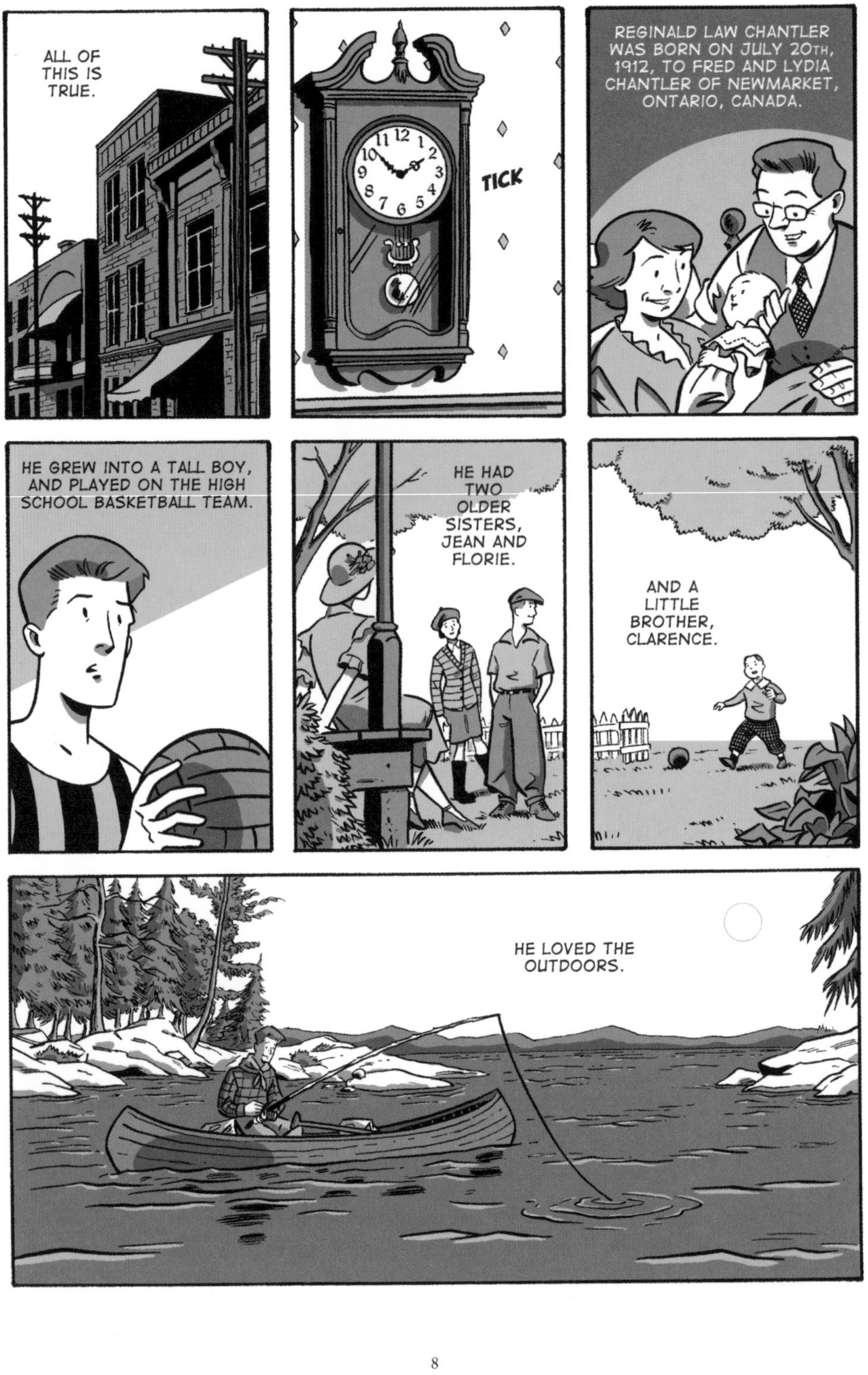
ALL OF THIS IS TRUE.
TICK
REGINALD LAW CHANTLER WAS BORN ON JULY 20TH, 1912, TO FRED AND LYDIA CHANTLER OF NEWMARKET, ONTARIO, CANADA.
HE GREW INTO A TALL BOY, AND PLAYED ON THE HIGH SCHOOL BASKETBALL TEAM.
HE HAD TWO OLDER SISTERS, JEAN AND FLORIE.
AND A LITTLE BROTHER, CLARENCE.
HE LOVED THE OUTDOORS.

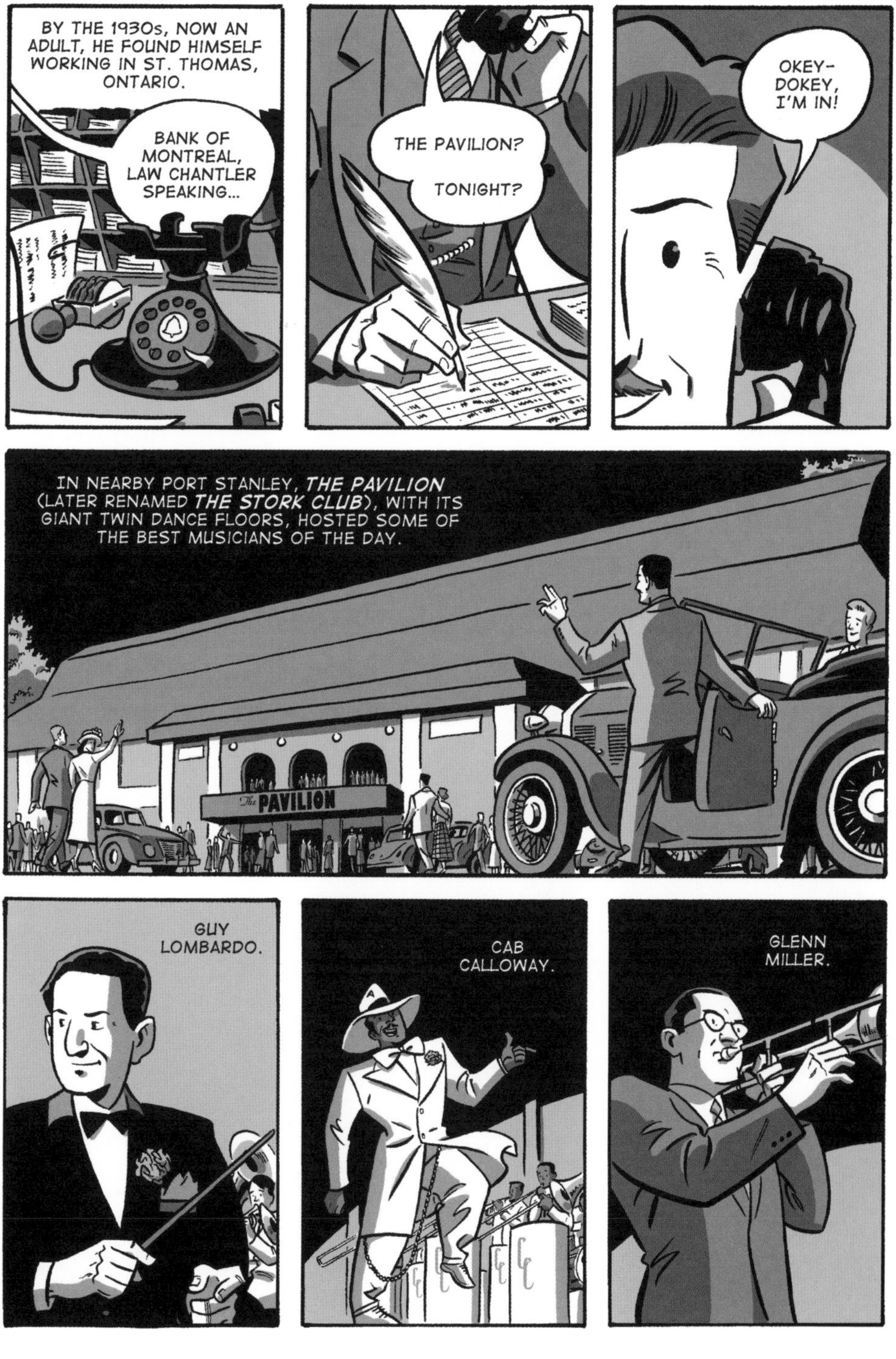
BY THE 1930s, NOW AN ADULT, HE FOUND HIMSELF WORKING IN ST. THOMAS, ONTARIO.
BANK OF MONTREAL, LAW CHANTLER SPEAKING...
THE PAVILION?
TONIGHT?
OKEY-DOKEY, I'M IN!
IN NEARBY PORT STANLEY, *THE PAVILION* (LATER RENAMED *THE STORK CLUB*), WITH ITS GIANT TWIN DANCE FLOORS, HOSTED SOME OF THE BEST MUSICIANS OF THE DAY.
The PAVILION
GUY LOMBARDO.
CAB CALLOWAY.
GLENN MILLER.

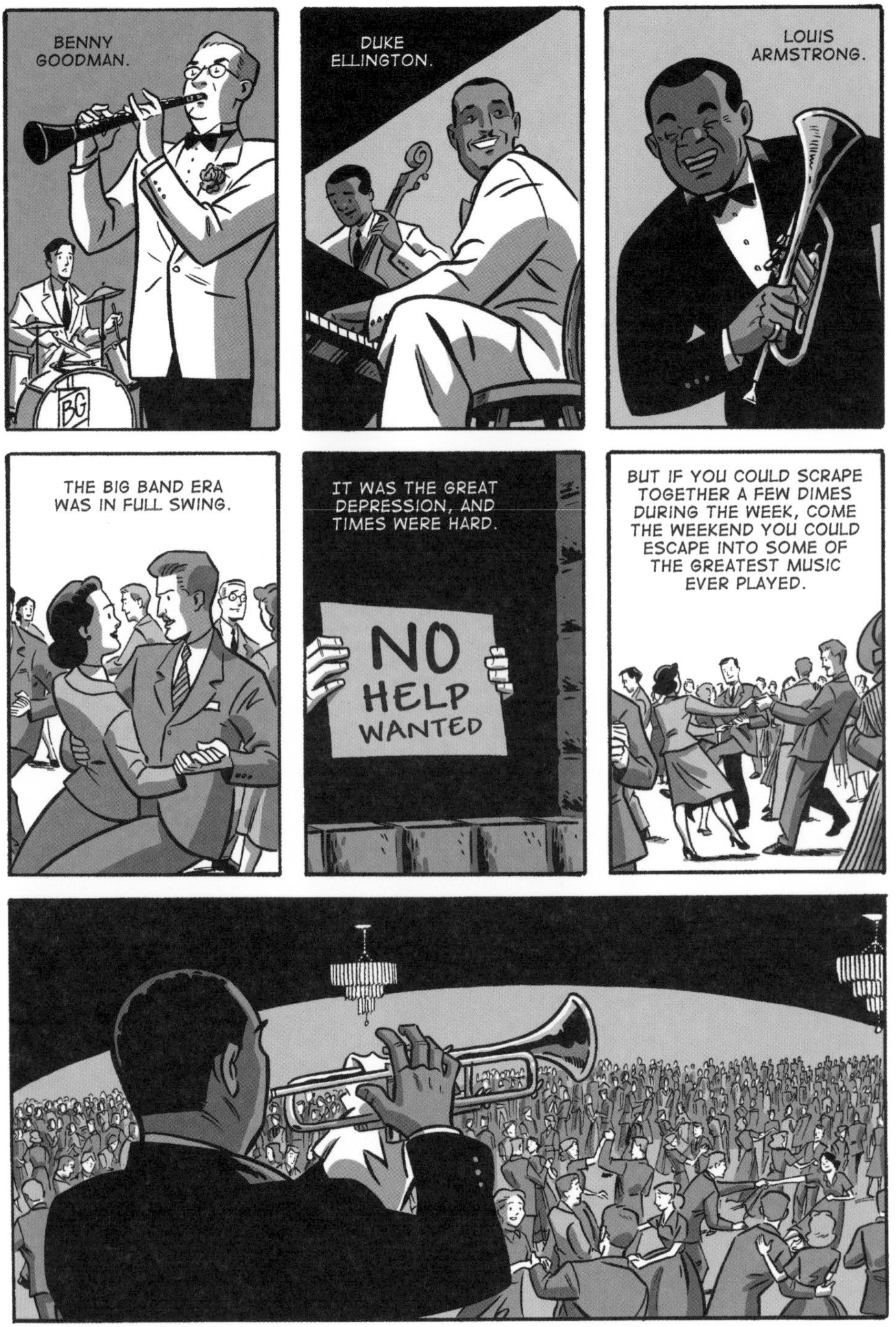
BENNY GOODMAN.
BG
DUKE ELLINGTON.
LOUIS ARMSTRONG.
THE BIG BAND ERA WAS IN FULL SWING.
IT WAS THE GREAT DEPRESSION, AND TIMES WERE HARD.
NO HELP WANTED
BUT IF YOU COULD SCRAPE TOGETHER A FEW DIMES DURING THE WEEK, COME THE WEEKEND YOU COULD ESCAPE INTO SOME OF THE GREATEST MUSIC EVER PLAYED.

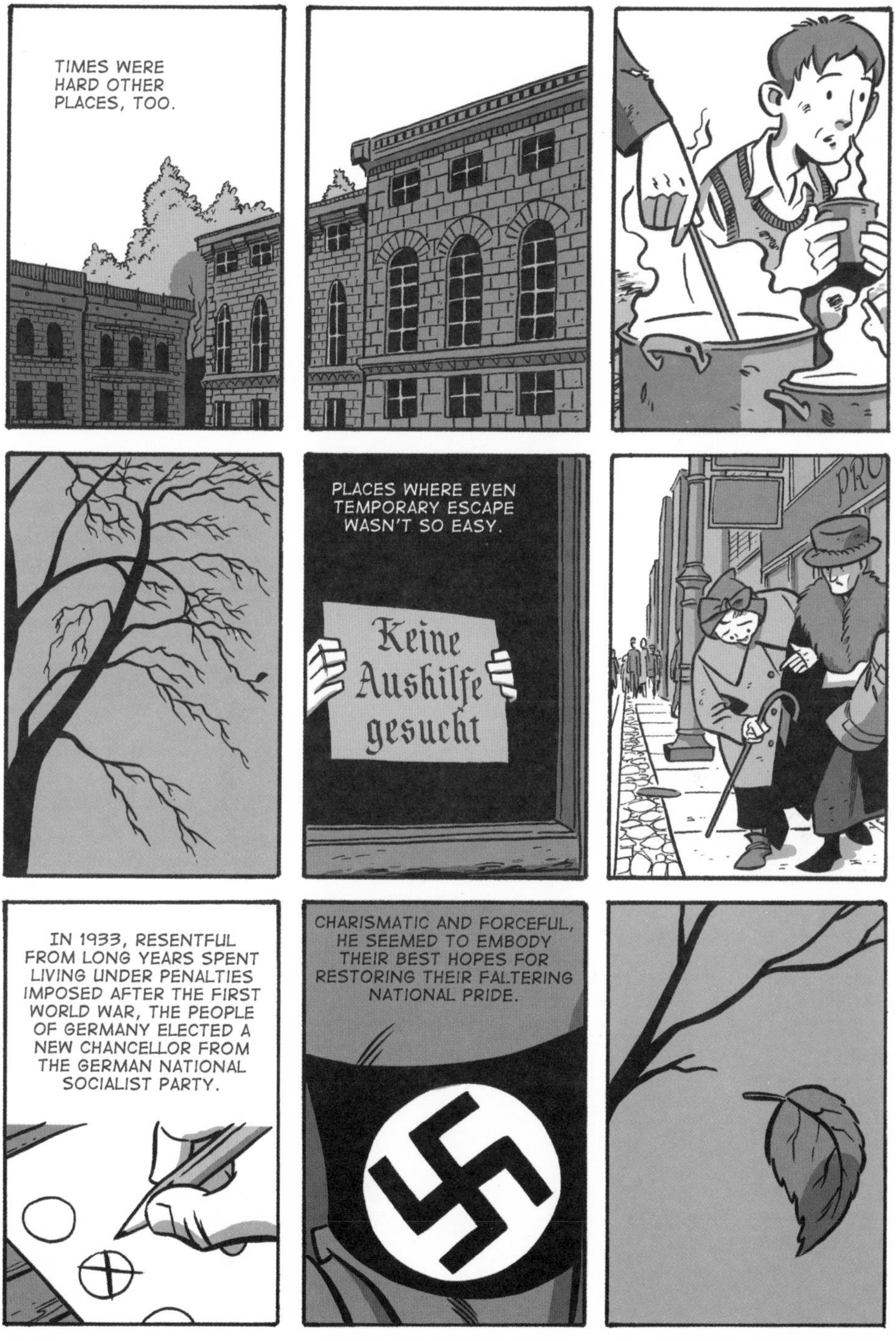
TIMES WERE HARD OTHER PLACES, TOO.
PLACES WHERE EVEN TEMPORARY ESCAPE WASN'T SO EASY.
Keine Aushilfe gesucht
IN 1933, RESENTFUL FROM LONG YEARS SPENT LIVING UNDER PENALTIES IMPOSED AFTER THE FIRST WORLD WAR, THE PEOPLE OF GERMANY ELECTED A NEW CHANCELLOR FROM THE GERMAN NATIONAL SOCIALIST PARTY.
CHARISMATIC AND FORCEFUL, HE SEEMED TO EMBODY THEIR BEST HOPES FOR RESTORING THEIR FALTERING NATIONAL PRIDE.

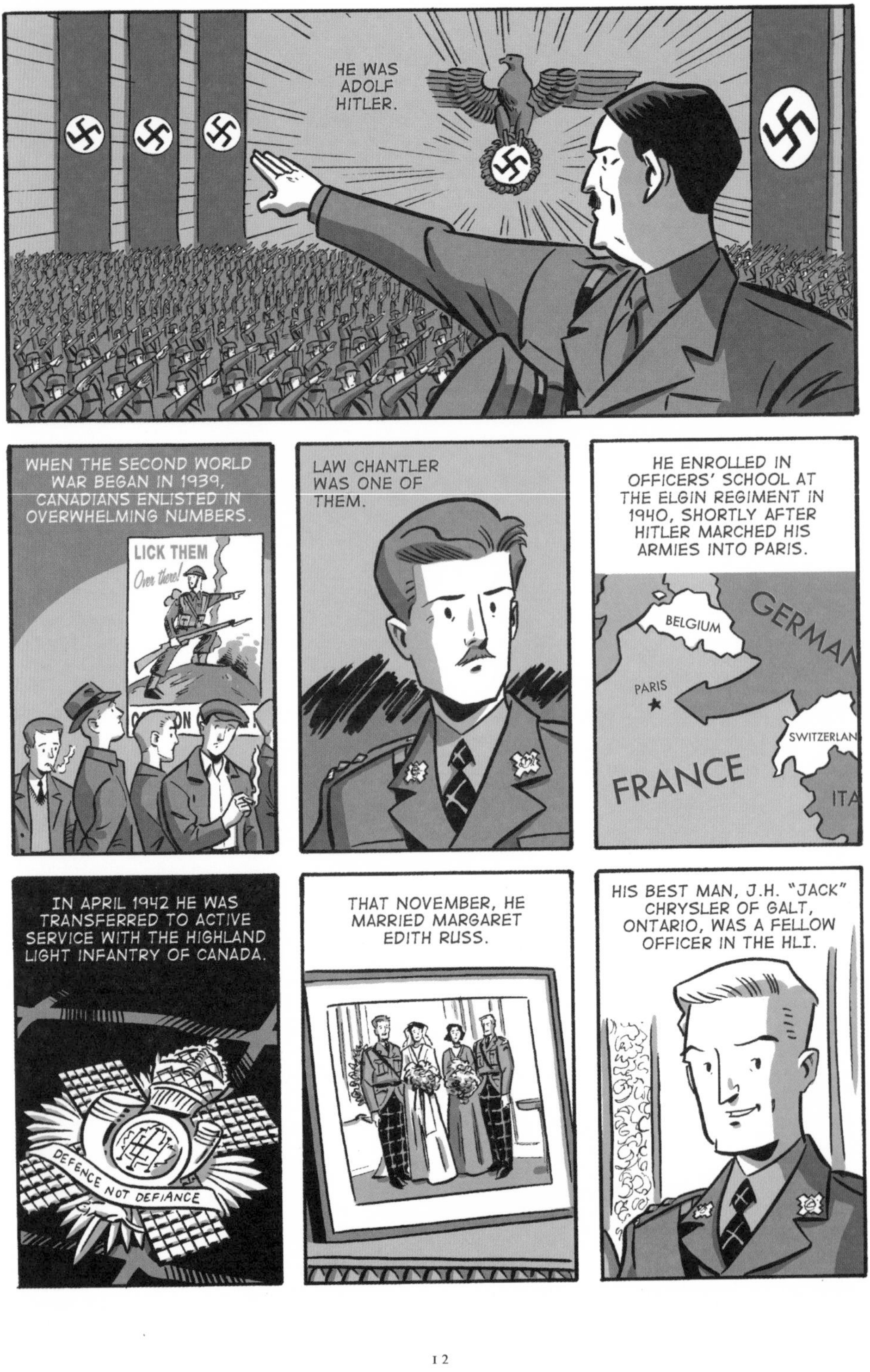

HE WAS ADOLF HITLER.
WHEN THE SECOND WORLD WAR BEGAN IN 1939, CANADIANS ENLISTED IN OVERWHELMING NUMBERS.
LICK THEM
Over there!
LAW CHANTLER WAS ONE OF THEM.
HE ENROLLED IN OFFICERS' SCHOOL AT THE ELGIN REGIMENT IN 1940, SHORTLY AFTER HITLER MARCHED HIS ARMIES INTO PARIS.
BELGIUM
GERMAN
PARIS
SWITZERLAN
FRANCE
ITA
IN APRIL 1942 HE WAS TRANSFERRED TO ACTIVE SERVICE WITH THE HIGHLAND LIGHT INFANTRY OF CANADA.
DEFENCE NOT DEFIANCE
THAT NOVEMBER, HE MARRIED MARGARET EDITH RUSS.
HIS BEST MAN, J.H. "JACK" CHRYSLER OF GALT, ONTARIO, WAS A FELLOW OFFICER IN THE HLI.

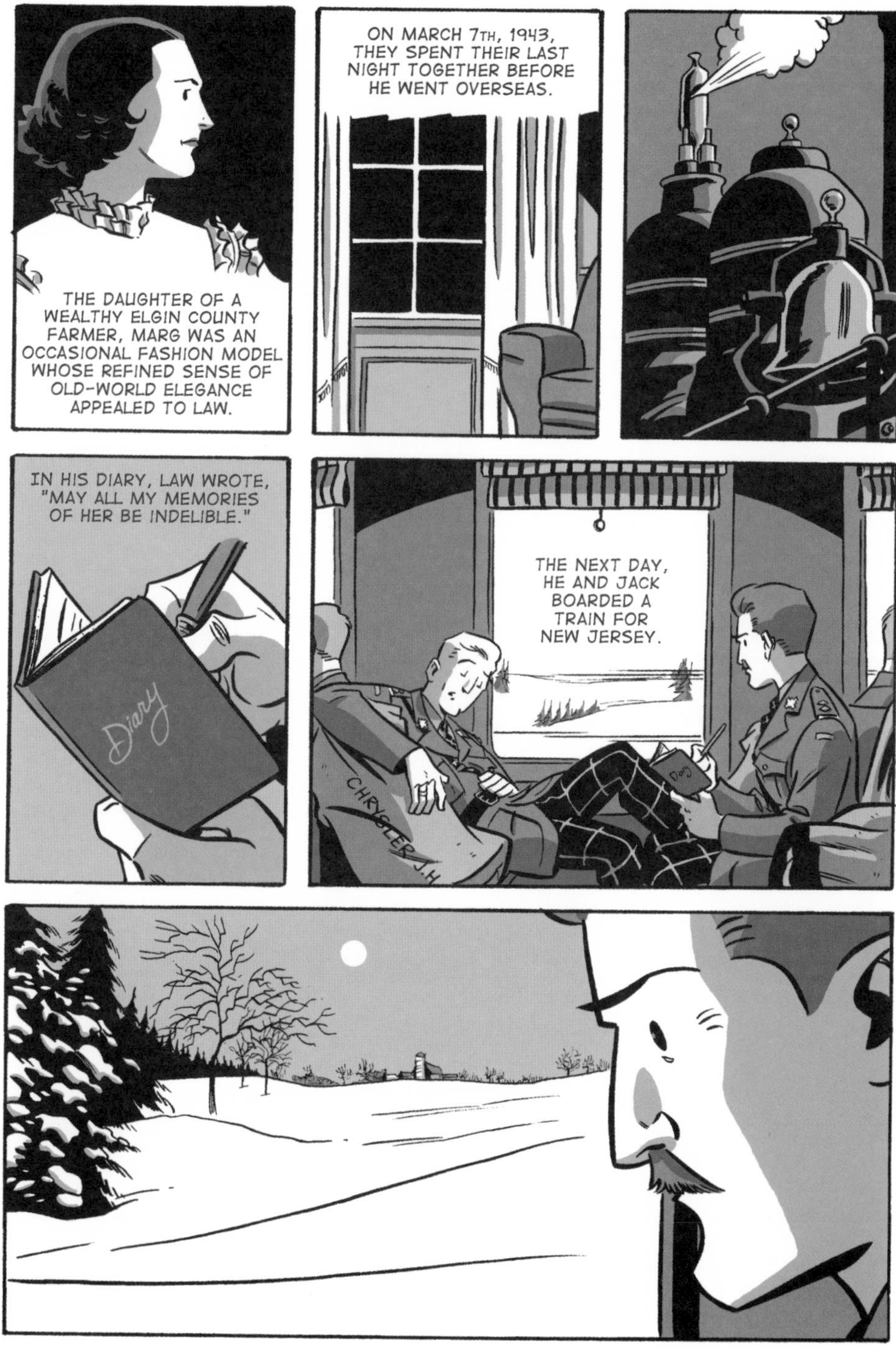
THE DAUGHTER OF A WEALTHY ELGIN COUNTY FARMER, MARG WAS AN OCCASIONAL FASHION MODEL WHOSE REFINED SENSE OF OLD-WORLD ELEGANCE APPEALED TO LAW.
ON MARCH 7TH, 1943, THEY SPENT THEIR LAST NIGHT TOGETHER BEFORE HE WENT OVERSEAS.
IN HIS DIARY, LAW WROTE, "MAY ALL MY MEMORIES OF HER BE INDELIBLE."
Diary
THE NEXT DAY, HE AND JACK BOARDED A TRAIN FOR NEW JERSEY.
Diary
CHRYSLER J.H

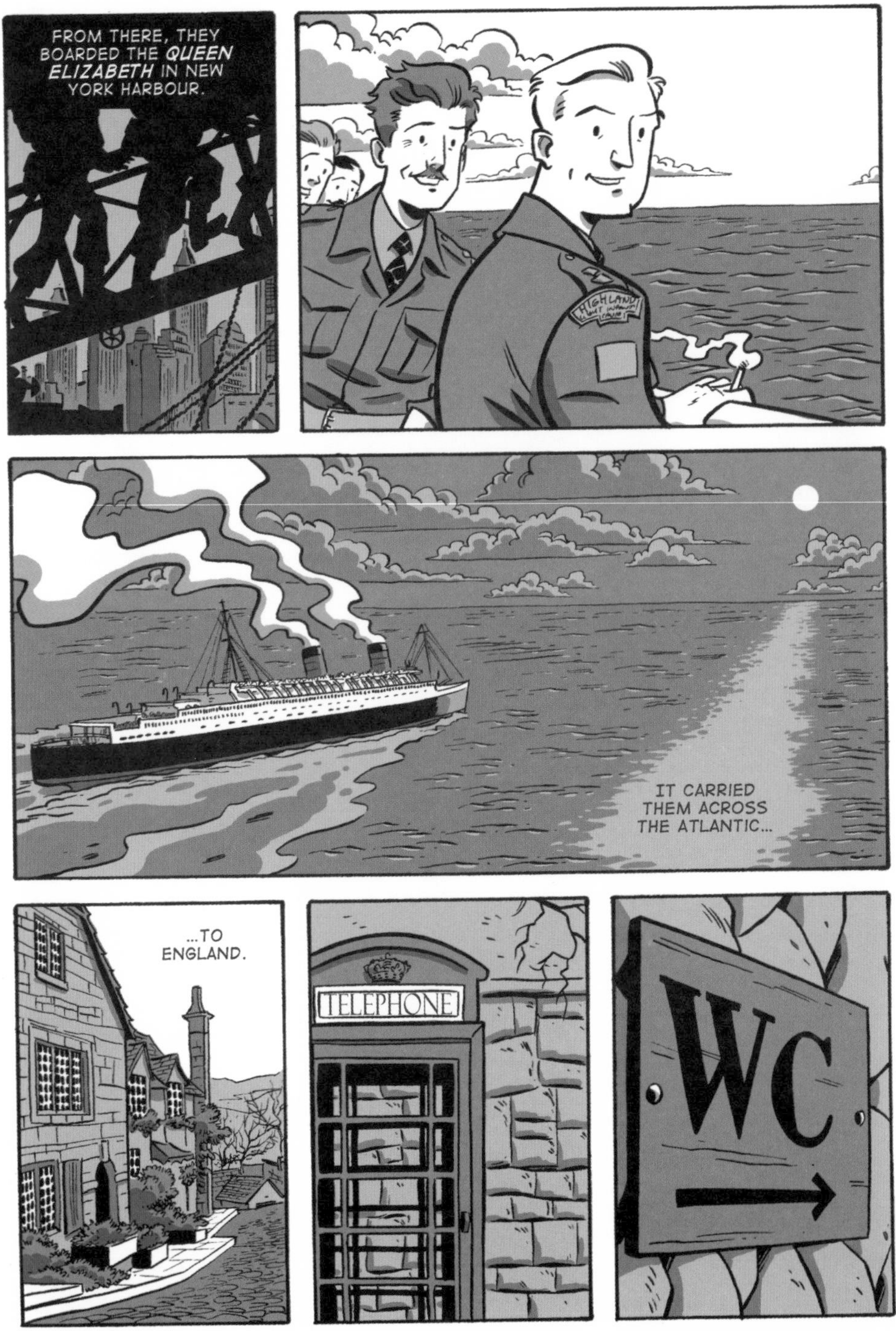
FROM THERE, THEY BOARDED THE *QUEEN ELIZABETH* IN NEW YORK HARBOUR.
IT CARRIED THEM ACROSS THE ATLANTIC...
...TO ENGLAND.
TELEPHONE
WC

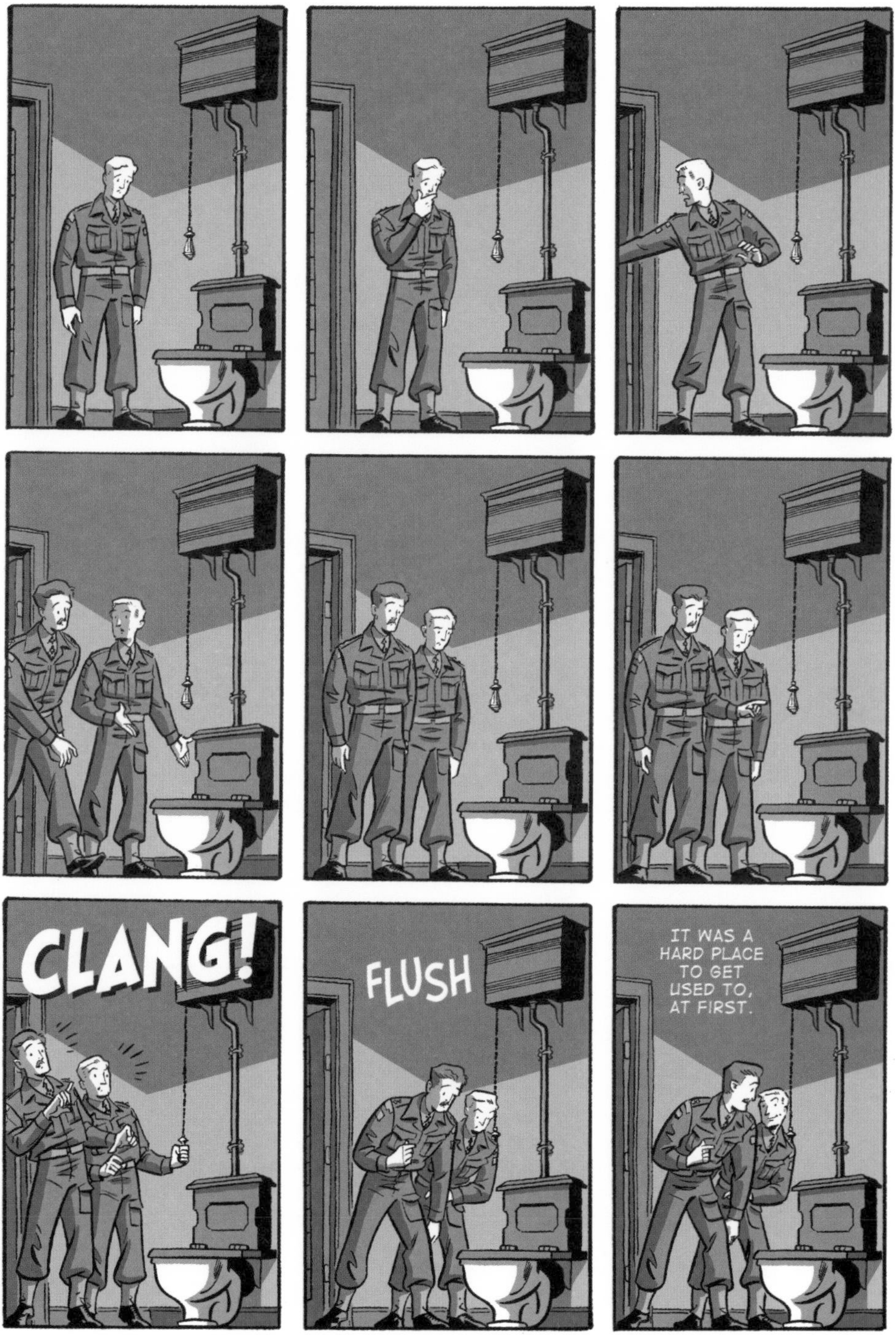
CLANG!
FLUSH
IT WAS A HARD PLACE TO GET USED TO, AT FIRST.

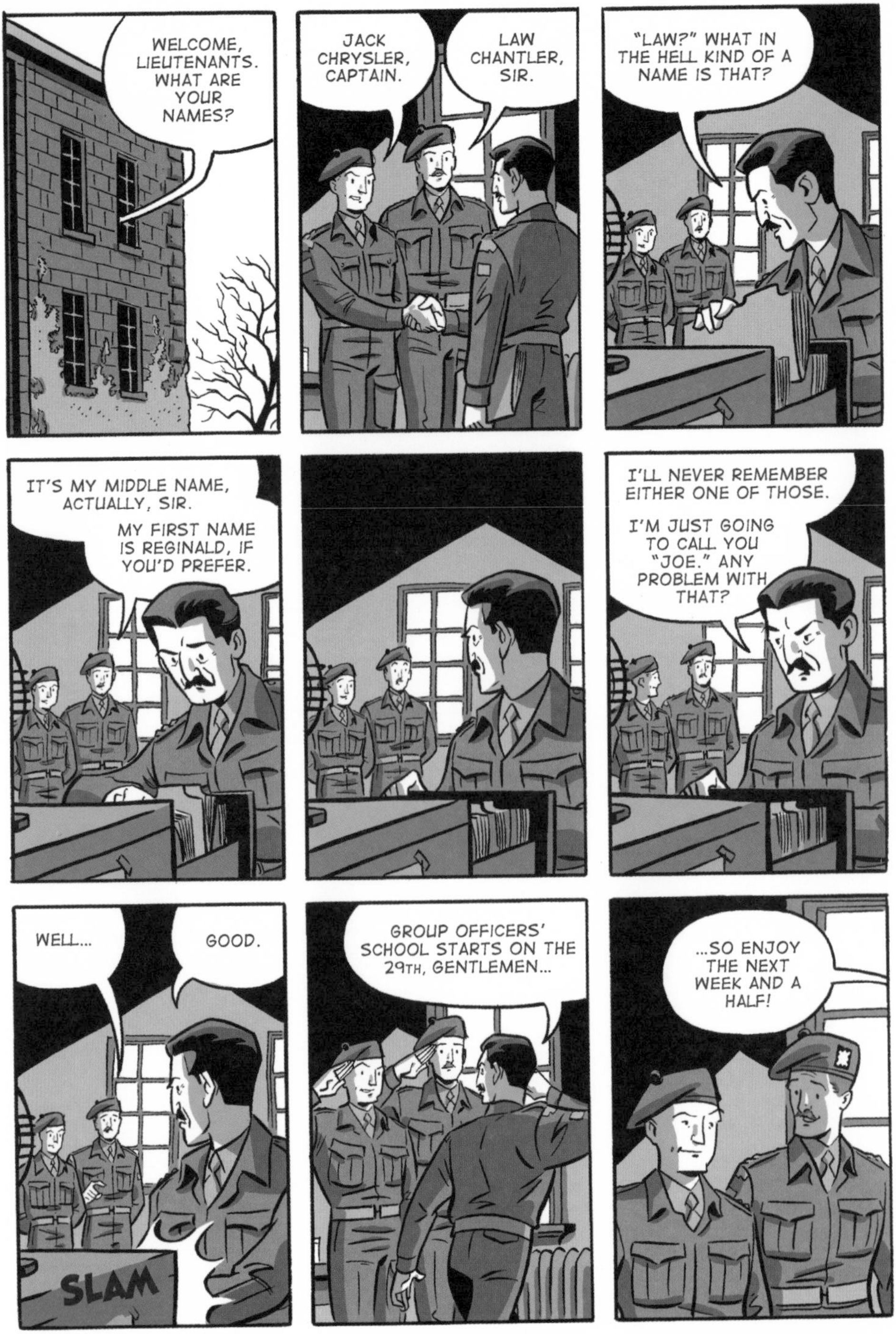
WELCOME, LIEUTENANTS. WHAT ARE YOUR NAMES?
JACK CHRYSLER, CAPTAIN.
LAW CHANTLER, SIR.
"LAW?" WHAT IN THE HELL KIND OF A NAME IS THAT?
IT'S MY MIDDLE NAME, ACTUALLY, SIR.
MY FIRST NAME IS REGINALD, IF YOU'D PREFER.
I'LL NEVER REMEMBER EITHER ONE OF THOSE.
I'M JUST GOING TO CALL YOU "JOE." ANY PROBLEM WITH THAT?
WELL...
GOOD.
SLAM
GROUP OFFICERS' SCHOOL STARTS ON THE 29TH, GENTLEMEN...
...SO ENJOY THE NEXT WEEK AND A HALF!

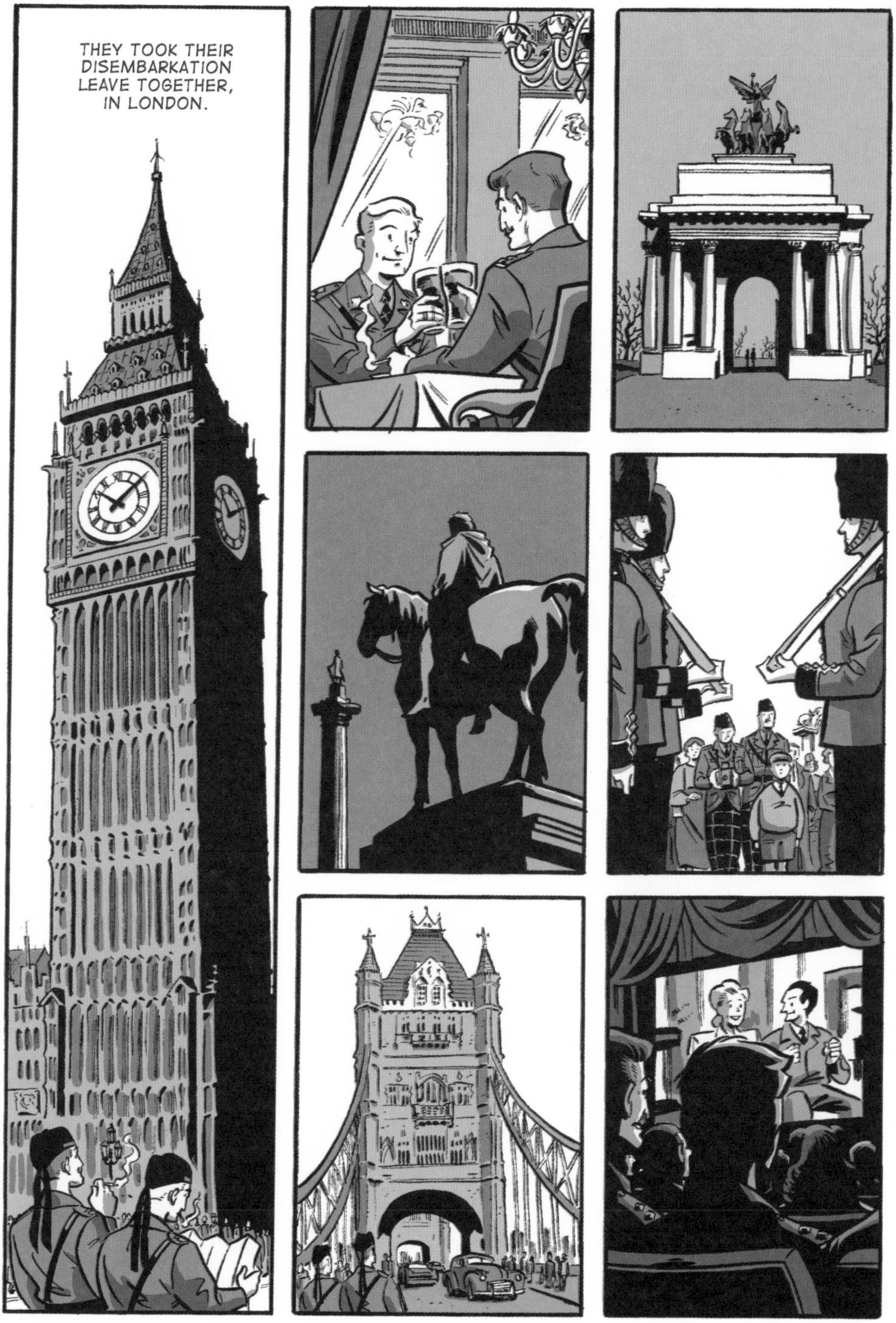
THEY TOOK THEIR DISEMBARKATION LEAVE TOGETHER, IN LONDON.

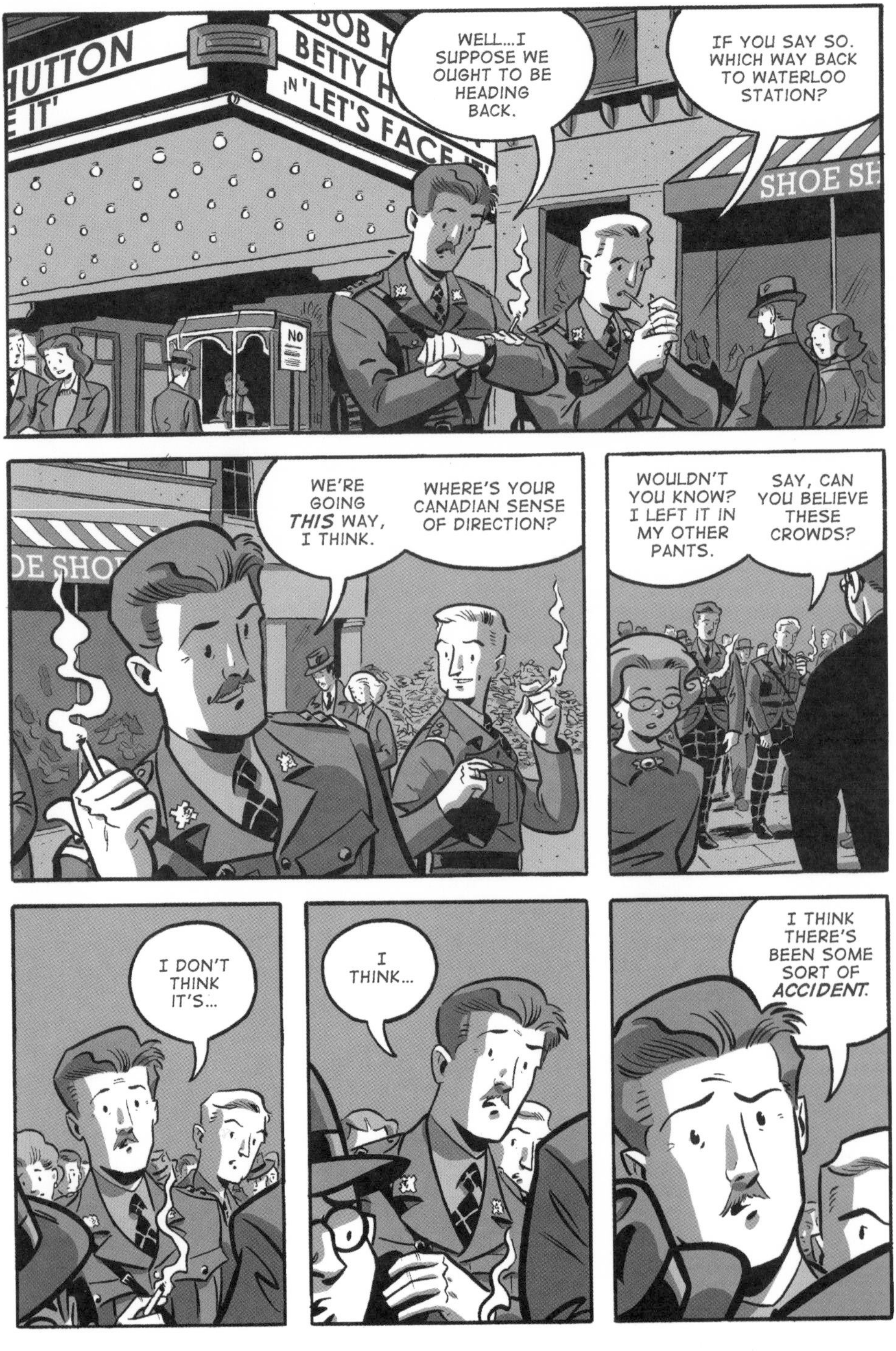
BOB H
BETTY H
HUTTON
IN 'LET'S FACE IT'
E IT'
WELL...I SUPPOSE WE OUGHT TO BE HEADING BACK.
IF YOU SAY SO. WHICH WAY BACK TO WATERLOO STATION?
SHOE SH
NO
DE SHO
WE'RE GOING ***THIS*** WAY, I THINK.
WHERE'S YOUR CANADIAN SENSE OF DIRECTION?
WOULDN'T YOU KNOW? I LEFT IT IN MY OTHER PANTS.
SAY, CAN YOU BELIEVE THESE CROWDS?
I DON'T THINK IT'S...
I THINK...
I THINK THERE'S BEEN SOME SORT OF ***ACCIDENT.***

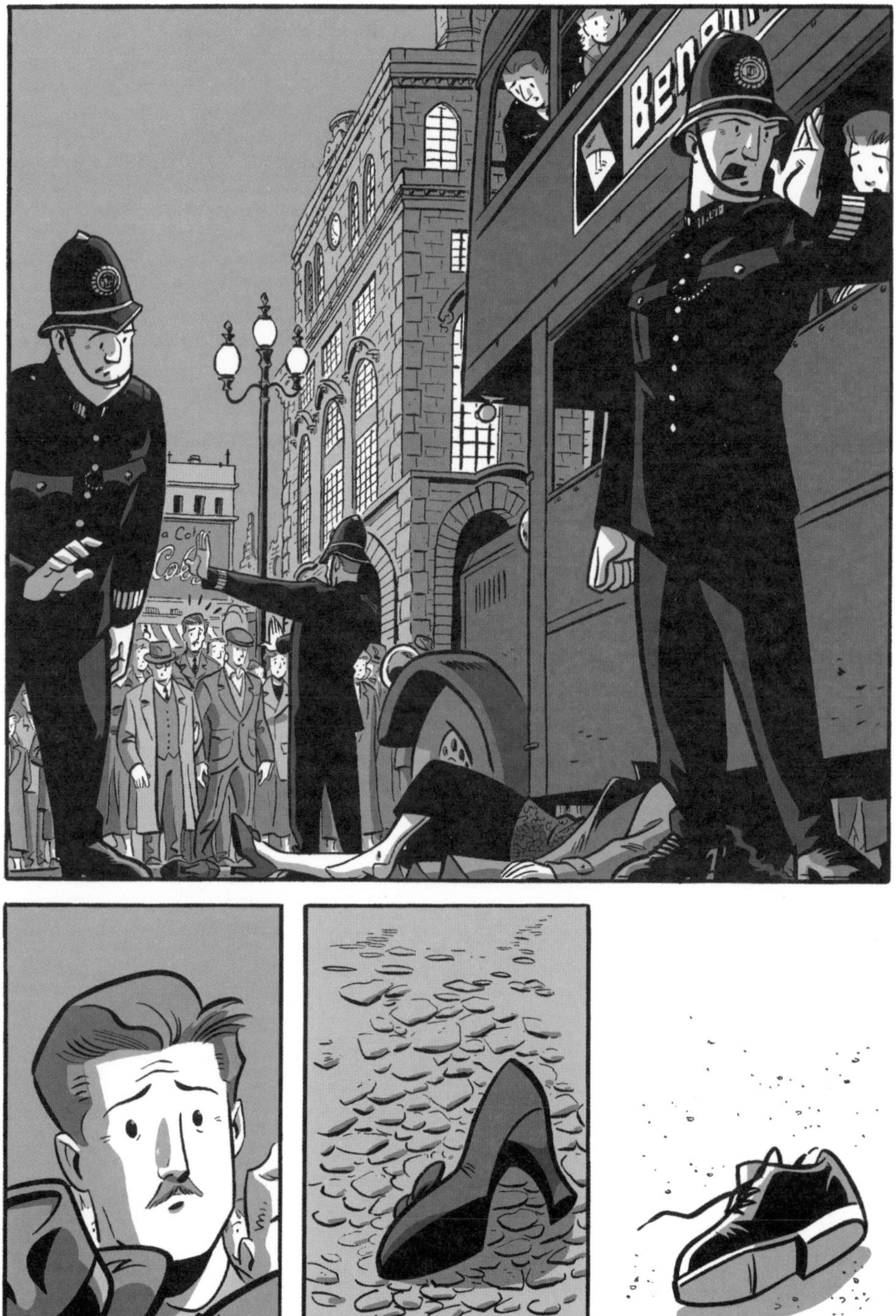

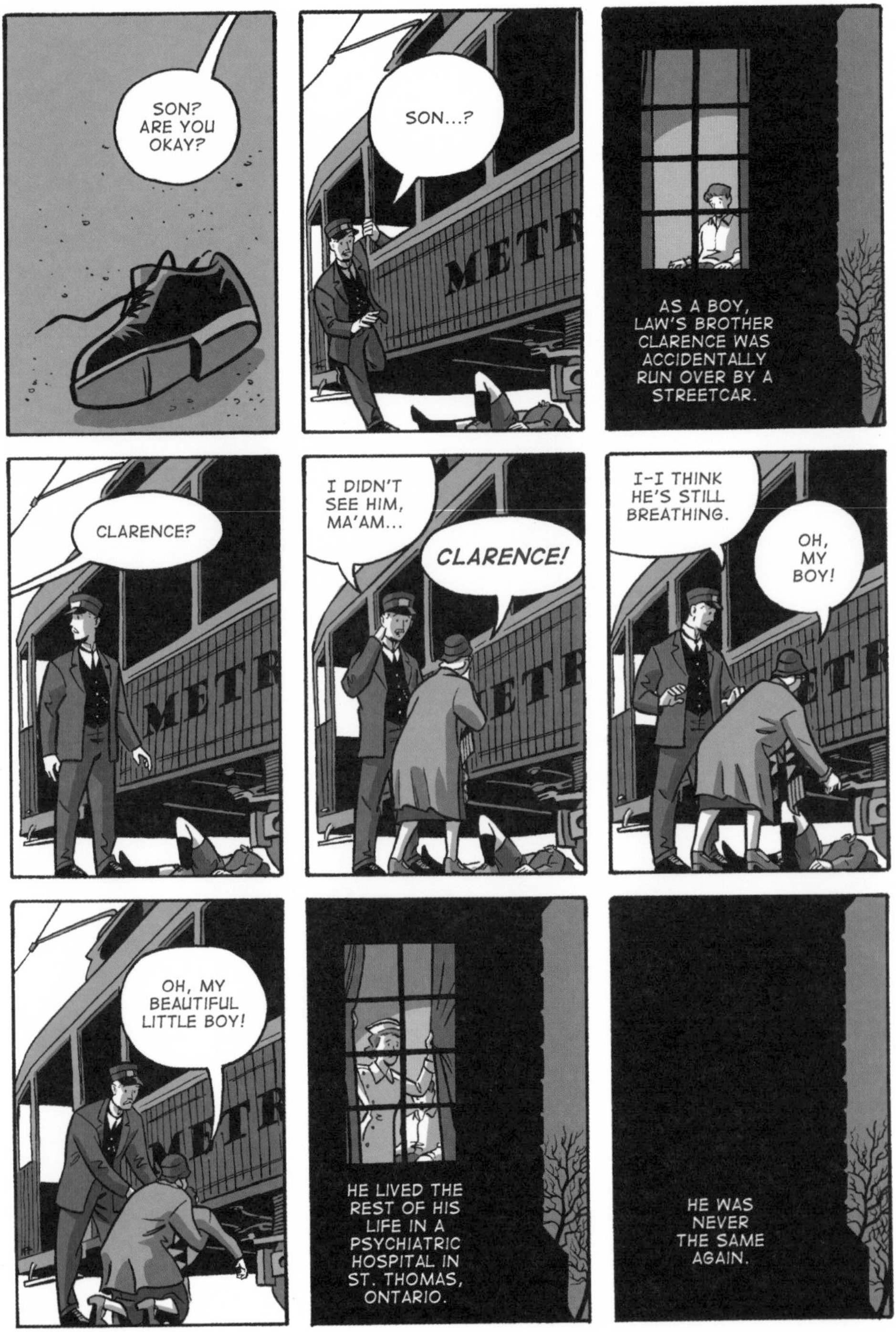
SON? ARE YOU OKAY?
SON...?
AS A BOY, LAW'S BROTHER CLARENCE WAS ACCIDENTALLY RUN OVER BY A STREETCAR.
CLARENCE?
I DIDN'T SEE HIM, MA'AM...
CLARENCE!
I-I THINK HE'S STILL BREATHING.
OH, MY BOY!
OH, MY BEAUTIFUL LITTLE BOY!
HE LIVED THE REST OF HIS LIFE IN A PSYCHIATRIC HOSPITAL IN ST. THOMAS, ONTARIO.
HE WAS NEVER THE SAME AGAIN.

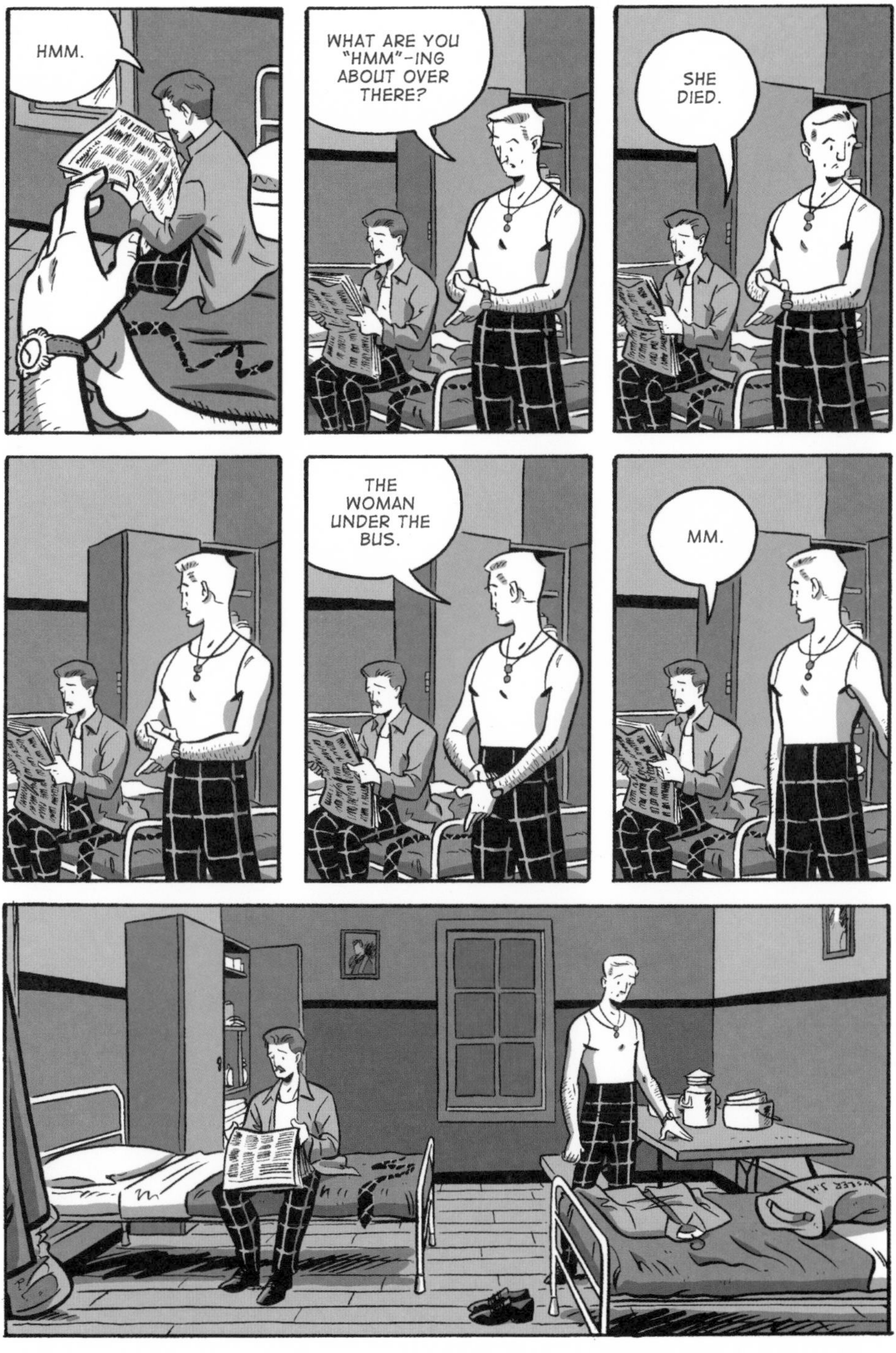
HMM.
WHAT ARE YOU "HMM"-ING ABOUT OVER THERE?
SHE DIED.
THE WOMAN UNDER THE BUS.
MM.

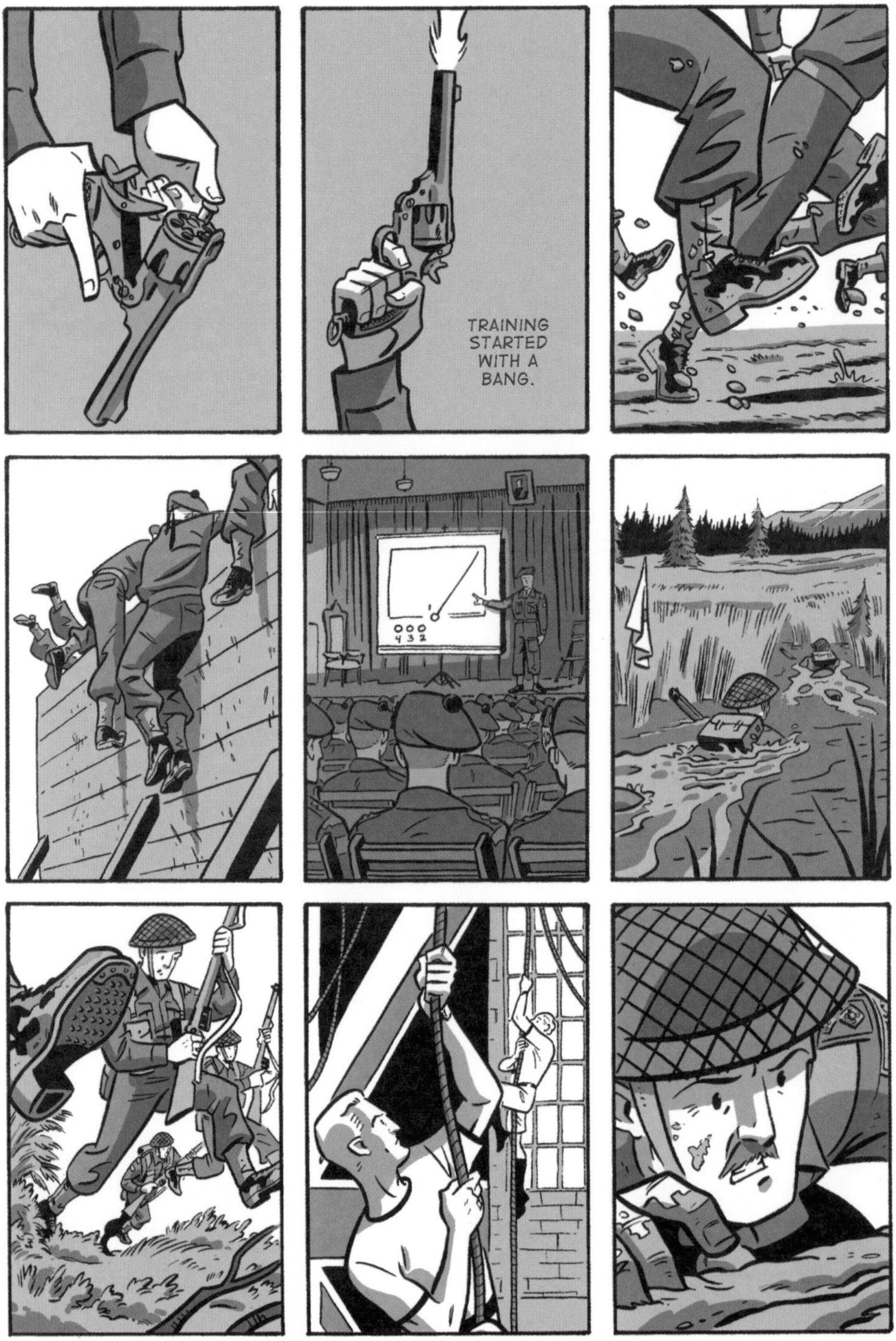
TRAINING STARTED WITH A BANG.
000
432

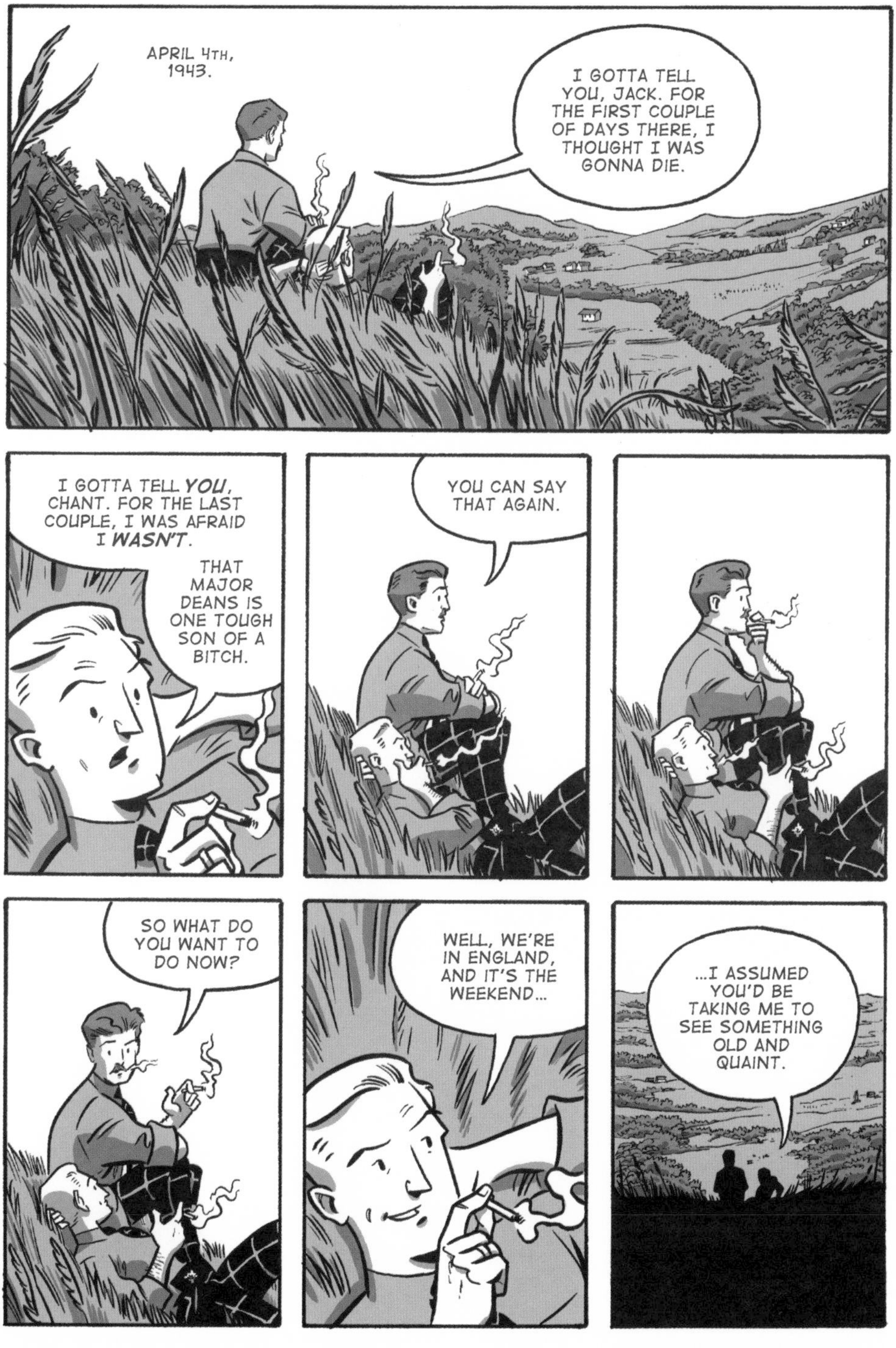
APRIL 4TH, 1943.
I GOTTA TELL YOU, JACK. FOR THE FIRST COUPLE OF DAYS THERE, I THOUGHT I WAS GONNA DIE.
I GOTTA TELL *YOU*, CHANT. FOR THE LAST COUPLE, I WAS AFRAID I *WASN'T*.
THAT MAJOR DEANS IS ONE TOUGH SON OF A BITCH.
YOU CAN SAY THAT AGAIN.
SO WHAT DO YOU WANT TO DO NOW?
WELL, WE'RE IN ENGLAND, AND IT'S THE WEEKEND...
...I ASSUMED YOU'D BE TAKING ME TO SEE SOMETHING OLD AND QUAINT.

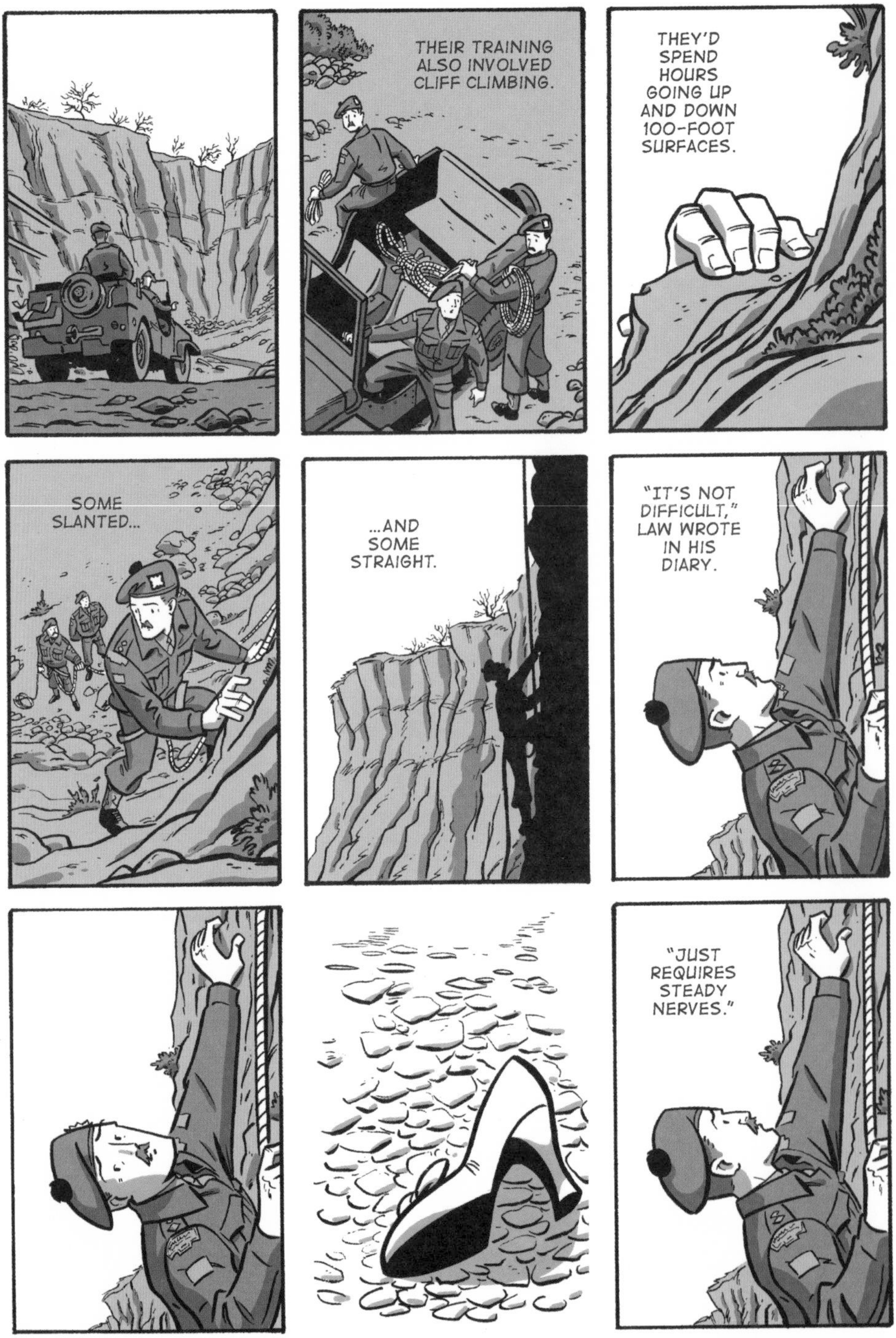
THEIR TRAINING ALSO INVOLVED CLIFF CLIMBING.
THEY'D SPEND HOURS GOING UP AND DOWN 100-FOOT SURFACES.
SOME SLANTED...
...AND SOME STRAIGHT.
"IT'S NOT DIFFICULT," LAW WROTE IN HIS DIARY.
"JUST REQUIRES STEADY NERVES."

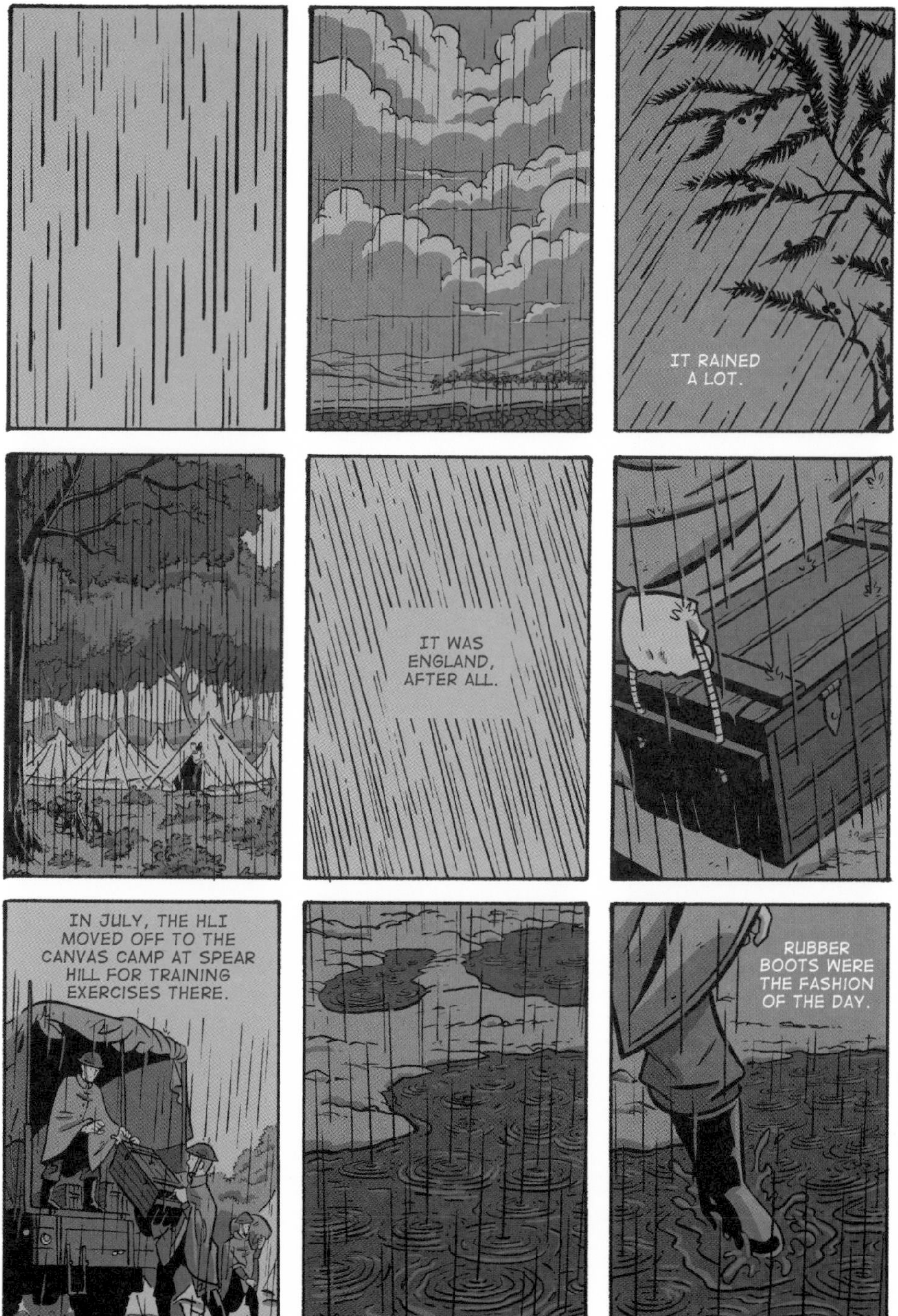
IT RAINED A LOT.
IT WAS ENGLAND, AFTER ALL.
IN JULY, THE HLI MOVED OFF TO THE CANVAS CAMP AT SPEAR HILL FOR TRAINING EXERCISES THERE.
RUBBER BOOTS WERE THE FASHION OF THE DAY.

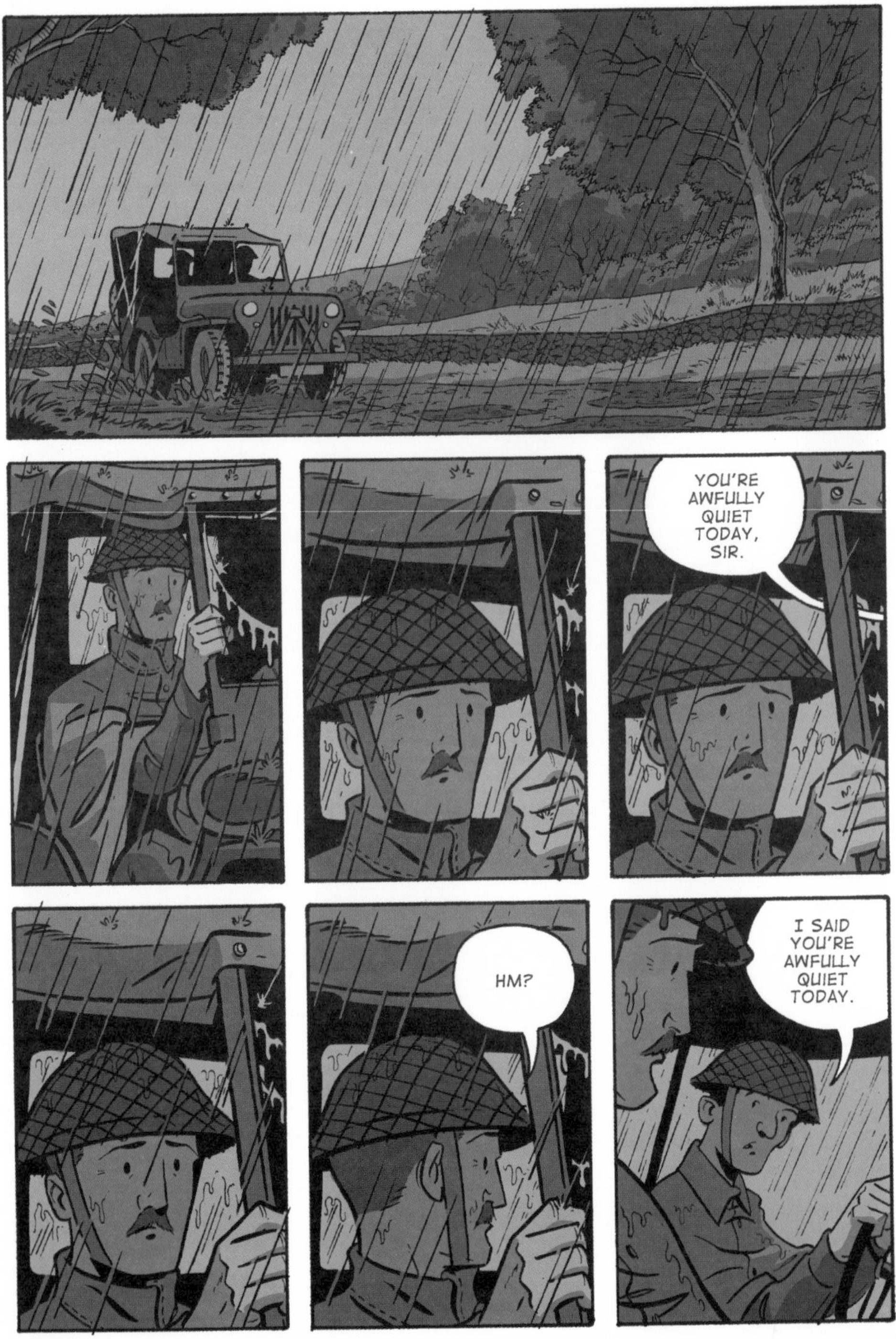
YOU'RE AWFULLY QUIET TODAY, SIR.
HM?
I SAID YOU'RE AWFULLY QUIET TODAY.

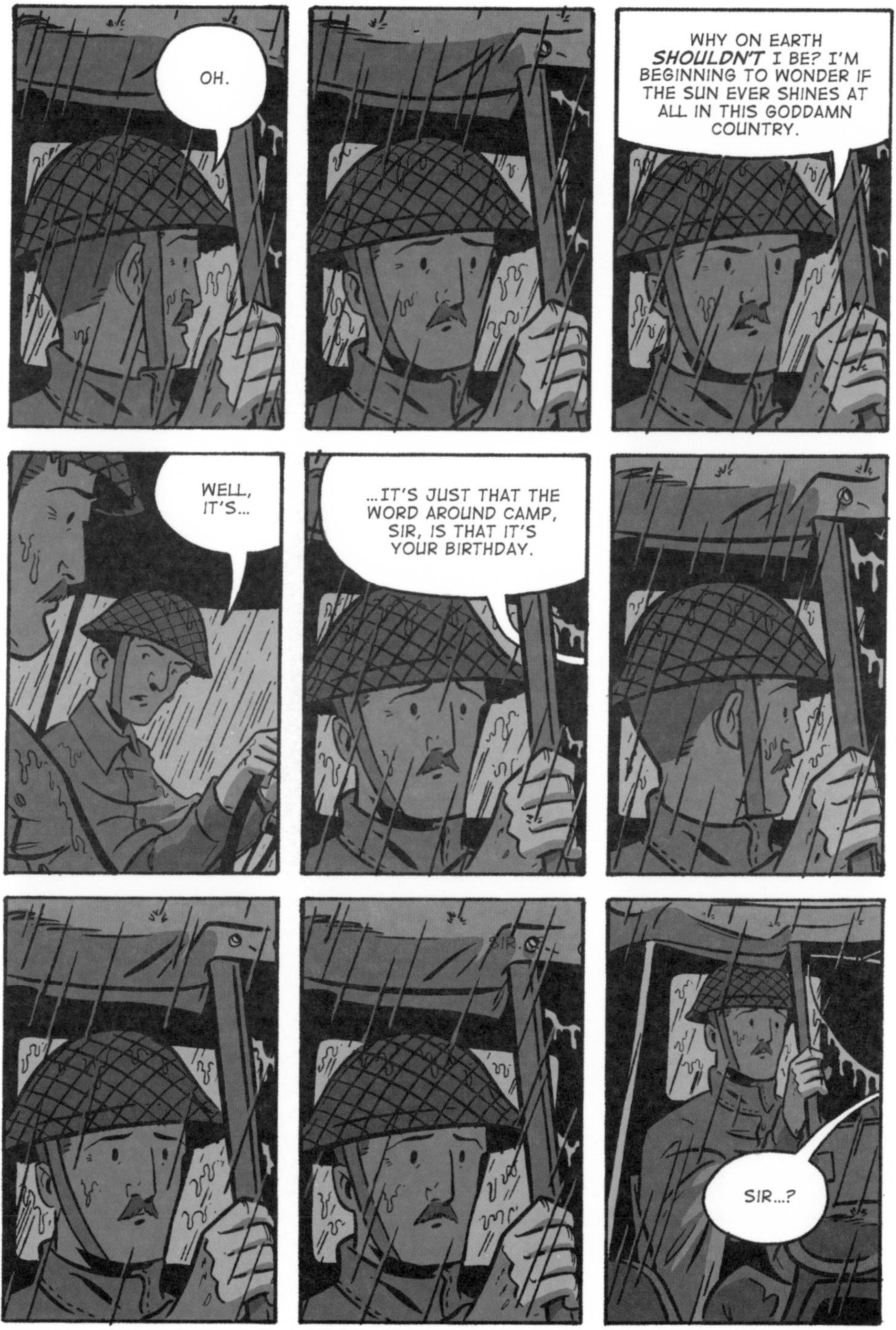
OH.
WHY ON EARTH **SHOULDN'T** I BE? I'M BEGINNING TO WONDER IF THE SUN EVER SHINES AT ALL IN THIS GODDAMN COUNTRY.
WELL, IT'S...
...IT'S JUST THAT THE WORD AROUND CAMP, SIR, IS THAT IT'S YOUR BIRTHDAY.
SIR...
SIR...?

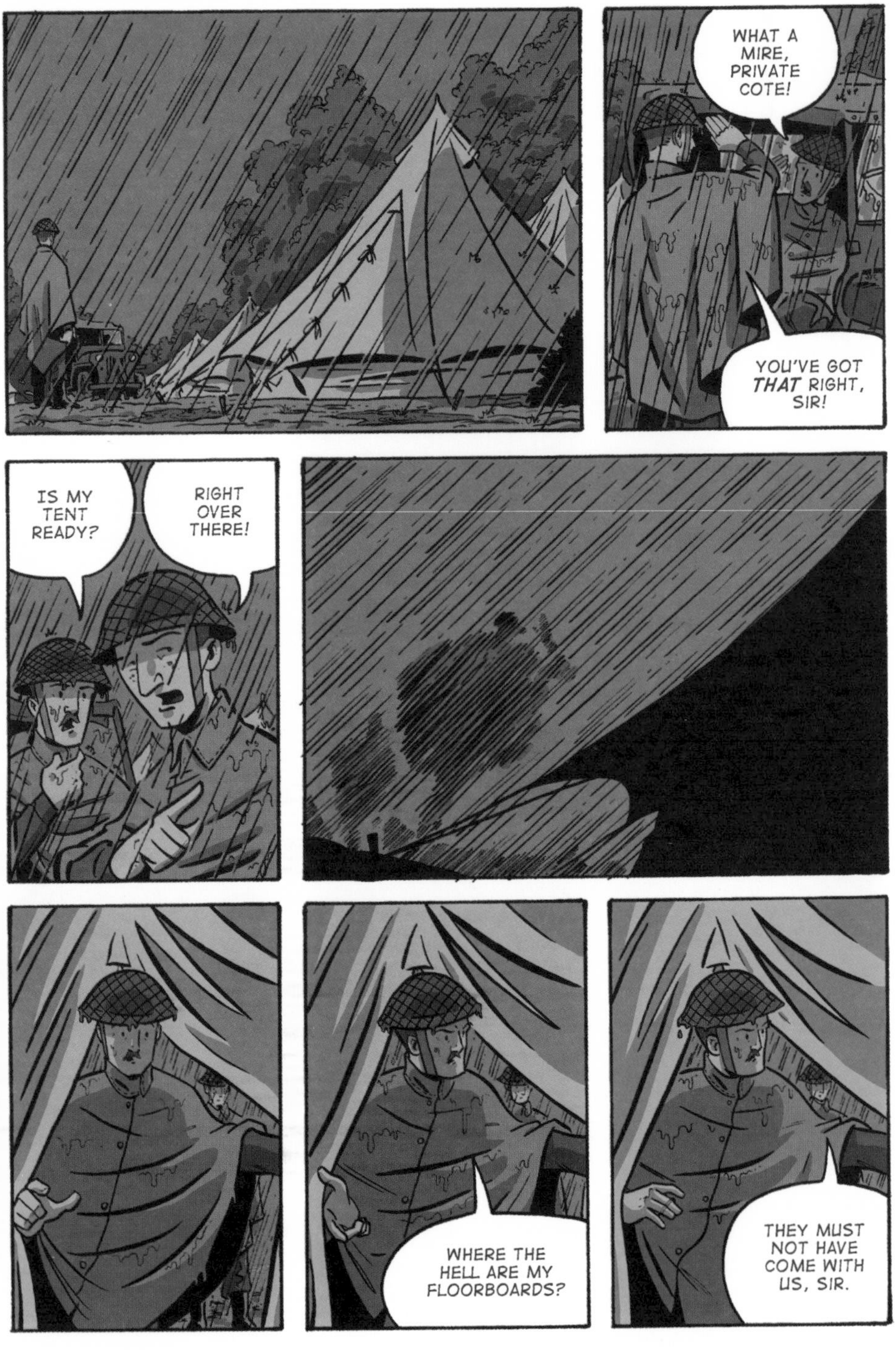
WHAT A MIRE, PRIVATE COTE!
YOU'VE GOT *THAT* RIGHT, SIR!
IS MY TENT READY?
RIGHT OVER THERE!
WHERE THE HELL ARE MY FLOORBOARDS?
THEY MUST NOT HAVE COME WITH US, SIR.

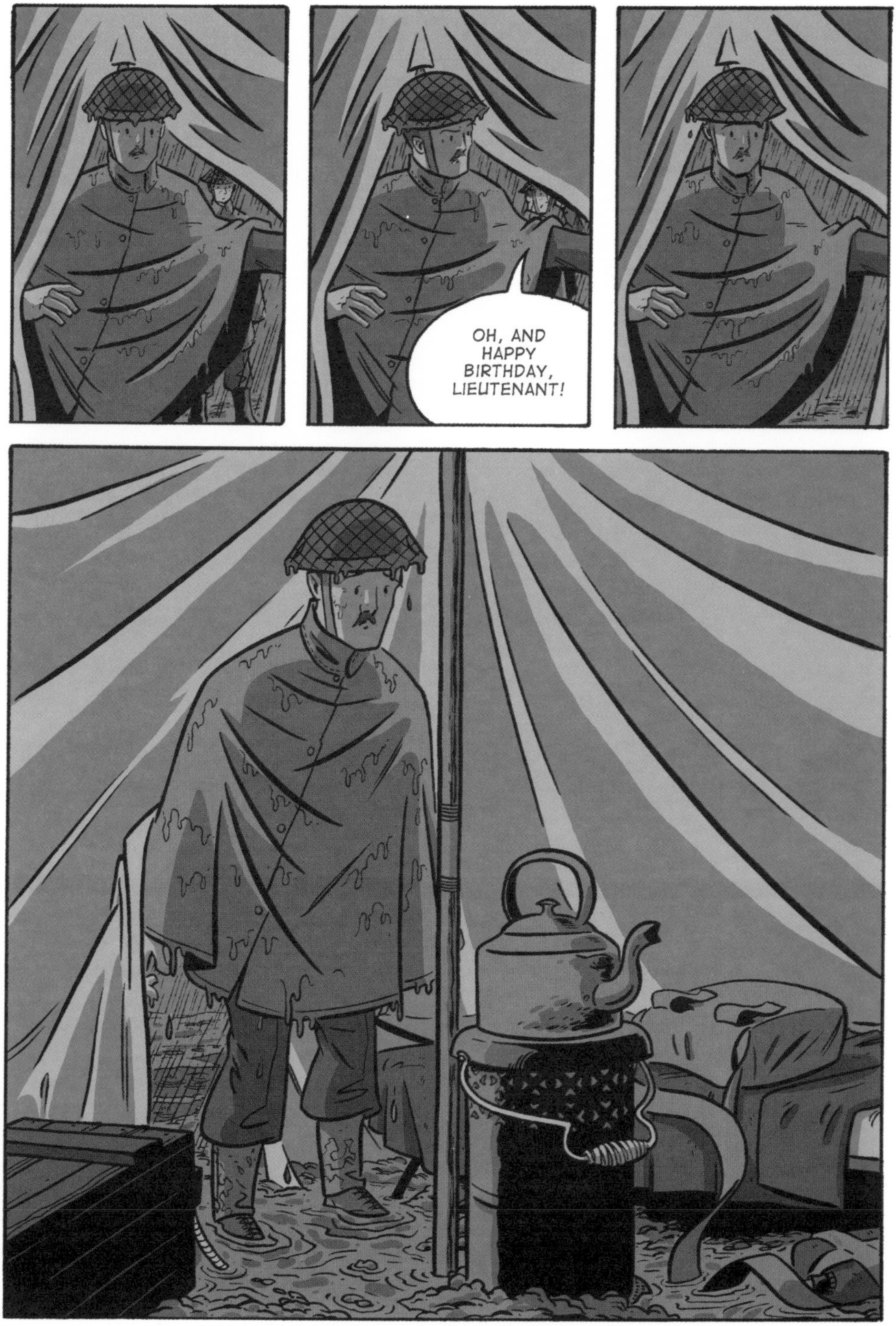
OH, AND HAPPY BIRTHDAY, LIEUTENANT!

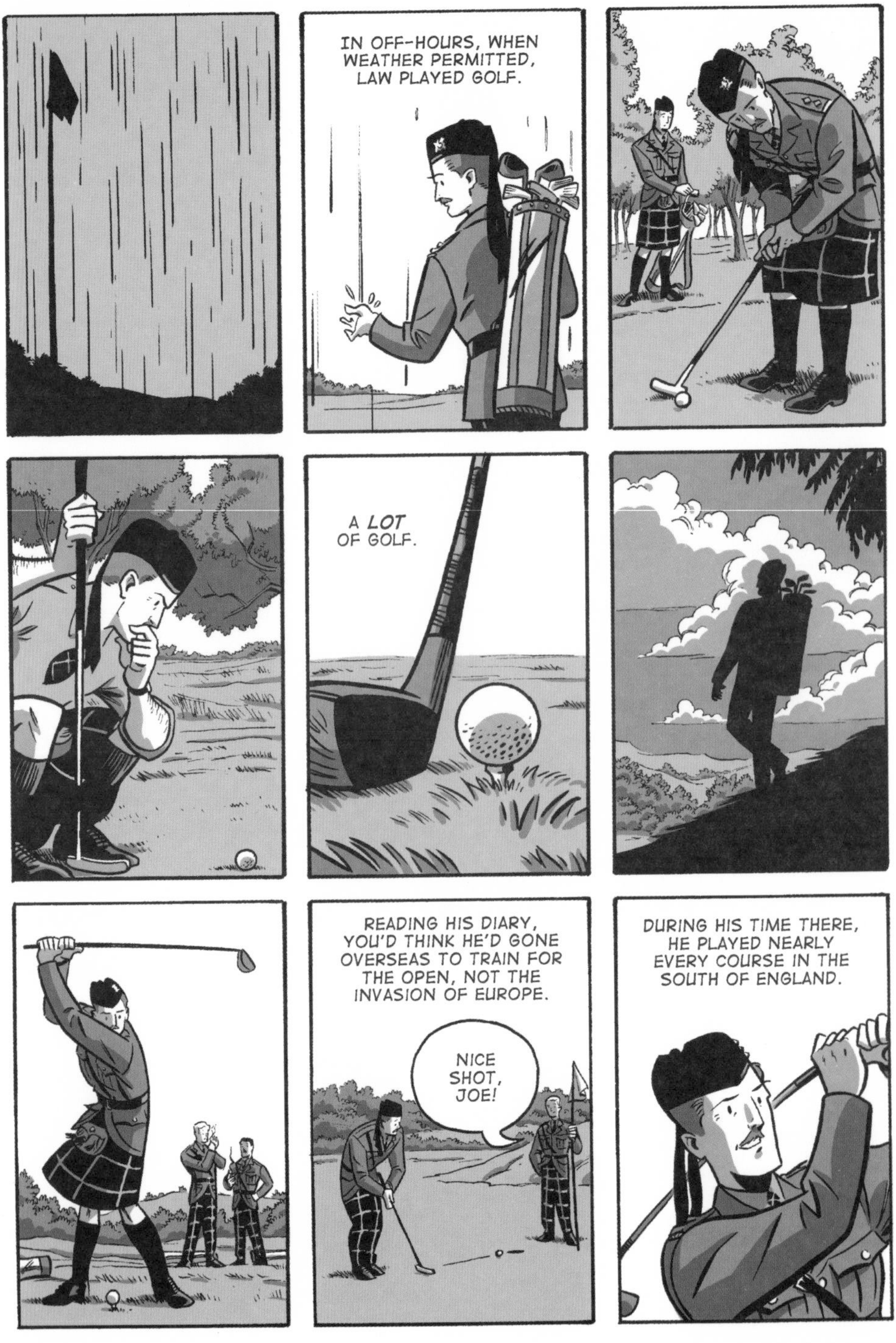
IN OFF-HOURS, WHEN WEATHER PERMITTED, LAW PLAYED GOLF.
A LOT OF GOLF.
READING HIS DIARY, YOU'D THINK HE'D GONE OVERSEAS TO TRAIN FOR THE OPEN, NOT THE INVASION OF EUROPE.
NICE SHOT, JOE!
DURING HIS TIME THERE, HE PLAYED NEARLY EVERY COURSE IN THE SOUTH OF ENGLAND.

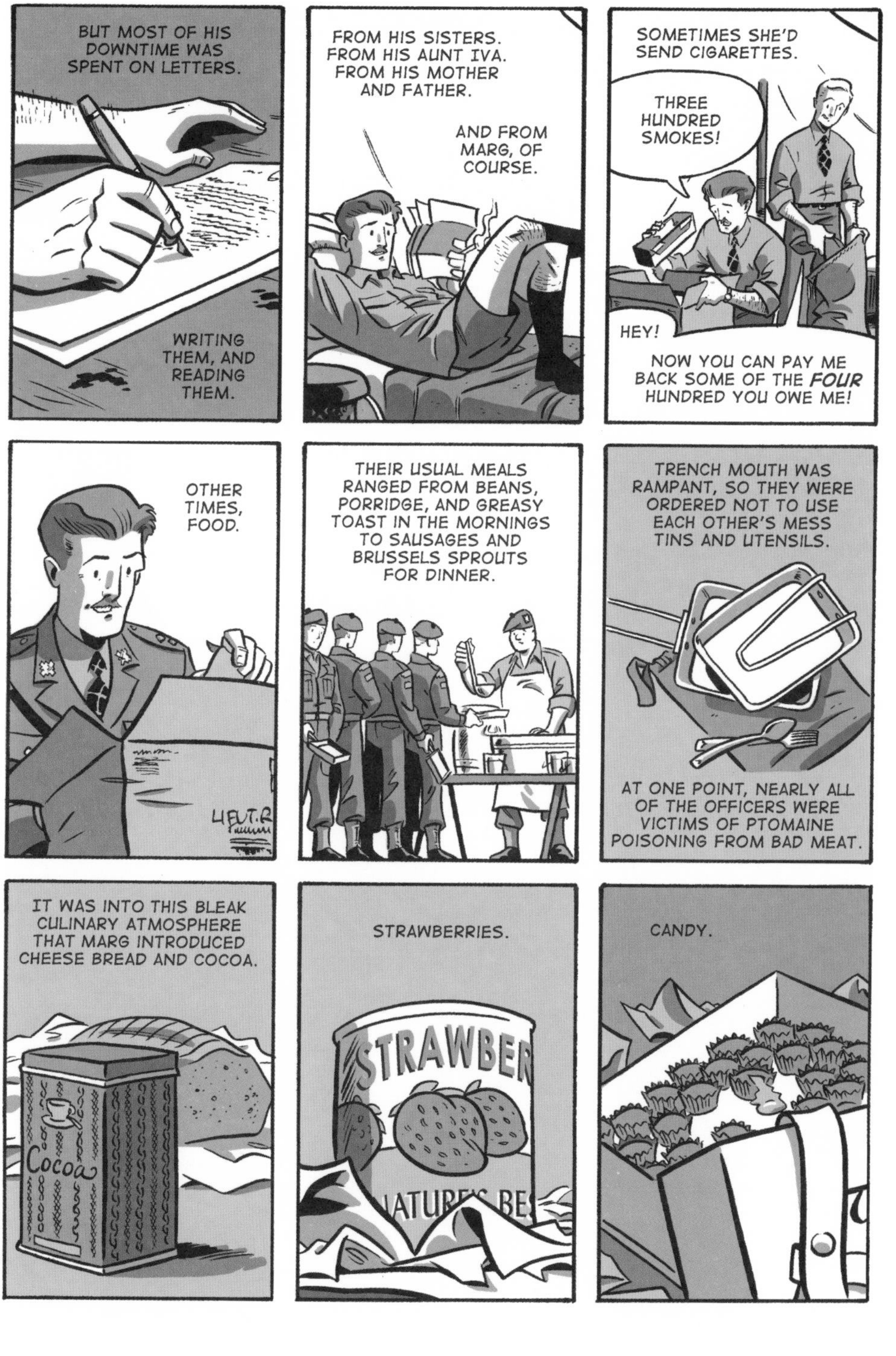
BUT MOST OF HIS DOWNTIME WAS SPENT ON LETTERS.
WRITING THEM, AND READING THEM.
FROM HIS SISTERS. FROM HIS AUNT IVA. FROM HIS MOTHER AND FATHER.
AND FROM MARG, OF COURSE.
SOMETIMES SHE'D SEND CIGARETTES.
THREE HUNDRED SMOKES!
HEY!
NOW YOU CAN PAY ME BACK SOME OF THE *FOUR* HUNDRED YOU OWE ME!
OTHER TIMES, FOOD.
THEIR USUAL MEALS RANGED FROM BEANS, PORRIDGE, AND GREASY TOAST IN THE MORNINGS TO SAUSAGES AND BRUSSELS SPROUTS FOR DINNER.
TRENCH MOUTH WAS RAMPANT, SO THEY WERE ORDERED NOT TO USE EACH OTHER'S MESS TINS AND UTENSILS.
AT ONE POINT, NEARLY ALL OF THE OFFICERS WERE VICTIMS OF PTOMAINE POISONING FROM BAD MEAT.
IT WAS INTO THIS BLEAK CULINARY ATMOSPHERE THAT MARG INTRODUCED CHEESE BREAD AND COCOA.
Cocoa
STRAWBERRIES.
STRAWBER
CANDY.

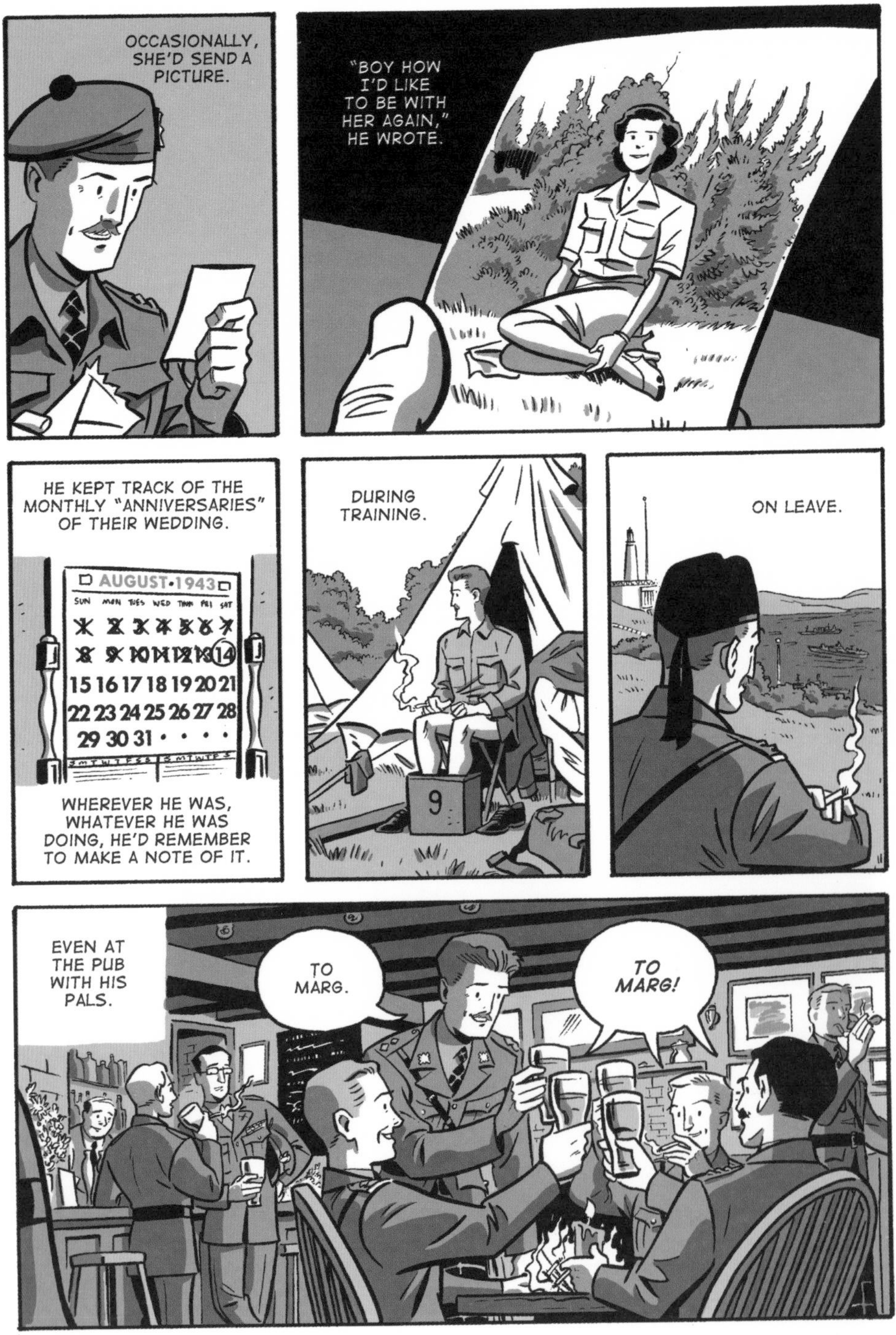
OCCASIONALLY, SHE'D SEND A PICTURE.
"BOY HOW I'D LIKE TO BE WITH HER AGAIN," HE WROTE.
HE KEPT TRACK OF THE MONTHLY "ANNIVERSARIES" OF THEIR WEDDING.
AUGUST•1943
SUN MON TUES WED THUR FRI SAT
1 2 3 4 5 6 7
8 9 10 11 12 13 14
15 16 17 18 19 20 21
22 23 24 25 26 27 28
29 30 31
WHEREVER HE WAS, WHATEVER HE WAS DOING, HE'D REMEMBER TO MAKE A NOTE OF IT.
DURING TRAINING.
9
ON LEAVE.
EVEN AT THE PUB WITH HIS PALS.
TO MARG.
TO MARG!

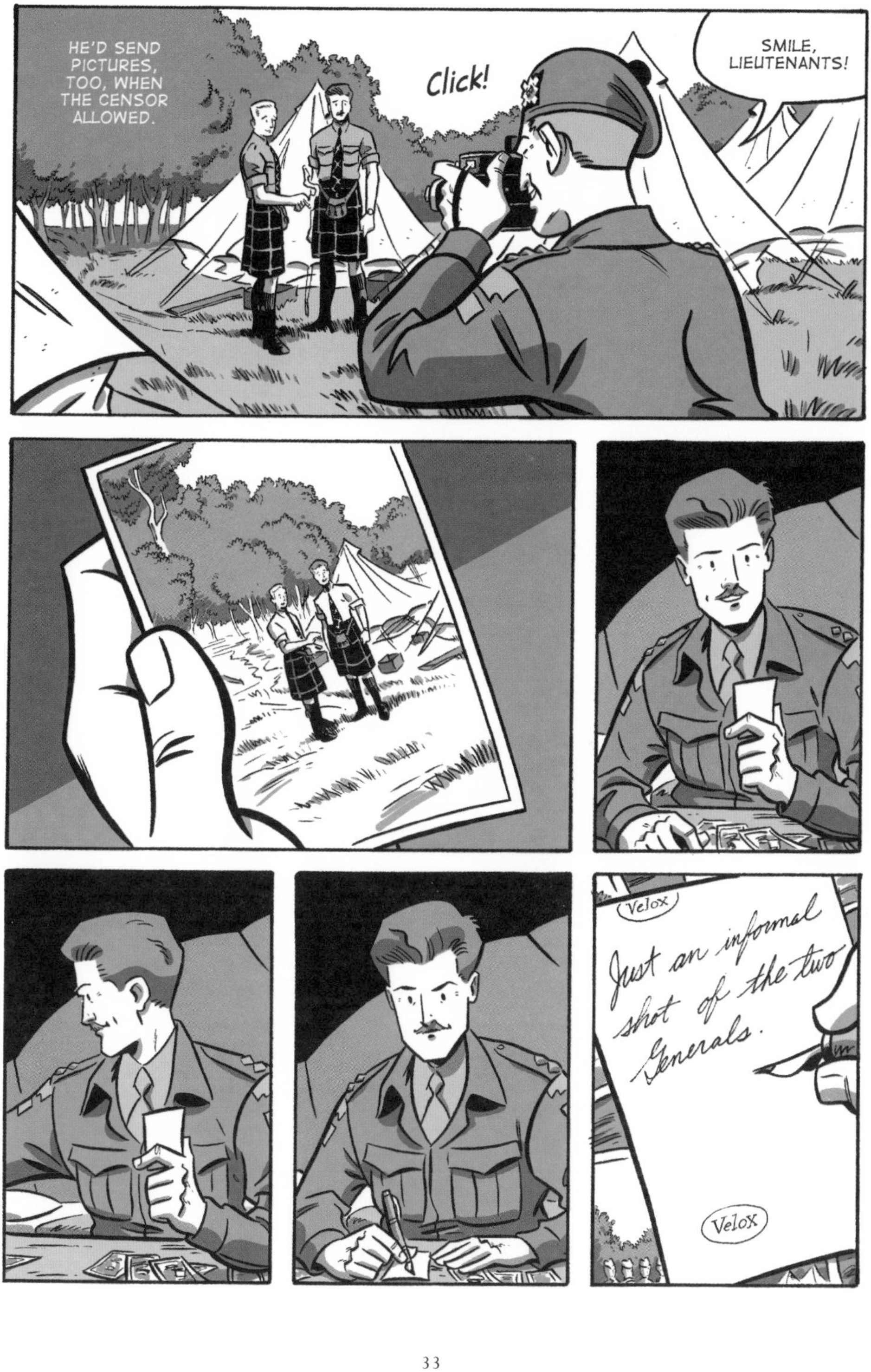
HE'D SEND PICTURES, TOO, WHEN THE CENSOR ALLOWED.
Click!
SMILE, LIEUTENANTS!
Velox
Just an informal shot of the two Generals.
Velox

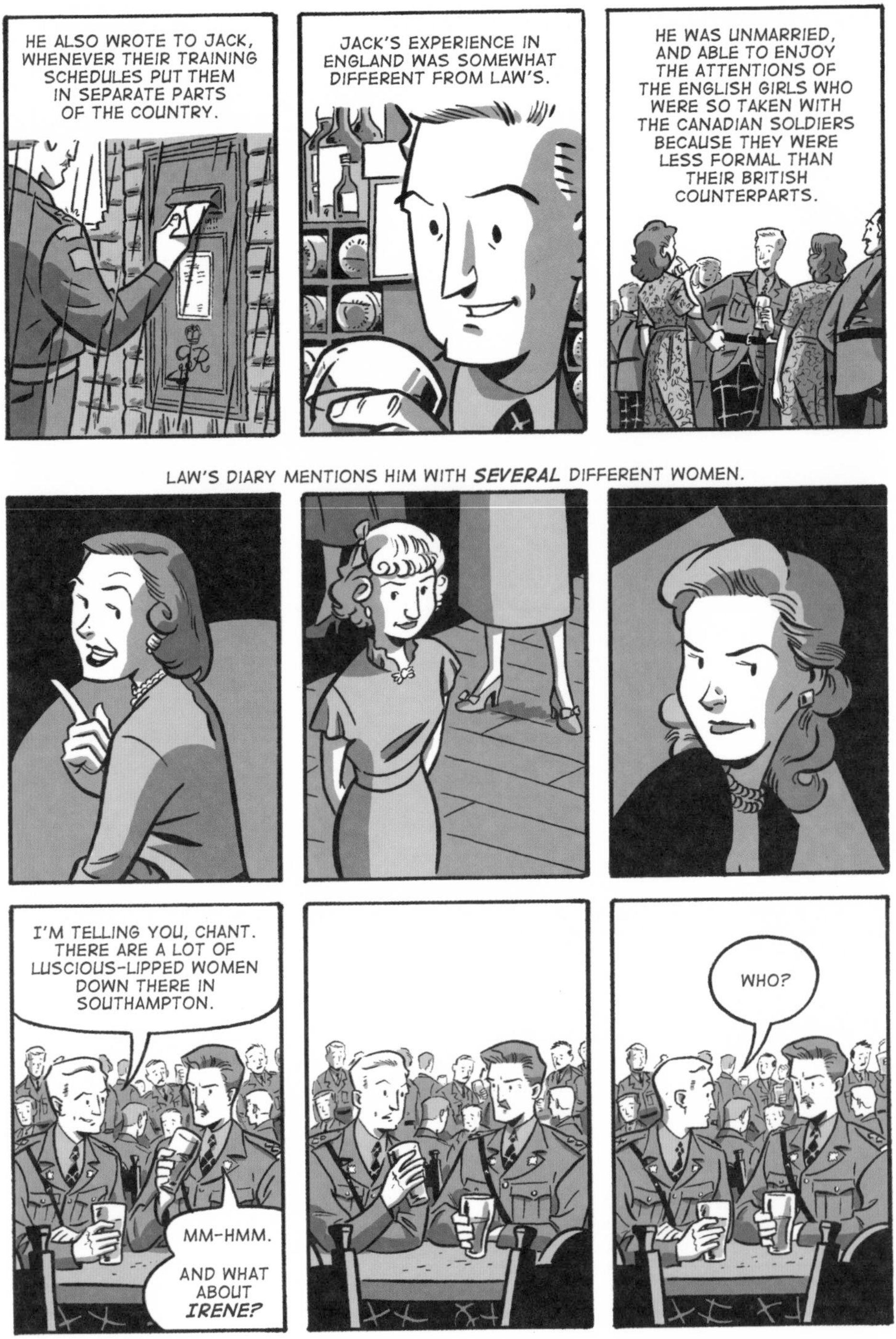
HE ALSO WROTE TO JACK, WHENEVER THEIR TRAINING SCHEDULES PUT THEM IN SEPARATE PARTS OF THE COUNTRY.
JACK'S EXPERIENCE IN ENGLAND WAS SOMEWHAT DIFFERENT FROM LAW'S.
HE WAS UNMARRIED, AND ABLE TO ENJOY THE ATTENTIONS OF THE ENGLISH GIRLS WHO WERE SO TAKEN WITH THE CANADIAN SOLDIERS BECAUSE THEY WERE LESS FORMAL THAN THEIR BRITISH COUNTERPARTS.
LAW'S DIARY MENTIONS HIM WITH *SEVERAL* DIFFERENT WOMEN.
I'M TELLING YOU, CHANT. THERE ARE A LOT OF LUSCIOUS-LIPPED WOMEN DOWN THERE IN SOUTHAMPTON.
MM-HMM.
AND WHAT ABOUT *IRENE?*
WHO?

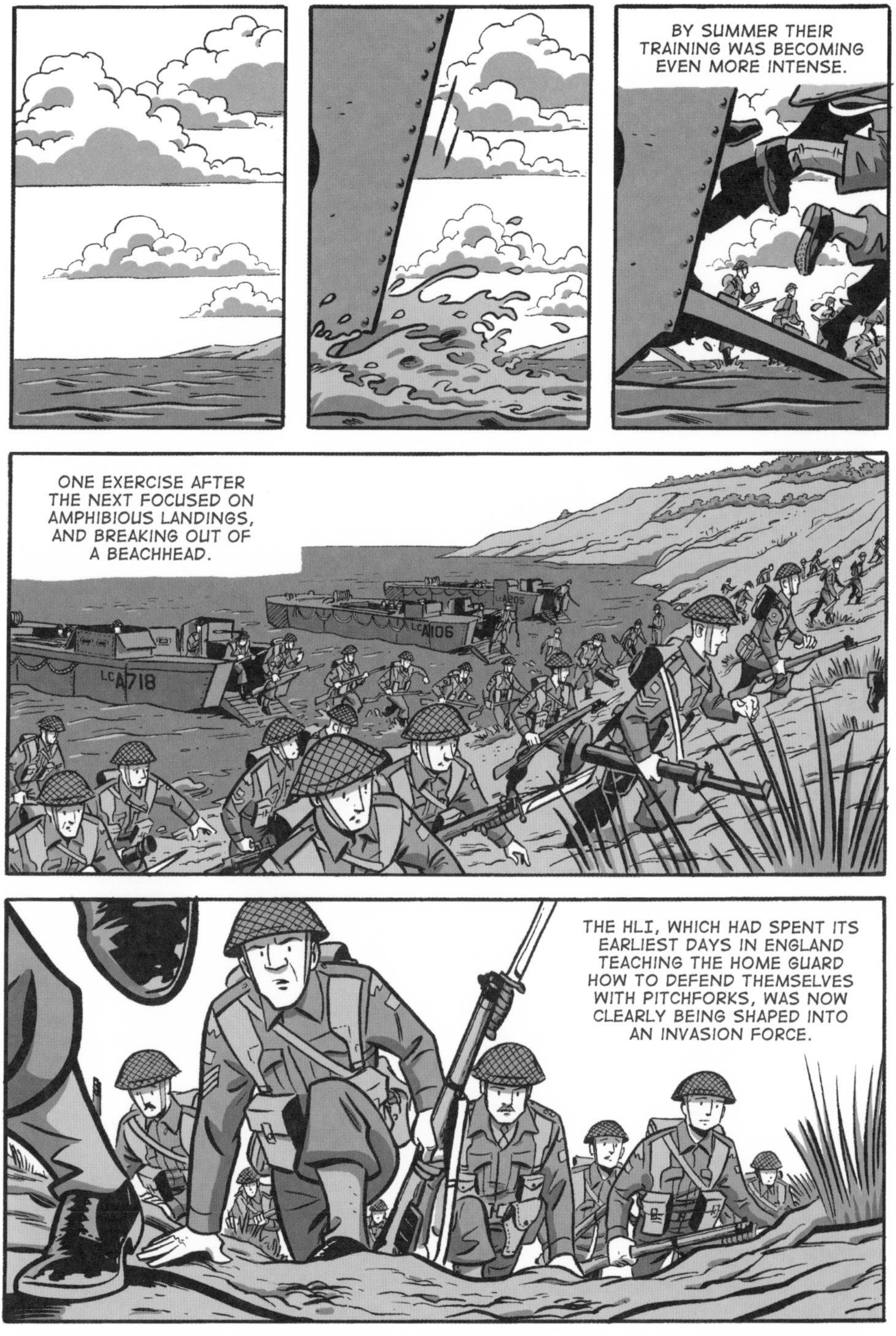
BY SUMMER THEIR TRAINING WAS BECOMING EVEN MORE INTENSE.
ONE EXERCISE AFTER THE NEXT FOCUSED ON AMPHIBIOUS LANDINGS, AND BREAKING OUT OF A BEACHHEAD.
THE HLI, WHICH HAD SPENT ITS EARLIEST DAYS IN ENGLAND TEACHING THE HOME GUARD HOW TO DEFEND THEMSELVES WITH PITCHFORKS, WAS NOW CLEARLY BEING SHAPED INTO AN INVASION FORCE.

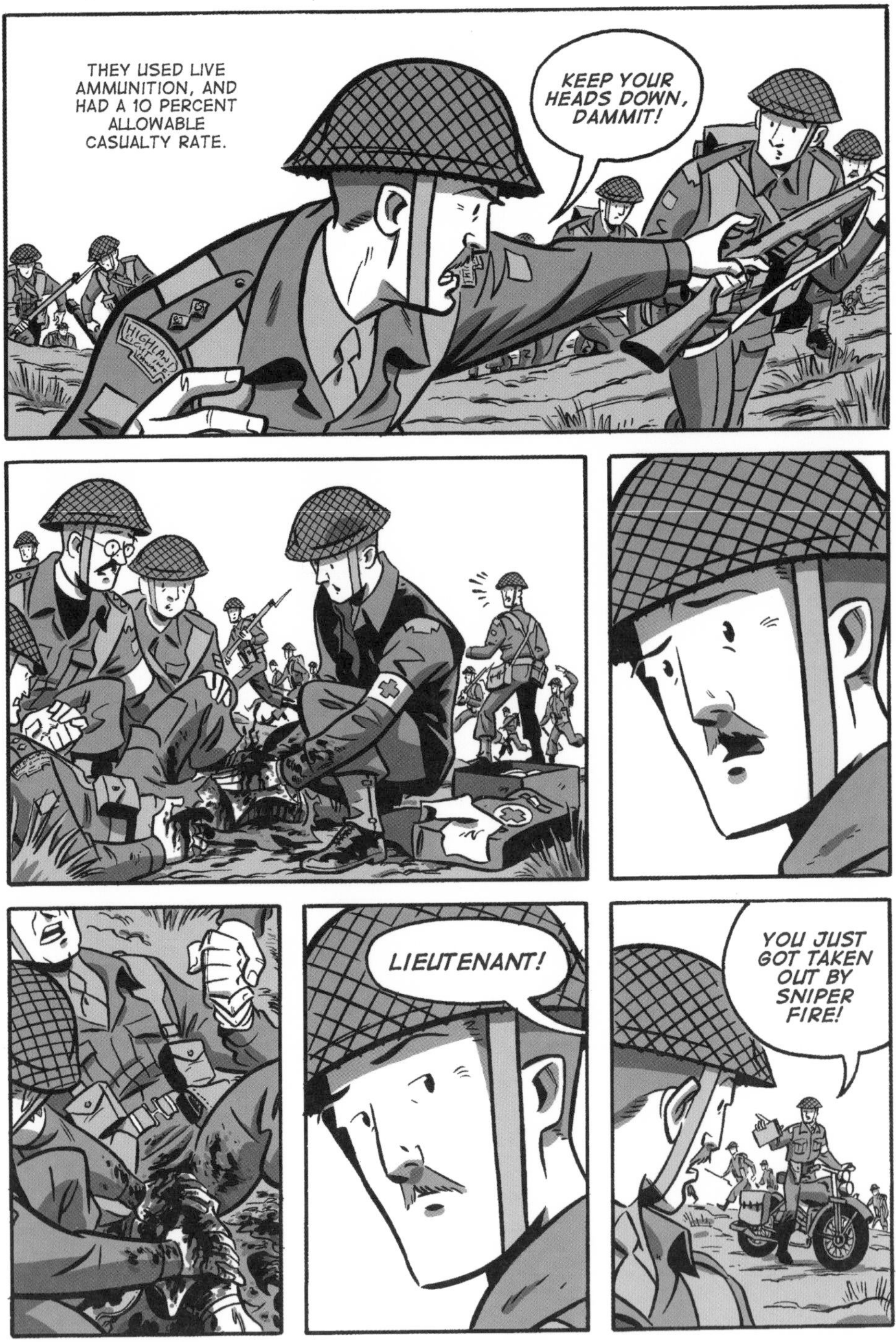
THEY USED LIVE AMMUNITION, AND HAD A 10 PERCENT ALLOWABLE CASUALTY RATE.
KEEP YOUR HEADS DOWN, DAMMIT!
LIEUTENANT!
YOU JUST GOT TAKEN OUT BY SNIPER FIRE!

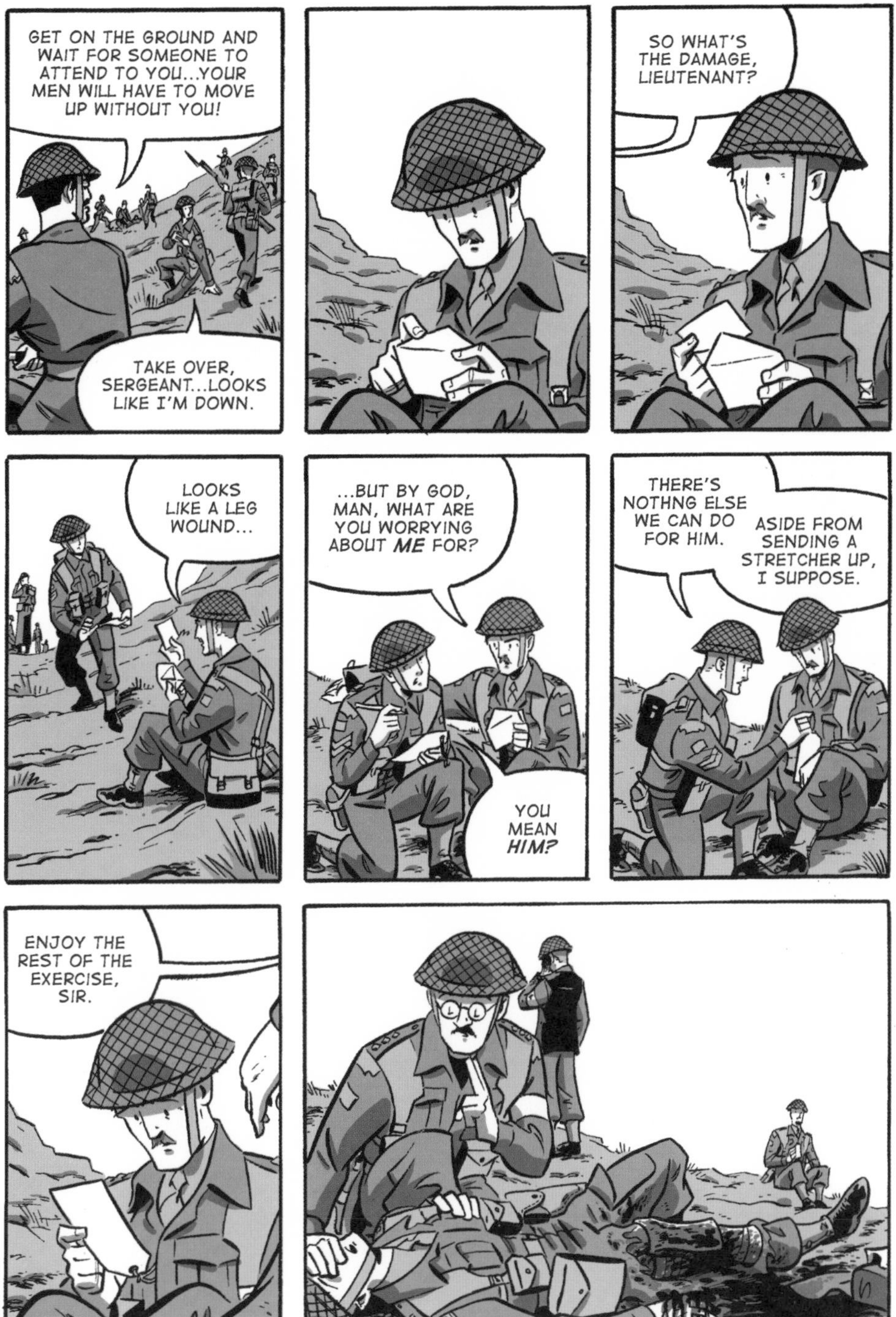
GET ON THE GROUND AND WAIT FOR SOMEONE TO ATTEND TO YOU...YOUR MEN WILL HAVE TO MOVE UP WITHOUT YOU!
TAKE OVER, SERGEANT...LOOKS LIKE I'M DOWN.
SO WHAT'S THE DAMAGE, LIEUTENANT?
LOOKS LIKE A LEG WOUND...
...BUT BY GOD, MAN, WHAT ARE YOU WORRYING ABOUT **ME** FOR?
YOU MEAN **HIM?**
THERE'S NOTHNG ELSE WE CAN DO FOR HIM.
ASIDE FROM SENDING A STRETCHER UP, I SUPPOSE.
ENJOY THE REST OF THE EXERCISE, SIR.

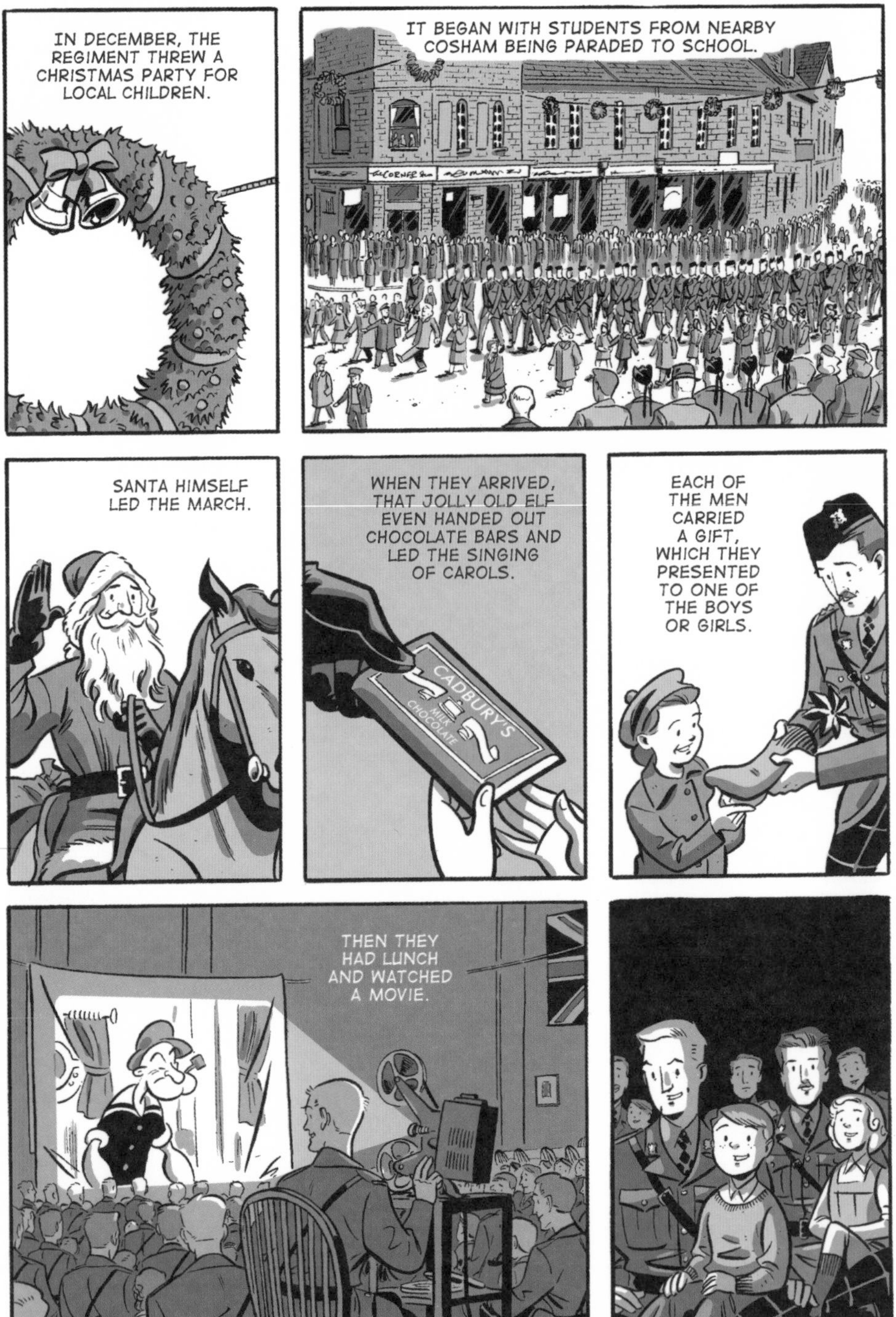
IN DECEMBER, THE REGIMENT THREW A CHRISTMAS PARTY FOR LOCAL CHILDREN.
IT BEGAN WITH STUDENTS FROM NEARBY COSHAM BEING PARADED TO SCHOOL.
SANTA HIMSELF LED THE MARCH.
WHEN THEY ARRIVED, THAT JOLLY OLD ELF EVEN HANDED OUT CHOCOLATE BARS AND LED THE SINGING OF CAROLS.
CADBURY'S
MILK CHOCOLATE
EACH OF THE MEN CARRIED A GIFT, WHICH THEY PRESENTED TO ONE OF THE BOYS OR GIRLS.
THEN THEY HAD LUNCH AND WATCHED A MOVIE.

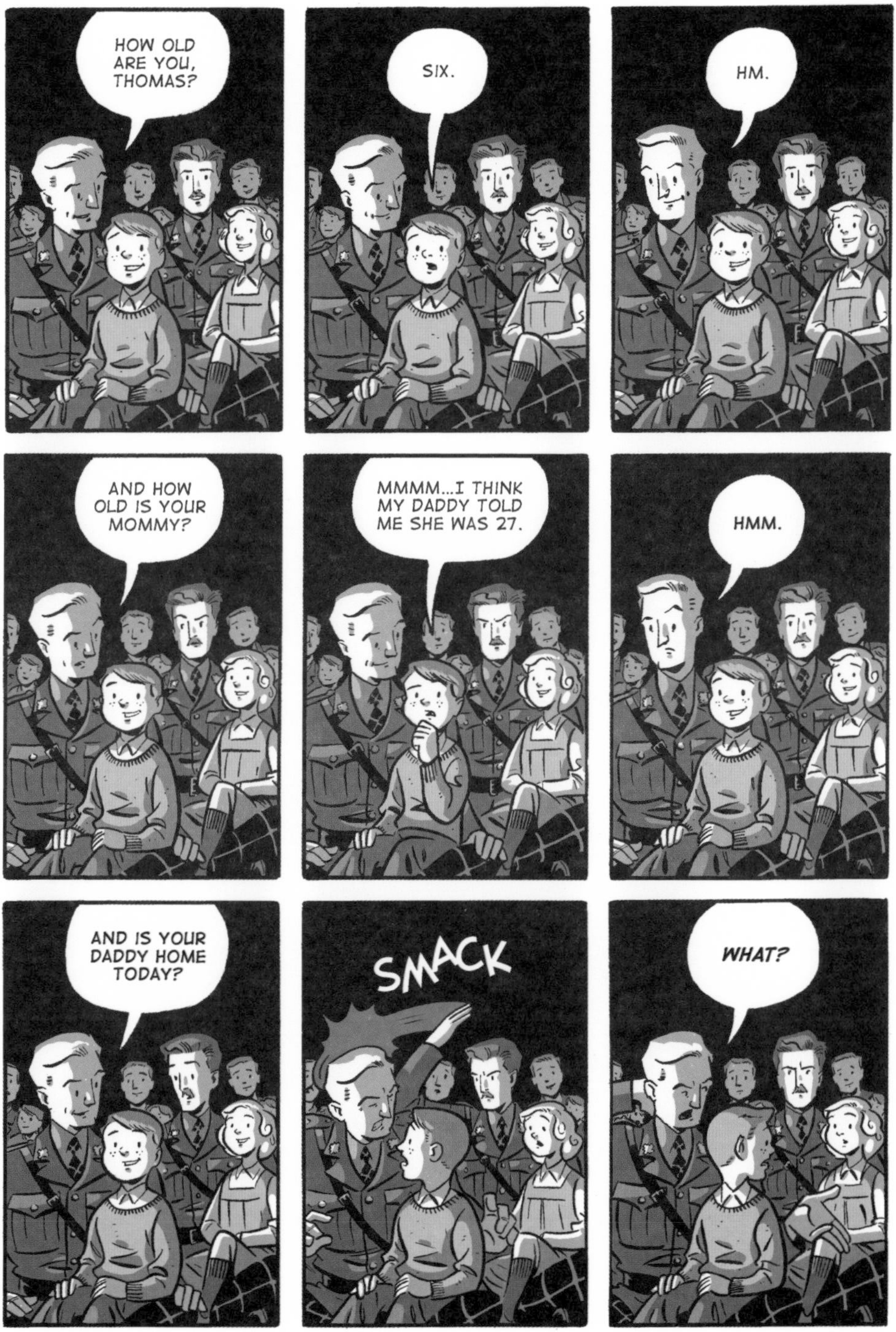
HOW OLD ARE YOU, THOMAS?
SIX.
HM.
AND HOW OLD IS YOUR MOMMY?
MMMM...I THINK MY DADDY TOLD ME SHE WAS 27.
HMM.
AND IS YOUR DADDY HOME TODAY?
SMACK
*WHAT?*

ALL OF THE MEN AGREED IT WAS THE HIGHLIGHT OF THE HLI'S HOLIDAY FESTIVITIES, AND THEY RETURNED TO CAMP IN GREAT SPIRITS.

FOR MANY, IT WOULD BE THEIR LAST CHRISTMAS.

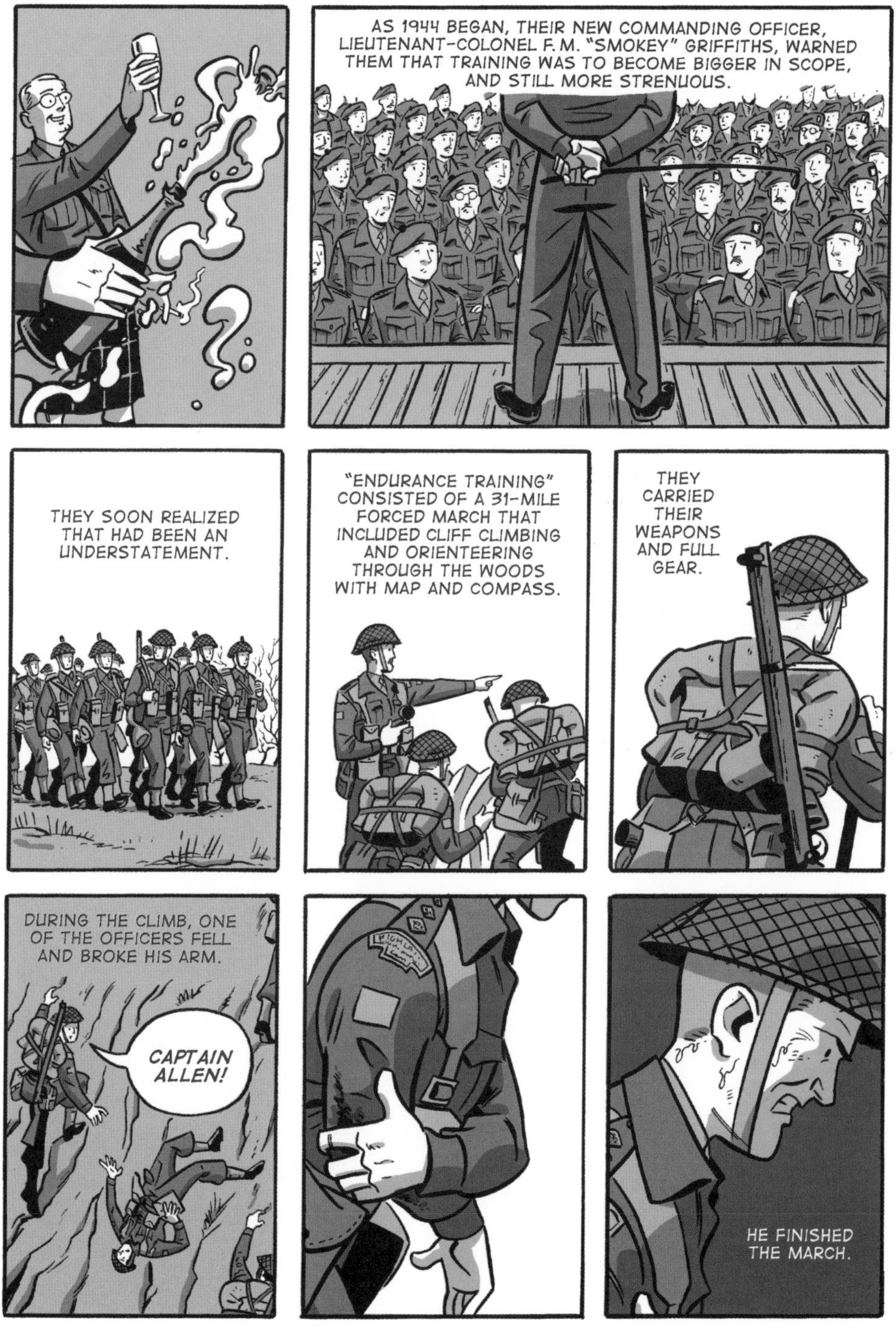
AS 1944 BEGAN, THEIR NEW COMMANDING OFFICER, LIEUTENANT-COLONEL F. M. "SMOKEY" GRIFFITHS, WARNED THEM THAT TRAINING WAS TO BECOME BIGGER IN SCOPE, AND STILL MORE STRENUOUS.
THEY SOON REALIZED THAT HAD BEEN AN UNDERSTATEMENT.
"ENDURANCE TRAINING" CONSISTED OF A 31-MILE FORCED MARCH THAT INCLUDED CLIFF CLIMBING AND ORIENTEERING THROUGH THE WOODS WITH MAP AND COMPASS.
THEY CARRIED THEIR WEAPONS AND FULL GEAR.
DURING THE CLIMB, ONE OF THE OFFICERS FELL AND BROKE HIS ARM.
CAPTAIN ALLEN!
HE FINISHED THE MARCH.

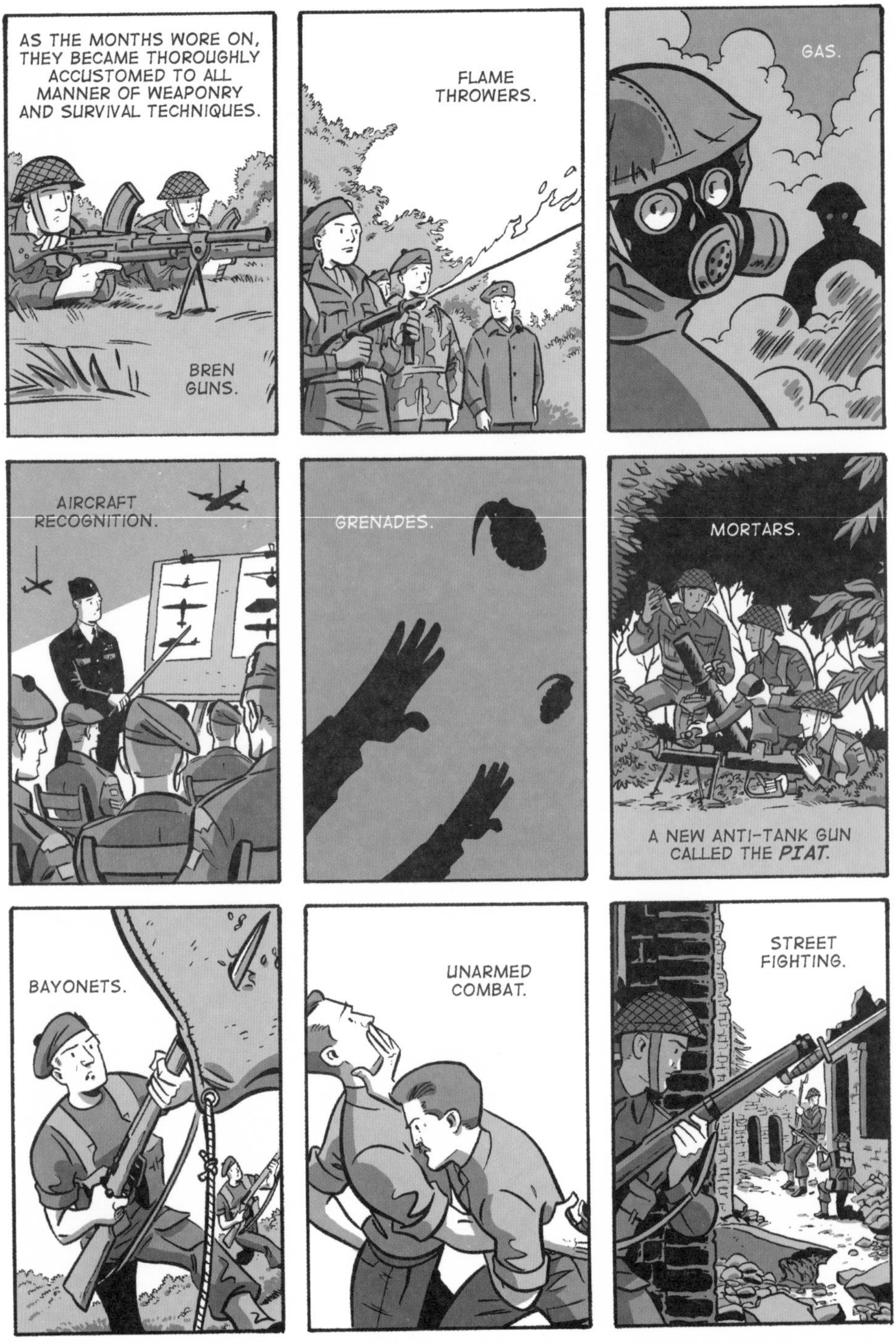
AS THE MONTHS WORE ON, THEY BECAME THOROUGHLY ACCUSTOMED TO ALL MANNER OF WEAPONRY AND SURVIVAL TECHNIQUES.
BREN GUNS.
FLAME THROWERS.
GAS.
AIRCRAFT RECOGNITION.
GRENADES.
MORTARS.
A NEW ANTI-TANK GUN CALLED THE *PIAT*.
BAYONETS.
UNARMED COMBAT.
STREET FIGHTING.

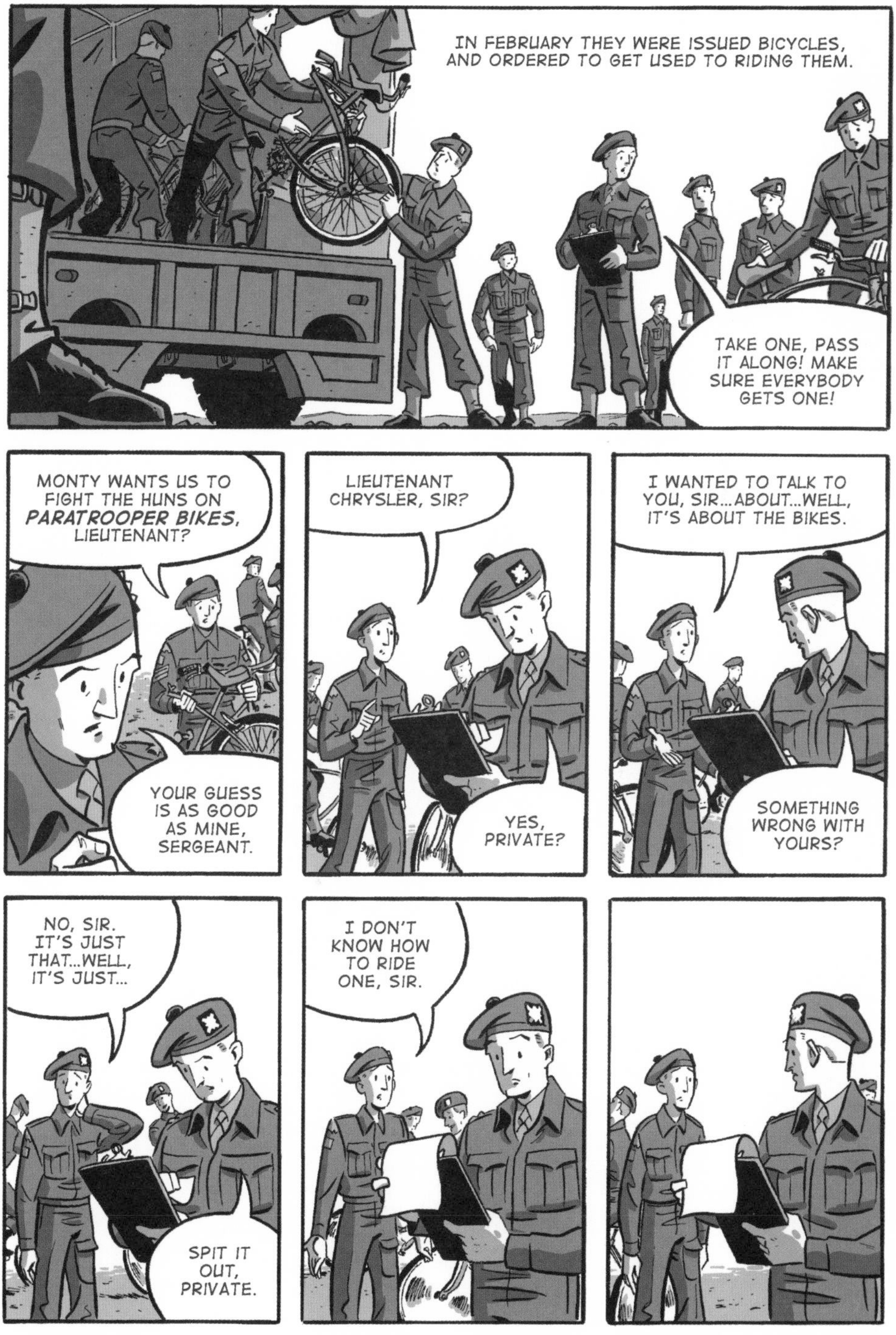

IN FEBRUARY THEY WERE ISSUED BICYCLES, AND ORDERED TO GET USED TO RIDING THEM.
TAKE ONE, PASS IT ALONG! MAKE SURE EVERYBODY GETS ONE!
MONTY WANTS US TO FIGHT THE HUNS ON *PARATROOPER BIKES*, LIEUTENANT?
YOUR GUESS IS AS GOOD AS MINE, SERGEANT.
LIEUTENANT CHRYSLER, SIR?
YES, PRIVATE?
I WANTED TO TALK TO YOU, SIR...ABOUT...WELL, IT'S ABOUT THE BIKES.
SOMETHING WRONG WITH YOURS?
NO, SIR. IT'S JUST THAT...WELL, IT'S JUST...
SPIT IT OUT, PRIVATE.
I DON'T KNOW HOW TO RIDE ONE, SIR.

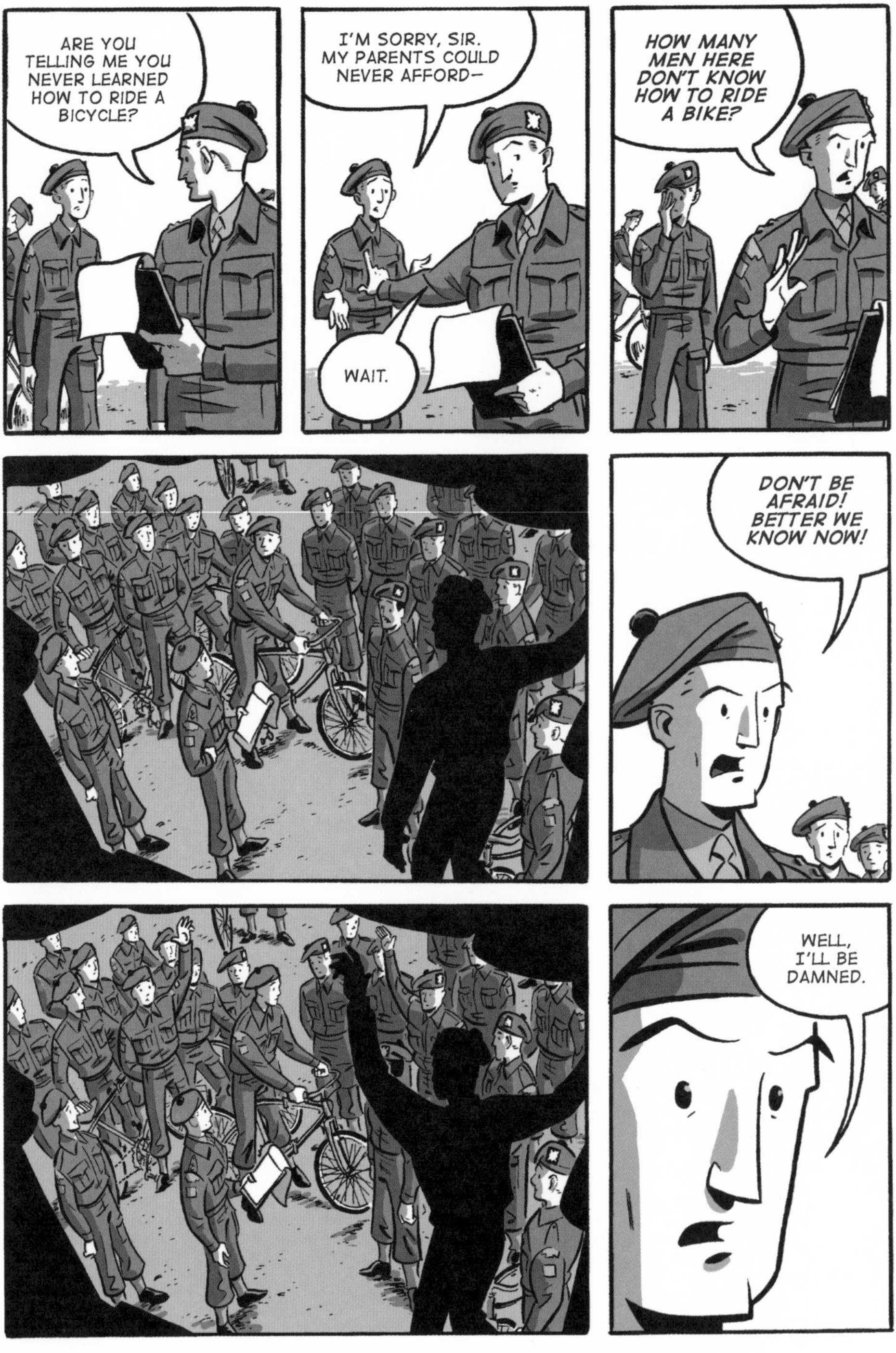
ARE YOU TELLING ME YOU NEVER LEARNED HOW TO RIDE A BICYCLE?
I'M SORRY, SIR. MY PARENTS COULD NEVER AFFORD—
WAIT.
HOW MANY MEN HERE DON'T KNOW HOW TO RIDE A BIKE?
DON'T BE AFRAID! BETTER WE KNOW NOW!
WELL, I'LL BE DAMNED.

SO TRAINING COVERED THAT, TOO.

OKAY, I'M LETTING GO...!

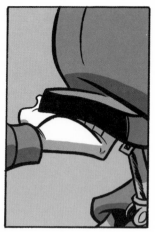

THE BICYCLES WERE COLLAPSIBLE, AND PUT TOGETHER WITH WING NUTS.

YOU ALL RIGHT, PRIVATE?

SOME VETERANS OF THE HLI CURSE THEM TO THIS DAY.

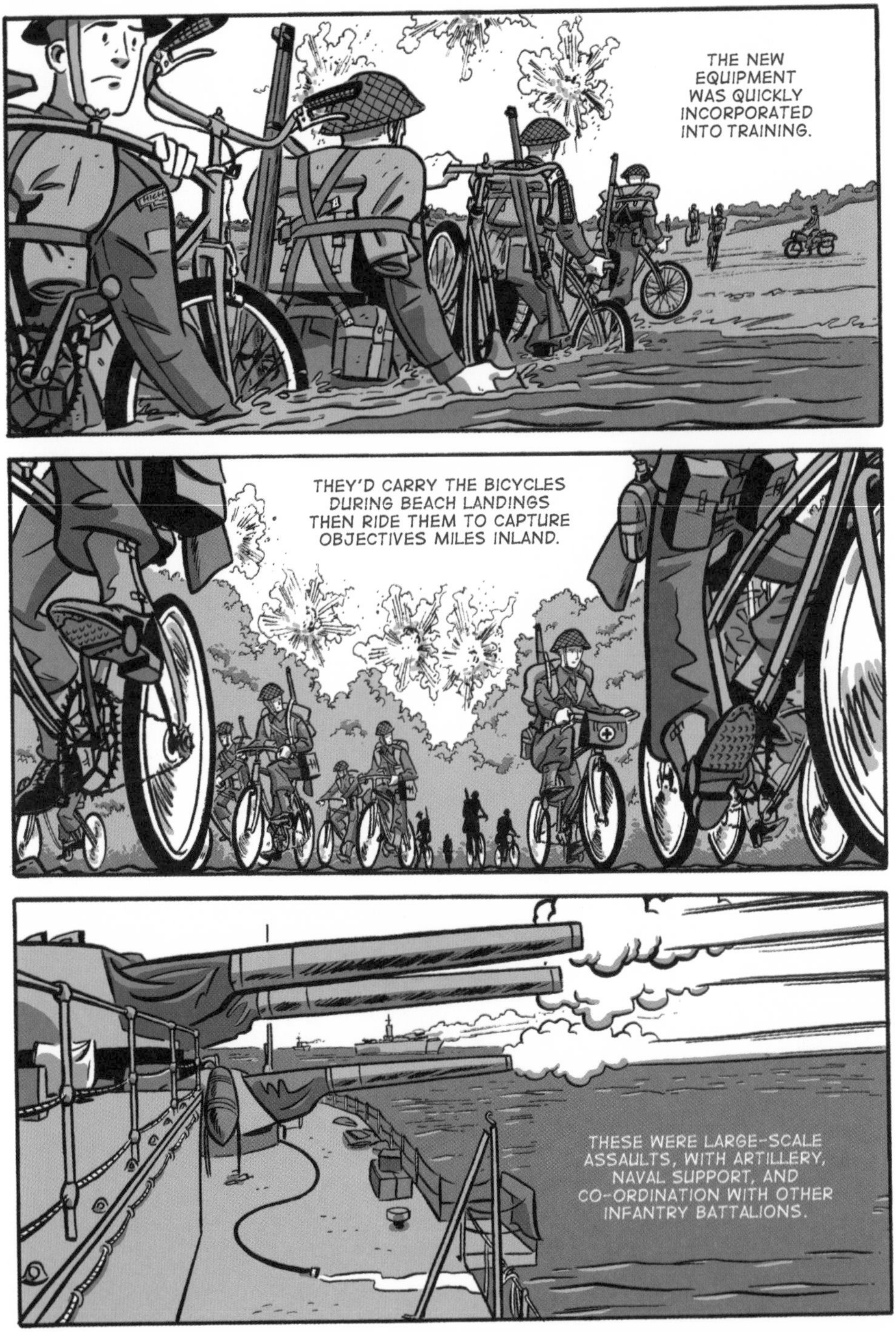
THE NEW EQUIPMENT WAS QUICKLY INCORPORATED INTO TRAINING.
THEY'D CARRY THE BICYCLES DURING BEACH LANDINGS THEN RIDE THEM TO CAPTURE OBJECTIVES MILES INLAND.
THESE WERE LARGE-SCALE ASSAULTS, WITH ARTILLERY, NAVAL SUPPORT, AND CO-ORDINATION WITH OTHER INFANTRY BATTALIONS.

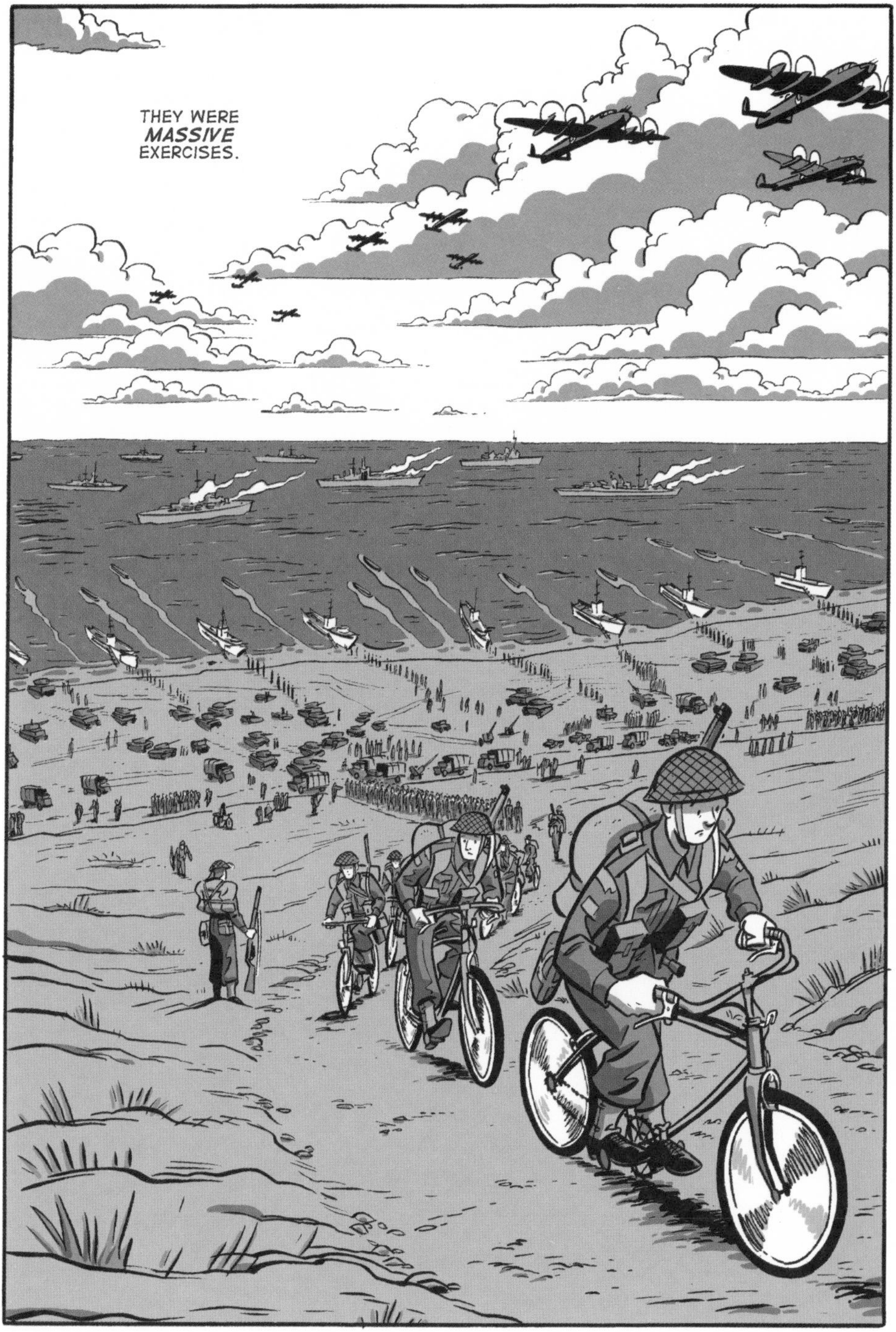
THEY WERE *MASSIVE* EXERCISES.

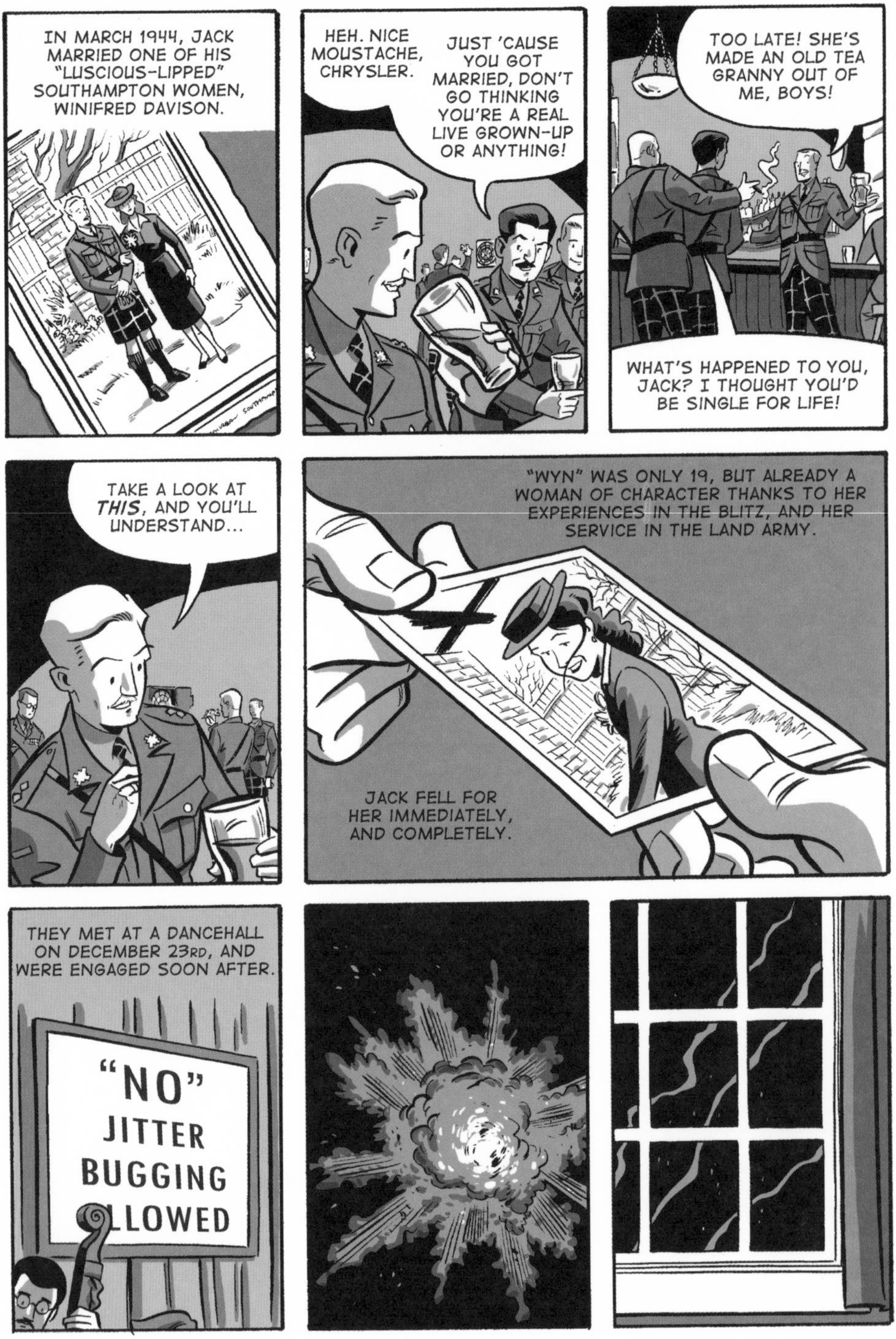
IN MARCH 1944, JACK MARRIED ONE OF HIS "LUSCIOUS-LIPPED" SOUTHAMPTON WOMEN, WINIFRED DAVISON.
HEH. NICE MOUSTACHE, CHRYSLER.
JUST 'CAUSE YOU GOT MARRIED, DON'T GO THINKING YOU'RE A REAL LIVE GROWN-UP OR ANYTHING!
TOO LATE! SHE'S MADE AN OLD TEA GRANNY OUT OF ME, BOYS!
WHAT'S HAPPENED TO YOU, JACK? I THOUGHT YOU'D BE SINGLE FOR LIFE!
TAKE A LOOK AT THIS, AND YOU'LL UNDERSTAND...
"WYN" WAS ONLY 19, BUT ALREADY A WOMAN OF CHARACTER THANKS TO HER EXPERIENCES IN THE BLITZ, AND HER SERVICE IN THE LAND ARMY.
JACK FELL FOR HER IMMEDIATELY, AND COMPLETELY.
THEY MET AT A DANCEHALL ON DECEMBER 23RD, AND WERE ENGAGED SOON AFTER.
"NO" JITTER BUGGING LLOWED

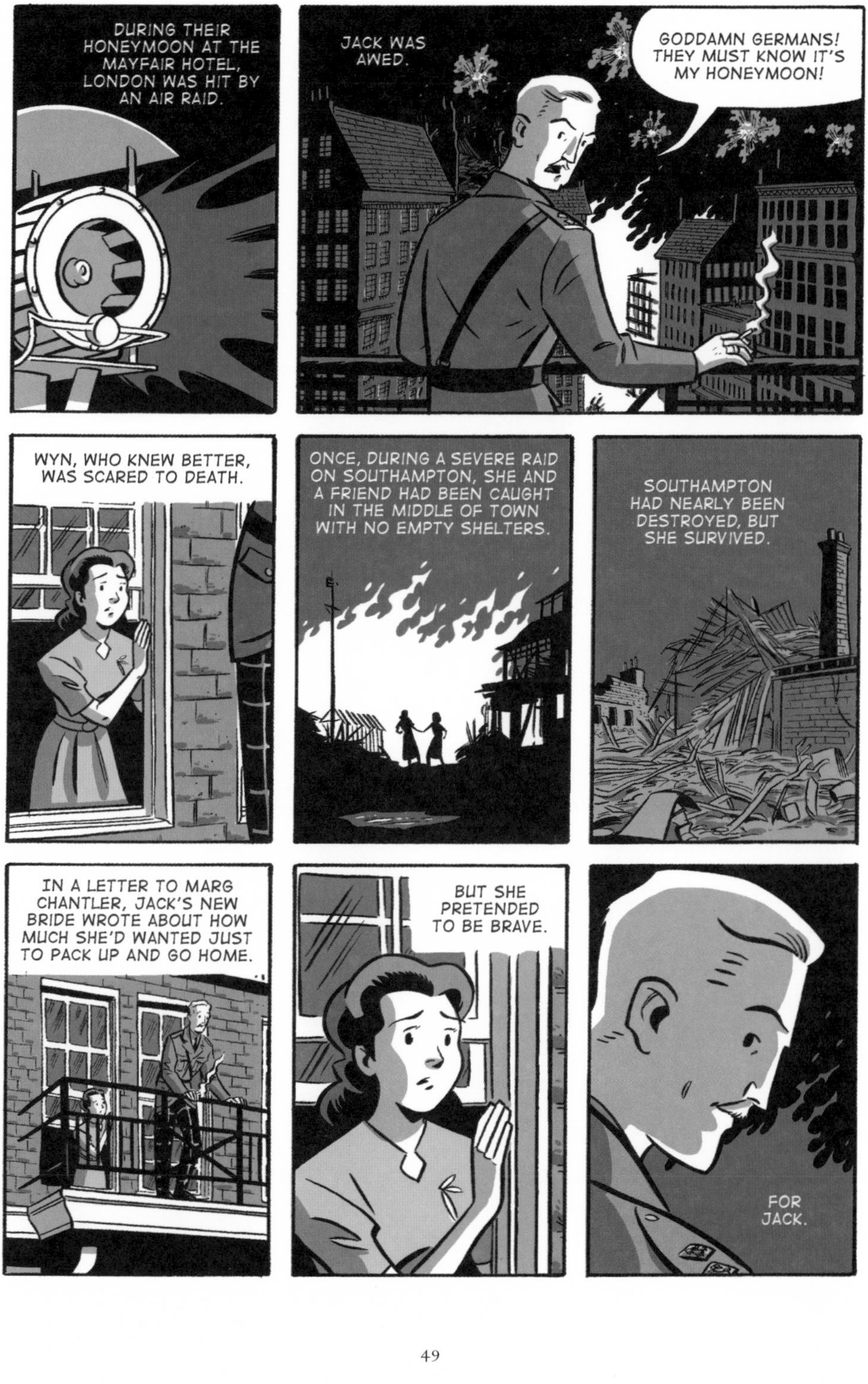
DURING THEIR HONEYMOON AT THE MAYFAIR HOTEL, LONDON WAS HIT BY AN AIR RAID.
JACK WAS AWED.
GODDAMN GERMANS! THEY MUST KNOW IT'S MY HONEYMOON!
WYN, WHO KNEW BETTER, WAS SCARED TO DEATH.
ONCE, DURING A SEVERE RAID ON SOUTHAMPTON, SHE AND A FRIEND HAD BEEN CAUGHT IN THE MIDDLE OF TOWN WITH NO EMPTY SHELTERS.
SOUTHAMPTON HAD NEARLY BEEN DESTROYED, BUT SHE SURVIVED.
IN A LETTER TO MARG CHANTLER, JACK'S NEW BRIDE WROTE ABOUT HOW MUCH SHE'D WANTED JUST TO PACK UP AND GO HOME.
BUT SHE PRETENDED TO BE BRAVE.
FOR JACK.

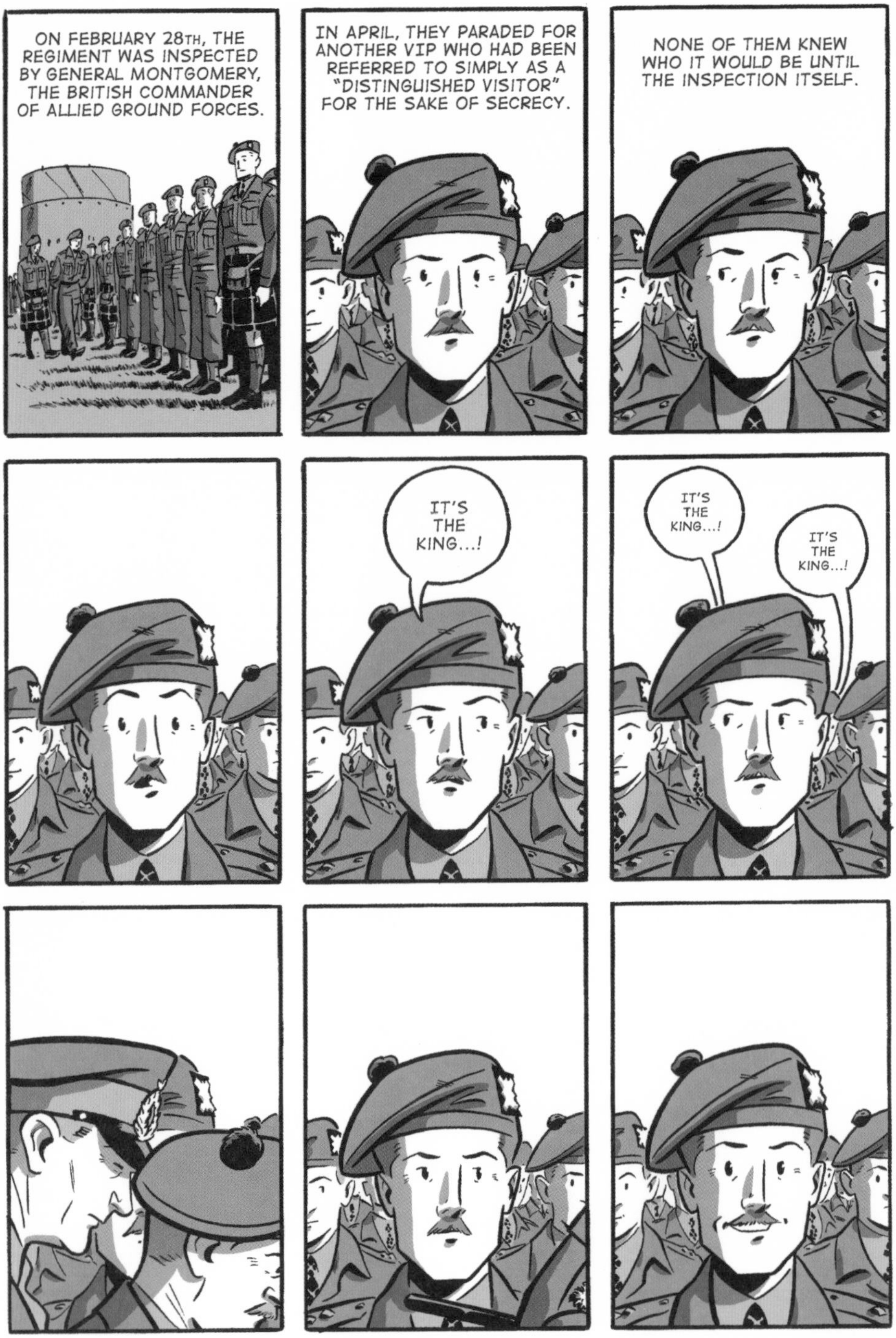
ON FEBRUARY 28TH, THE REGIMENT WAS INSPECTED BY GENERAL MONTGOMERY, THE BRITISH COMMANDER OF ALLIED GROUND FORCES.
IN APRIL, THEY PARADED FOR ANOTHER VIP WHO HAD BEEN REFERRED TO SIMPLY AS A "DISTINGUISHED VISITOR" FOR THE SAKE OF SECRECY.
NONE OF THEM KNEW WHO IT WOULD BE UNTIL THE INSPECTION ITSELF.
IT'S THE KING...!
IT'S THE KING...!
IT'S THE KING...!

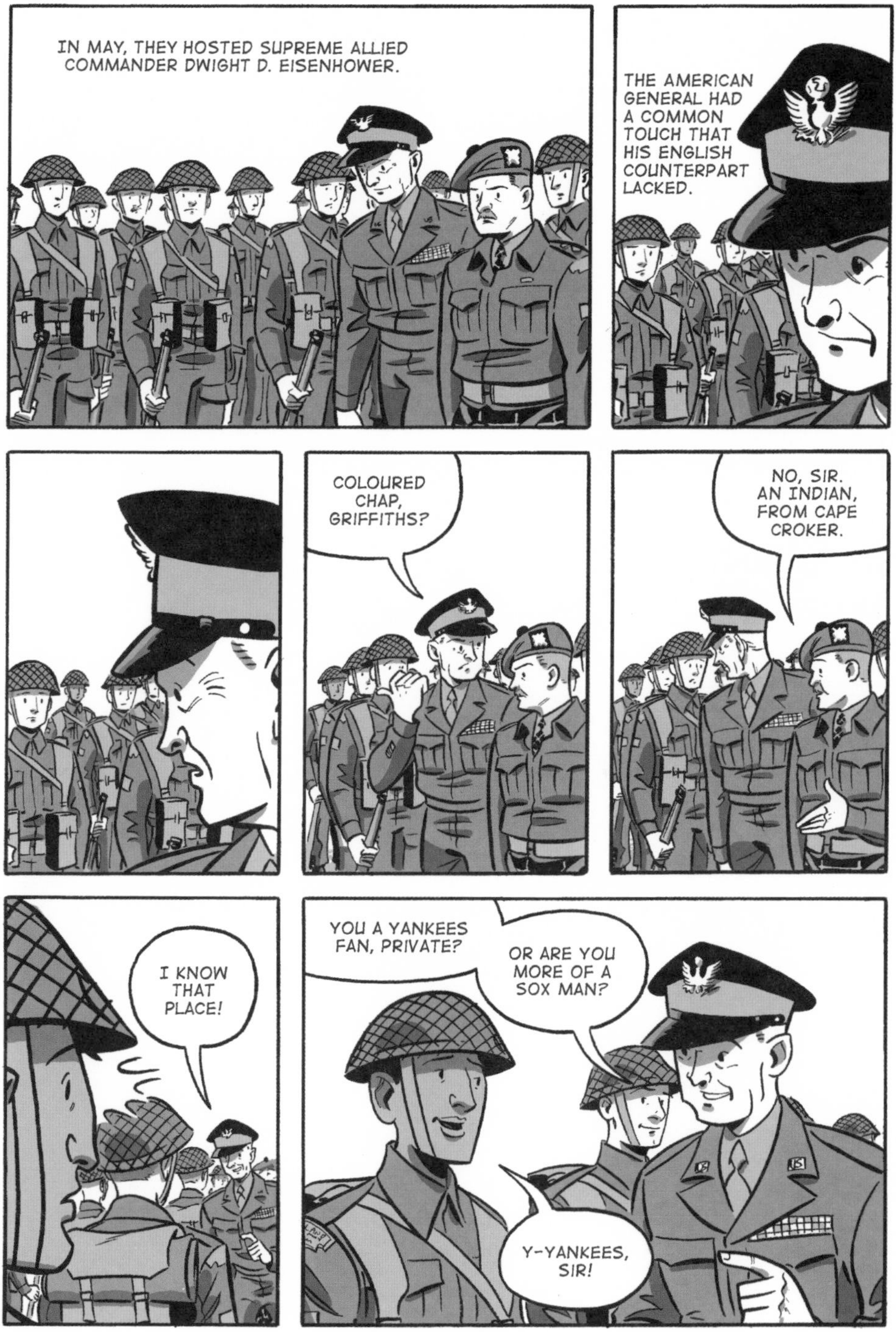
IN MAY, THEY HOSTED SUPREME ALLIED COMMANDER DWIGHT D. EISENHOWER.
THE AMERICAN GENERAL HAD A COMMON TOUCH THAT HIS ENGLISH COUNTERPART LACKED.
COLOURED CHAP, GRIFFITHS?
NO, SIR. AN INDIAN, FROM CAPE CROKER.
I KNOW THAT PLACE!
YOU A YANKEES FAN, PRIVATE?
OR ARE YOU MORE OF A SOX MAN?
Y-YANKEES, SIR!

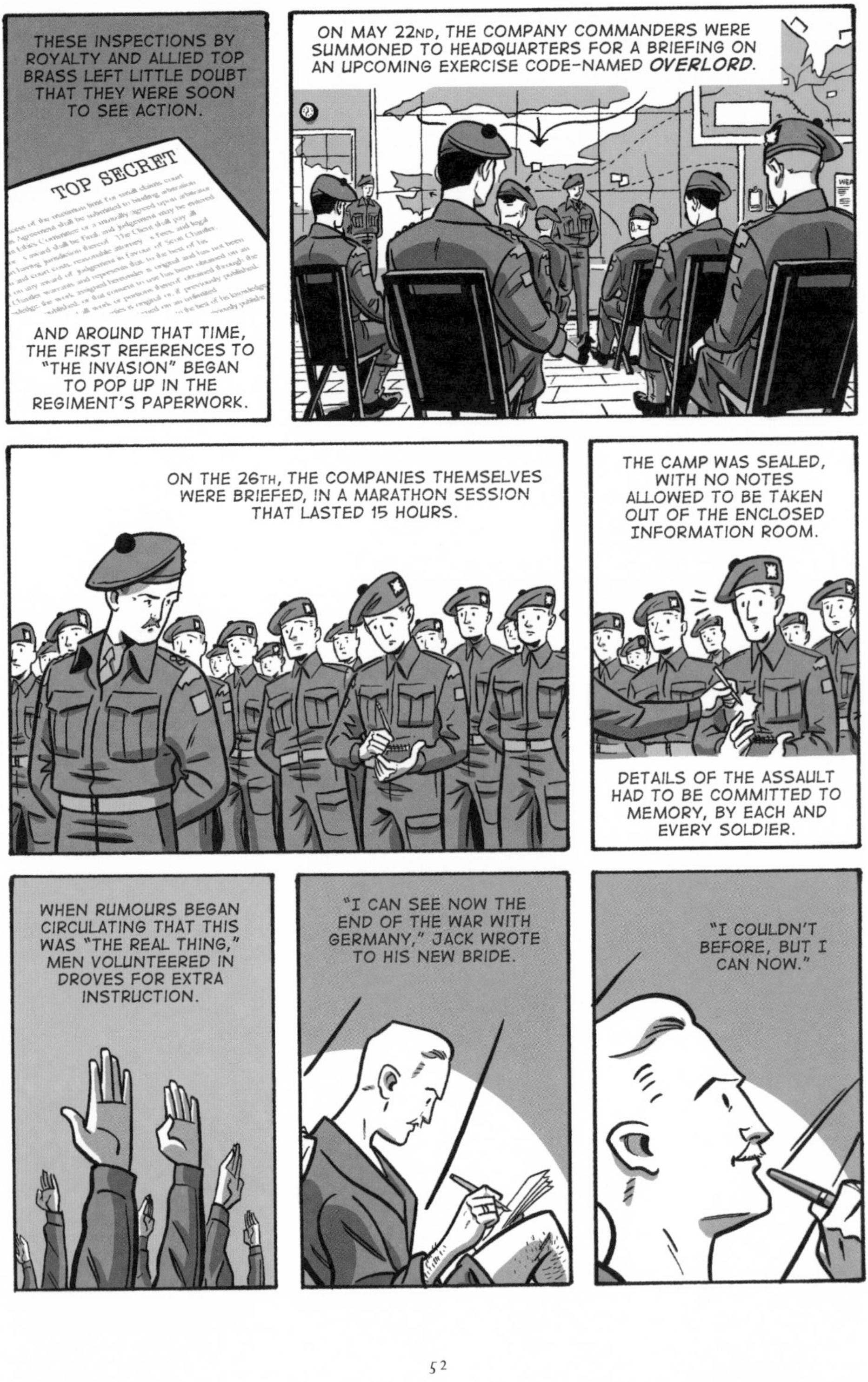
THESE INSPECTIONS BY ROYALTY AND ALLIED TOP BRASS LEFT LITTLE DOUBT THAT THEY WERE SOON TO SEE ACTION.
TOP SECRET
AND AROUND THAT TIME, THE FIRST REFERENCES TO "THE INVASION" BEGAN TO POP UP IN THE REGIMENT'S PAPERWORK.
ON MAY 22ND, THE COMPANY COMMANDERS WERE SUMMONED TO HEADQUARTERS FOR A BRIEFING ON AN UPCOMING EXERCISE CODE-NAMED OVERLORD.
ON THE 26TH, THE COMPANIES THEMSELVES WERE BRIEFED, IN A MARATHON SESSION THAT LASTED 15 HOURS.
THE CAMP WAS SEALED, WITH NO NOTES ALLOWED TO BE TAKEN OUT OF THE ENCLOSED INFORMATION ROOM.
DETAILS OF THE ASSAULT HAD TO BE COMMITTED TO MEMORY, BY EACH AND EVERY SOLDIER.
WHEN RUMOURS BEGAN CIRCULATING THAT THIS WAS "THE REAL THING," MEN VOLUNTEERED IN DROVES FOR EXTRA INSTRUCTION.
"I CAN SEE NOW THE END OF THE WAR WITH GERMANY," JACK WROTE TO HIS NEW BRIDE.
"I COULDN'T BEFORE, BUT I CAN NOW."

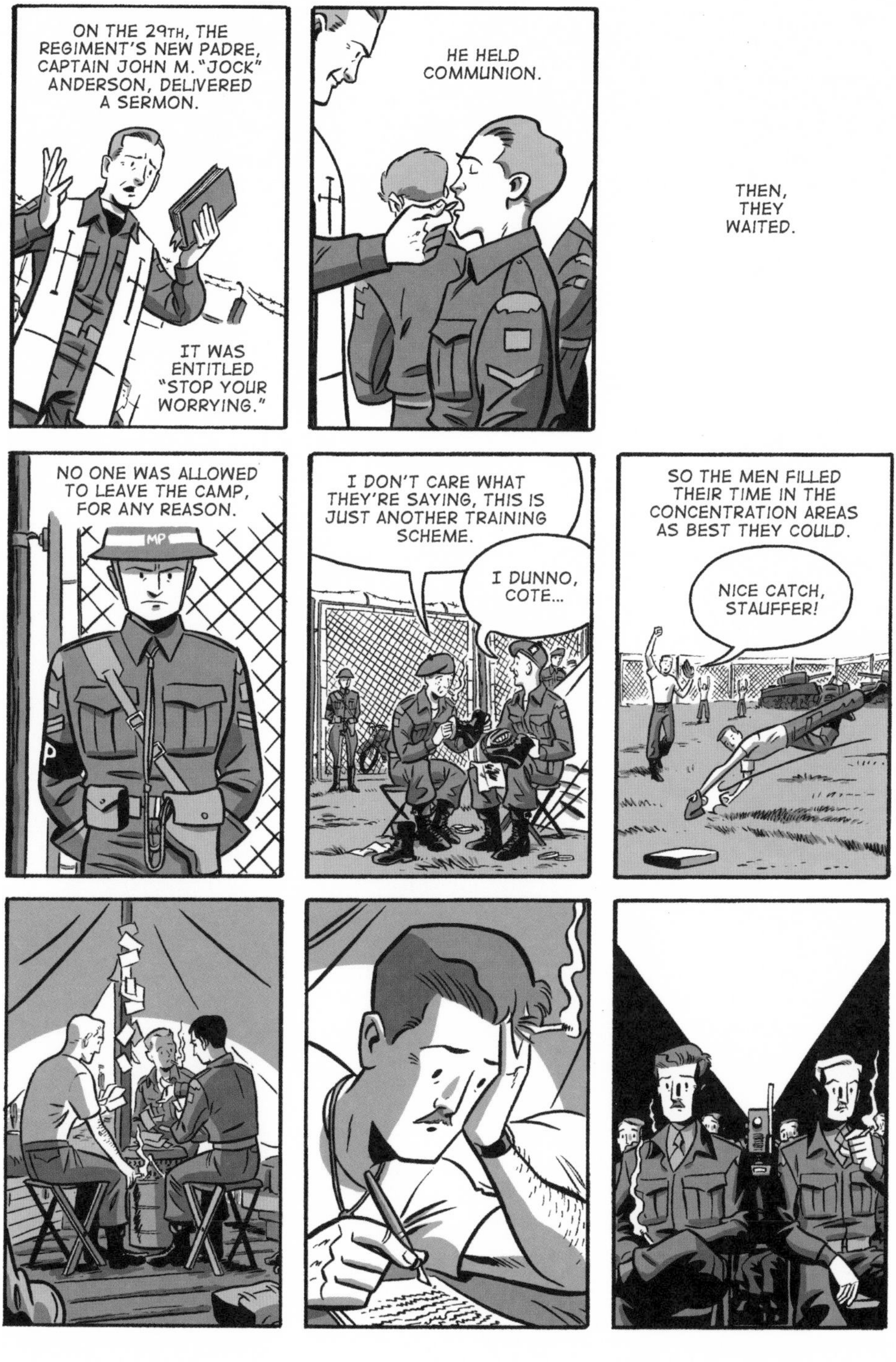
ON THE 29TH, THE REGIMENT'S NEW PADRE, CAPTAIN JOHN M. "JOCK" ANDERSON, DELIVERED A SERMON.
IT WAS ENTITLED "STOP YOUR WORRYING."
HE HELD COMMUNION.
THEN, THEY WAITED.
NO ONE WAS ALLOWED TO LEAVE THE CAMP, FOR ANY REASON.
MP
P
I DON'T CARE WHAT THEY'RE SAYING, THIS IS JUST ANOTHER TRAINING SCHEME.
I DUNNO, COTE...
SO THE MEN FILLED THEIR TIME IN THE CONCENTRATION AREAS AS BEST THEY COULD.
NICE CATCH, STAUFFER!

JUNE 3RD, 1944, WAS ONE OF THE HOTTEST DAYS IN DECADES IN THE SOUTH OF ENGLAND.

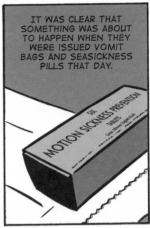

IT WAS CLEAR THAT SOMETHING WAS ABOUT TO HAPPEN WHEN THEY WERE ISSUED VOMIT BAGS AND SEASICKNESS PILLS THAT DAY.

MOTION SICKNESS PREVENTION TABLETS

SIR!

LIEUTENANT CHANTLER!

HM.

WAKE UP, SIR!

CHRIST...I ...IT'S TWO IN THE MORNING.

I KNOW, SIR.

THIS IS IT.

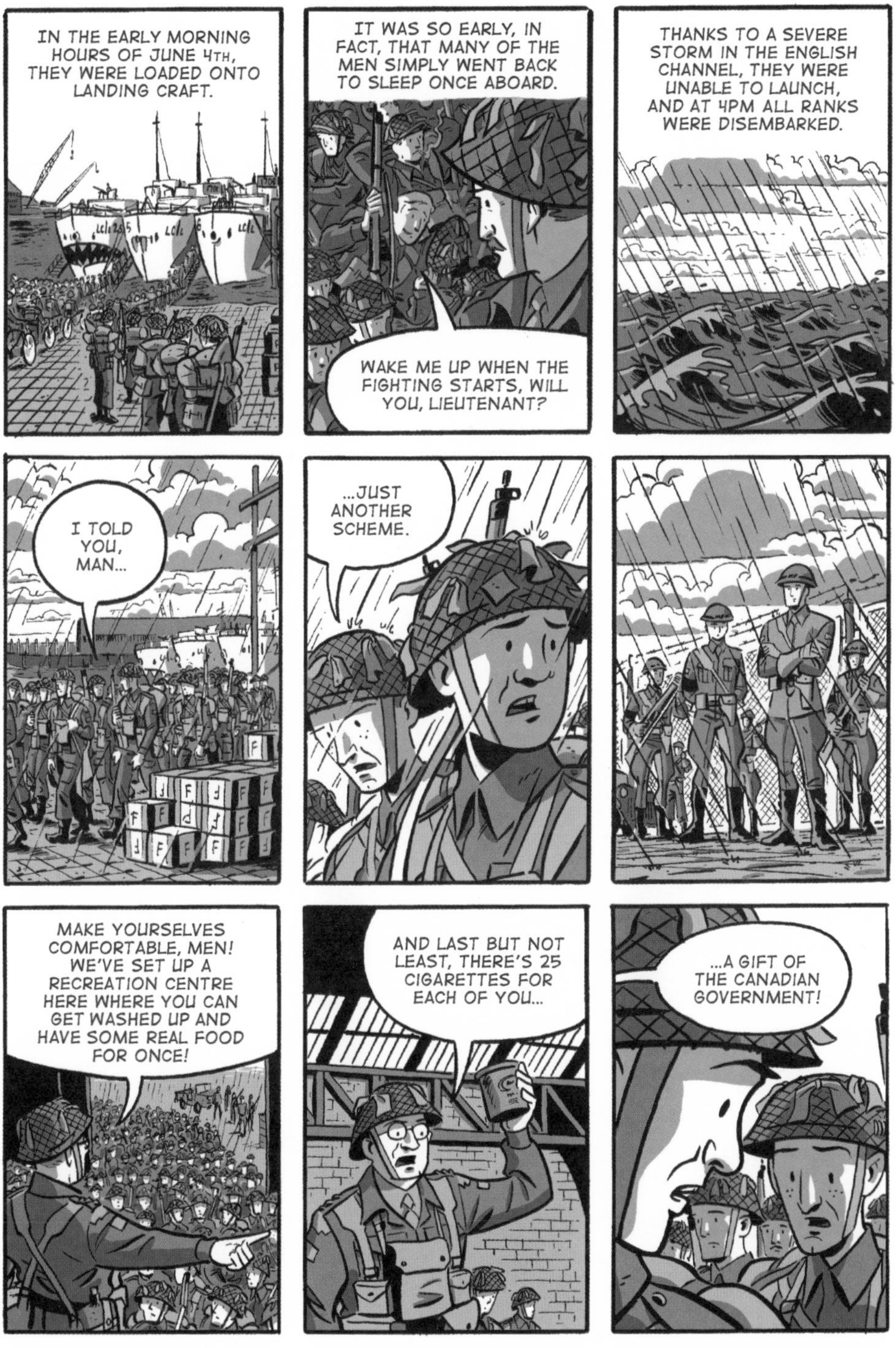
IN THE EARLY MORNING HOURS OF JUNE 4TH, THEY WERE LOADED ONTO LANDING CRAFT.
IT WAS SO EARLY, IN FACT, THAT MANY OF THE MEN SIMPLY WENT BACK TO SLEEP ONCE ABOARD.
WAKE ME UP WHEN THE FIGHTING STARTS, WILL YOU, LIEUTENANT?
THANKS TO A SEVERE STORM IN THE ENGLISH CHANNEL, THEY WERE UNABLE TO LAUNCH, AND AT 4PM ALL RANKS WERE DISEMBARKED.
I TOLD YOU, MAN...
...JUST ANOTHER SCHEME.
MAKE YOURSELVES COMFORTABLE, MEN! WE'VE SET UP A RECREATION CENTRE HERE WHERE YOU CAN GET WASHED UP AND HAVE SOME REAL FOOD FOR ONCE!
AND LAST BUT NOT LEAST, THERE'S 25 CIGARETTES FOR EACH OF YOU...
...A GIFT OF THE CANADIAN GOVERNMENT!

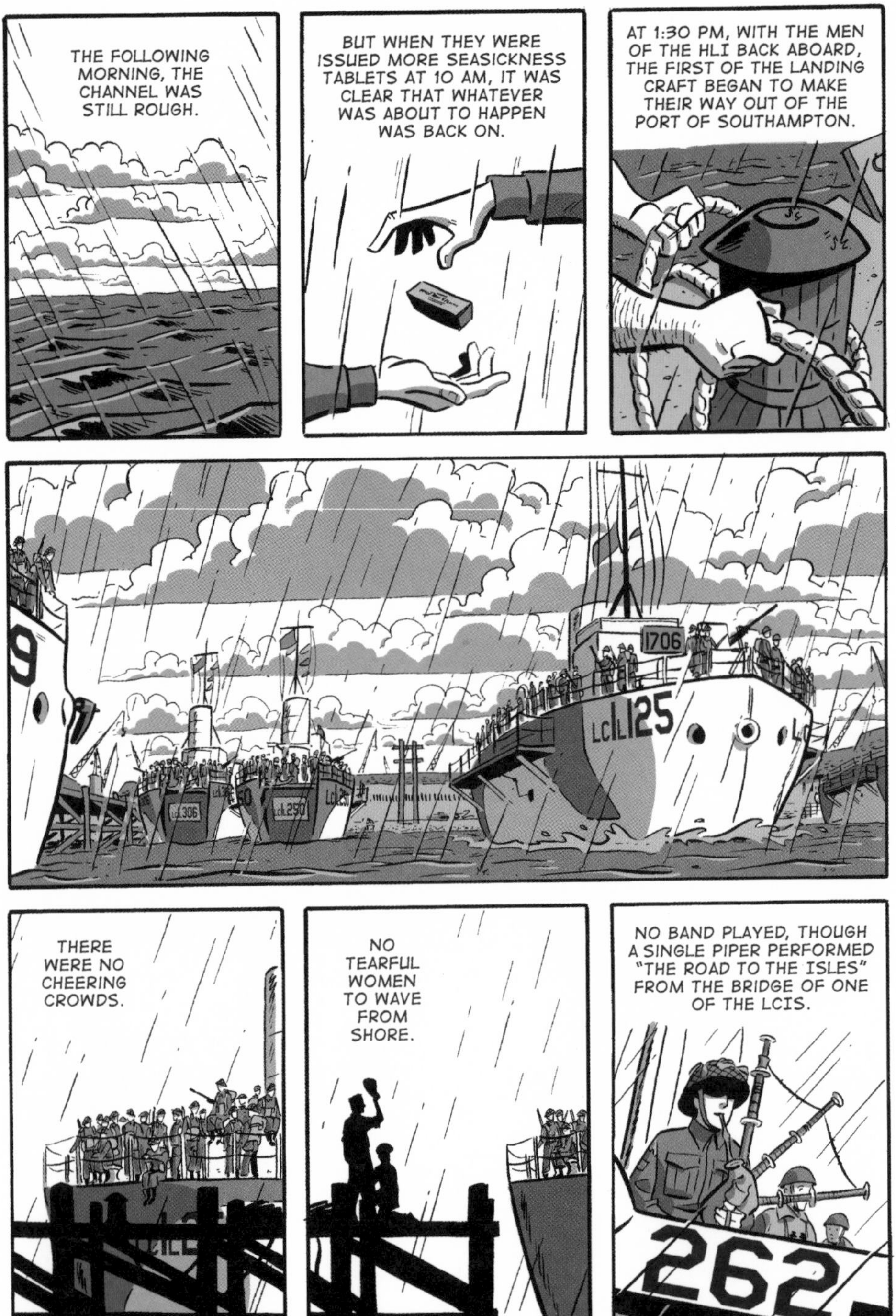
THE FOLLOWING MORNING, THE CHANNEL WAS STILL ROUGH.
BUT WHEN THEY WERE ISSUED MORE SEASICKNESS TABLETS AT 10 AM, IT WAS CLEAR THAT WHATEVER WAS ABOUT TO HAPPEN WAS BACK ON.
AT 1:30 PM, WITH THE MEN OF THE HLI BACK ABOARD, THE FIRST OF THE LANDING CRAFT BEGAN TO MAKE THEIR WAY OUT OF THE PORT OF SOUTHAMPTON.
1706
LCIL 125
LCIL 306
LCIL 250
THERE WERE NO CHEERING CROWDS.
NO TEARFUL WOMEN TO WAVE FROM SHORE.
NO BAND PLAYED, THOUGH A SINGLE PIPER PERFORMED "THE ROAD TO THE ISLES" FROM THE BRIDGE OF ONE OF THE LCIS.
262

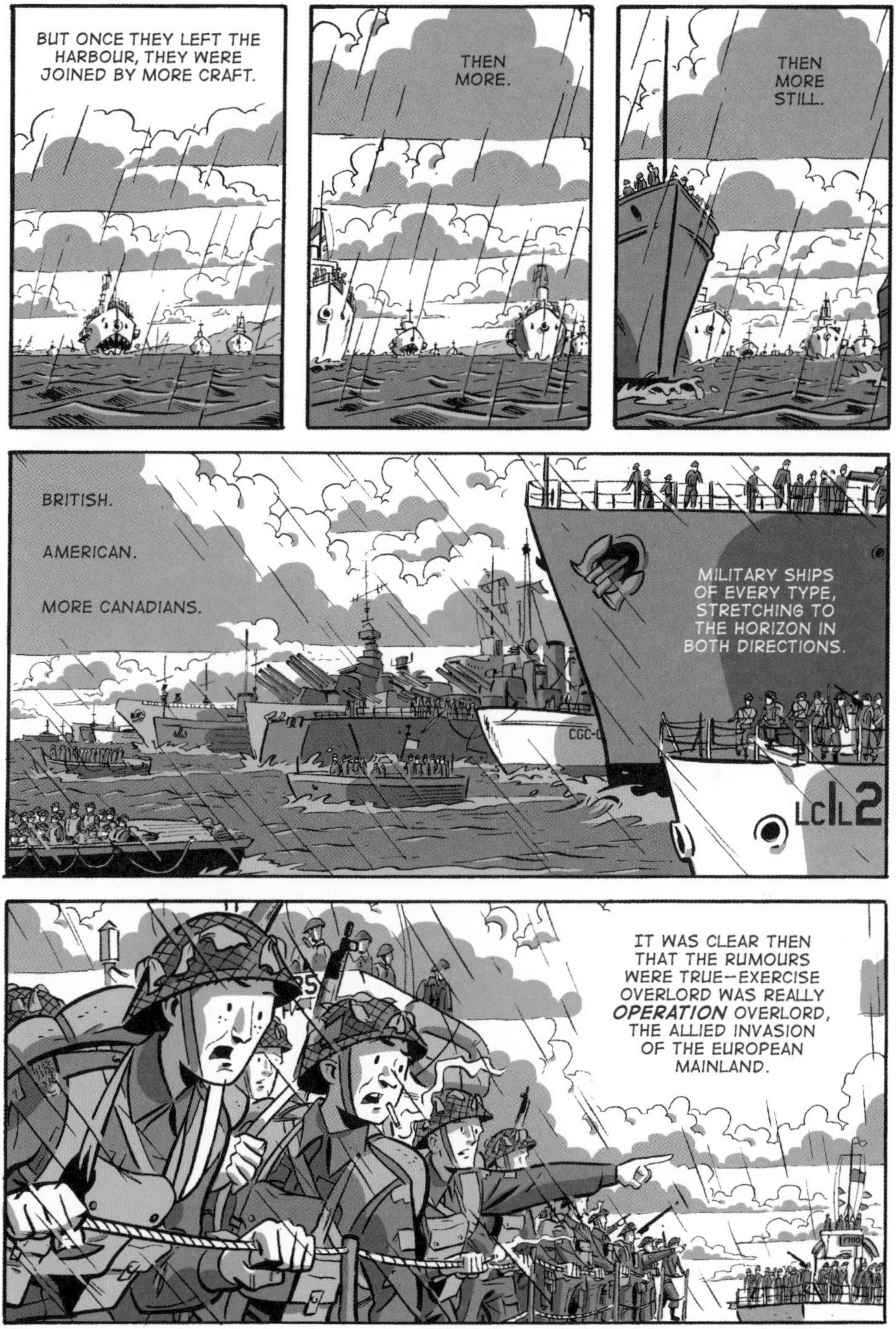
BUT ONCE THEY LEFT THE HARBOUR, THEY WERE JOINED BY MORE CRAFT.
THEN MORE.
THEN MORE STILL.
BRITISH.
AMERICAN.
MORE CANADIANS.
MILITARY SHIPS OF EVERY TYPE, STRETCHING TO THE HORIZON IN BOTH DIRECTIONS.
IT WAS CLEAR THEN THAT THE RUMOURS WERE TRUE—EXERCISE OVERLORD WAS REALLY *OPERATION* OVERLORD, THE ALLIED INVASION OF THE EUROPEAN MAINLAND.

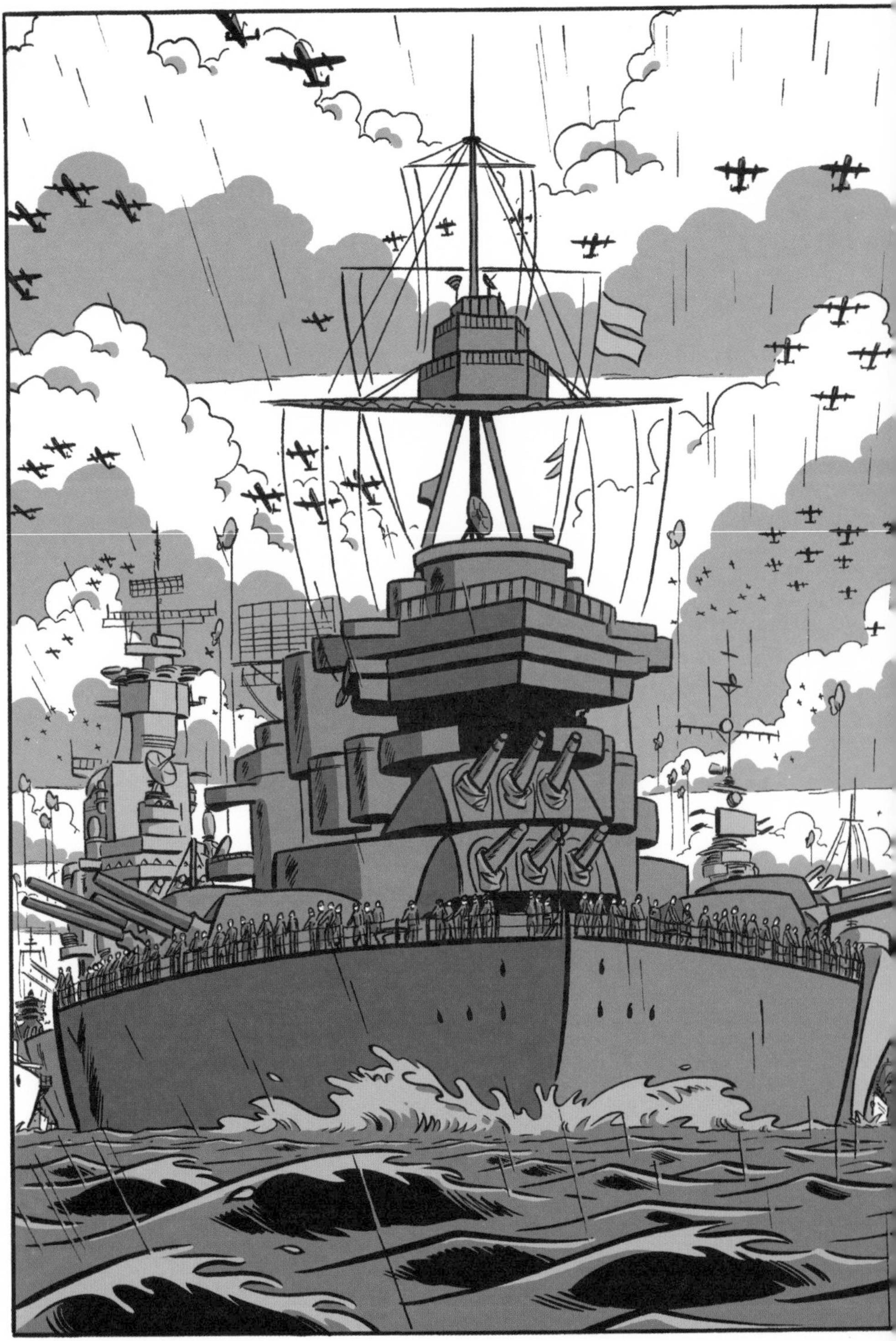

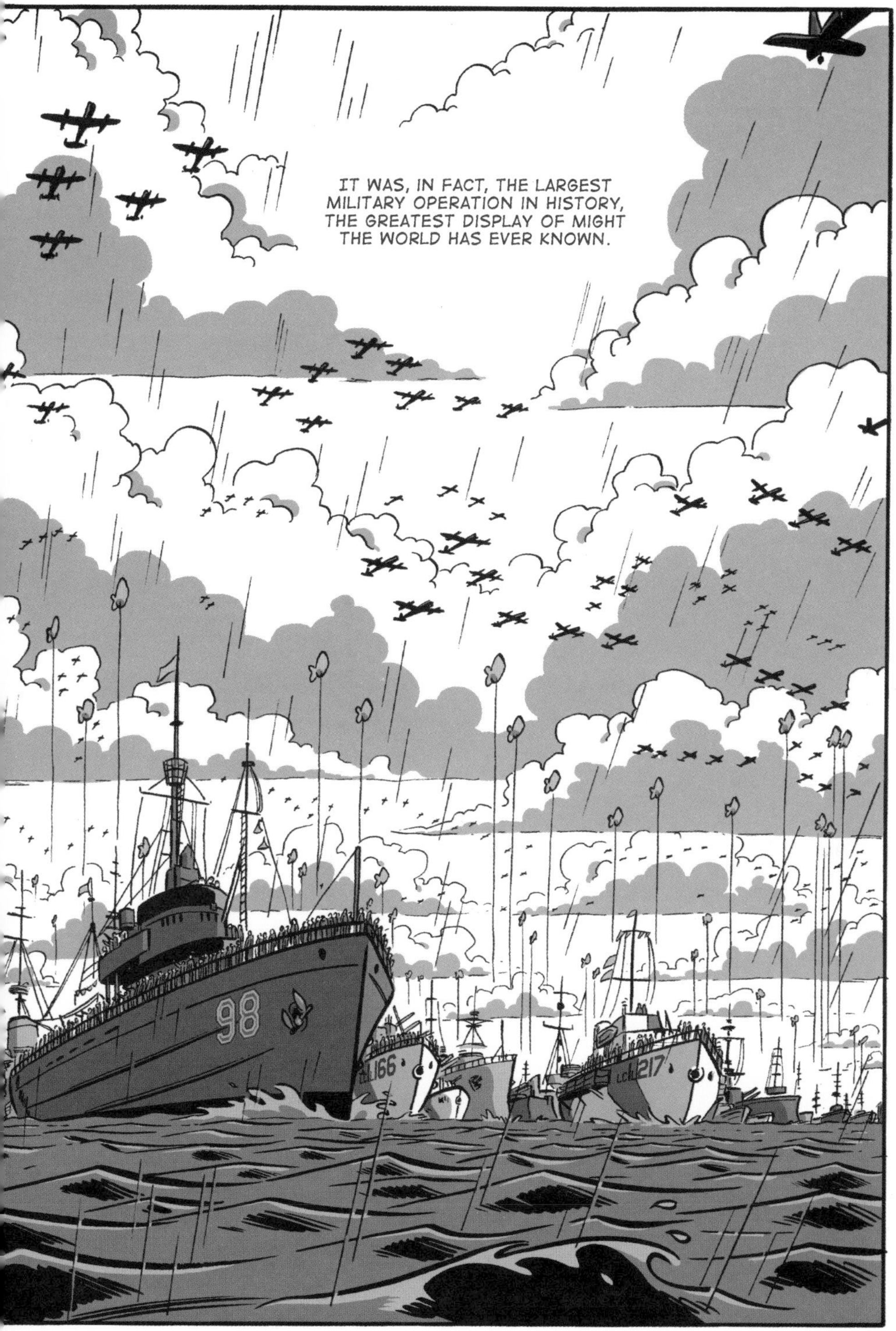
IT WAS, IN FACT, THE LARGEST MILITARY OPERATION IN HISTORY, THE GREATEST DISPLAY OF MIGHT THE WORLD HAS EVER KNOWN.
98
LCI L 166
LCH 217

GATHER 'ROUND, MEN.

I'M SUPPOSED TO READ THIS TO YOU, SO LISTEN UP.

"THE TIME HAS COME TO DEAL THE ENEMY A TERRIFIC BLOW IN WESTERN EUROPE."

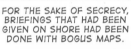

FOR THE SAKE OF SECRECY, BRIEFINGS THAT HAD BEEN GIVEN ON SHORE HAD BEEN DONE WITH BOGUS MAPS.

"ON THE EVE OF THIS GREAT ADVENTURE I SEND MY BEST WISHES TO EVERY SOLDIER IN THE ALLIED TEAM."

THE TERRAIN, LANDMARKS, AND DEFENCES WERE ACCURATE, BUT PHONY NAMES HAD BEEN USED, IN CASE THE TRAINING MAPS HAD FALLEN INTO ENEMY HANDS.

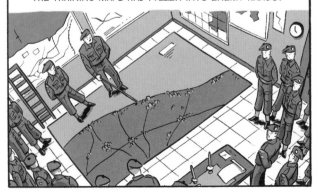

"TO US IS GIVEN THE HONOUR OF STRIKING A BLOW FOR FREEDOM WHICH WILL LIVE IN HISTORY..."

"...AND IN THE BETTER DAYS THAT LIE AHEAD MEN WILL SPEAK WITH PRIDE OF OUR DOINGS."

"WE HAVE A GREAT AND RIGHTEOUS CAUSE."

"WITH STOUT HEARTS, AND WITH ENTHUSIASM FOR THE CONTEST, LET US GO FORWARD TO VICTORY."

IT WAS ONLY AS THEY LEFT ENGLISH WATERS THAT THE REAL MAPS WERE ORDERED OPENED AND DISTRIBUTED.

POLAND

ONLY THEN THAT THEY LEARNED THAT THE OBJECTIVE MARKED "POLAND" ON THEIR TRAINING MAPS...

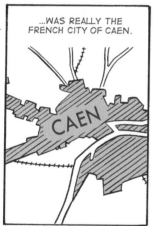

...WAS REALLY THE FRENCH CITY OF CAEN.

CAEN

"GOOD LUCK TO EACH ONE OF YOU. AND GOOD HUNTING ON THE MAINLAND OF EUROPE."

SIGNED, GENERAL B.L. MONTGOMERY, C-IN-C 21ST ARMY GROUP.

THEY WERE ABOUT TO INVADE NORMANDY.

299

# PART TWO

## NOW FADES THE GLIMM'RING LANDSCAPE

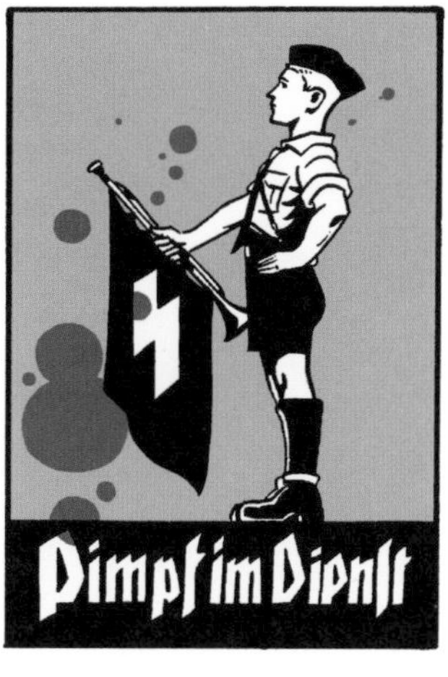
Pimpf im Dienst

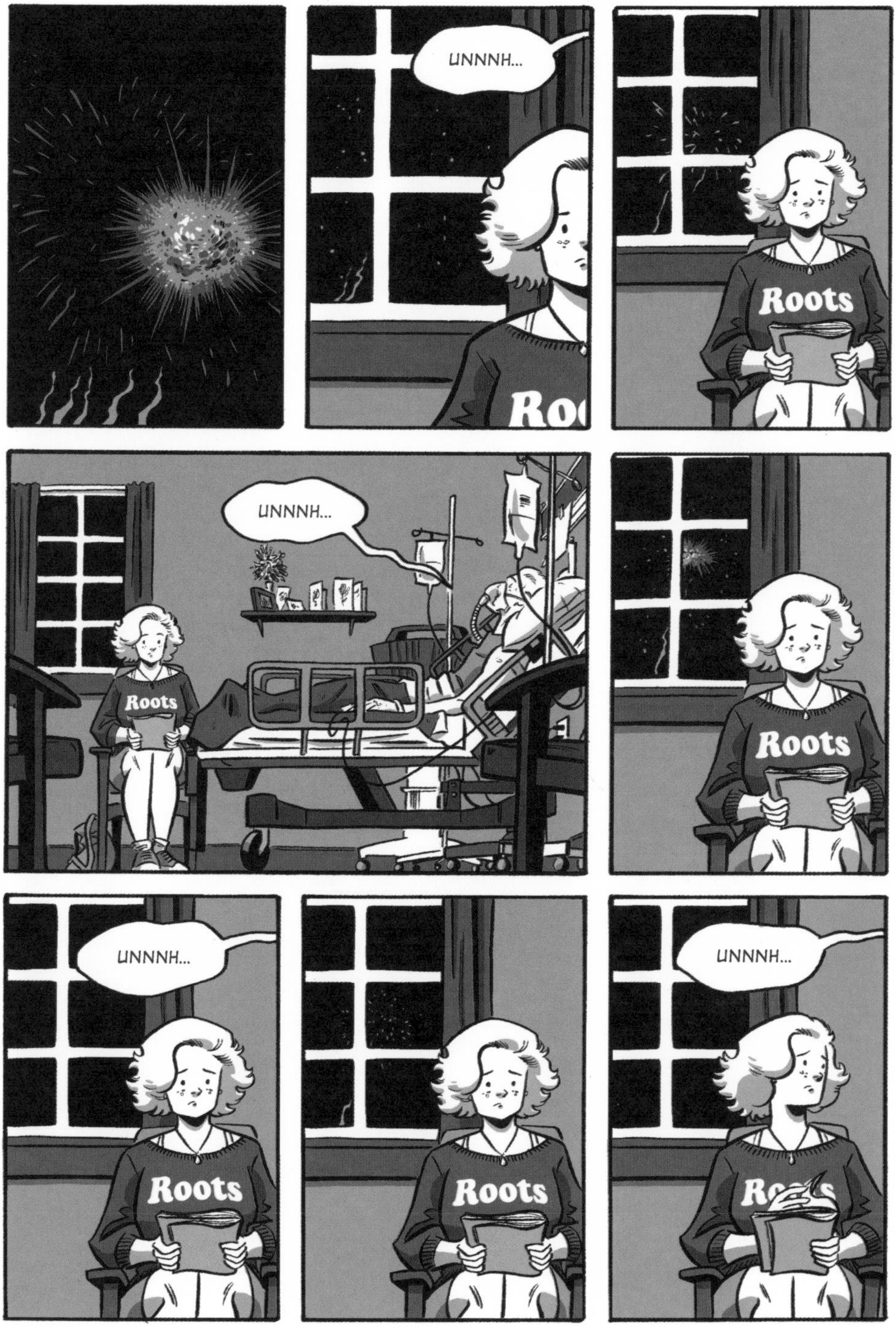
UNNNH...
UNNNH...
UNNNH...
UNNNH...

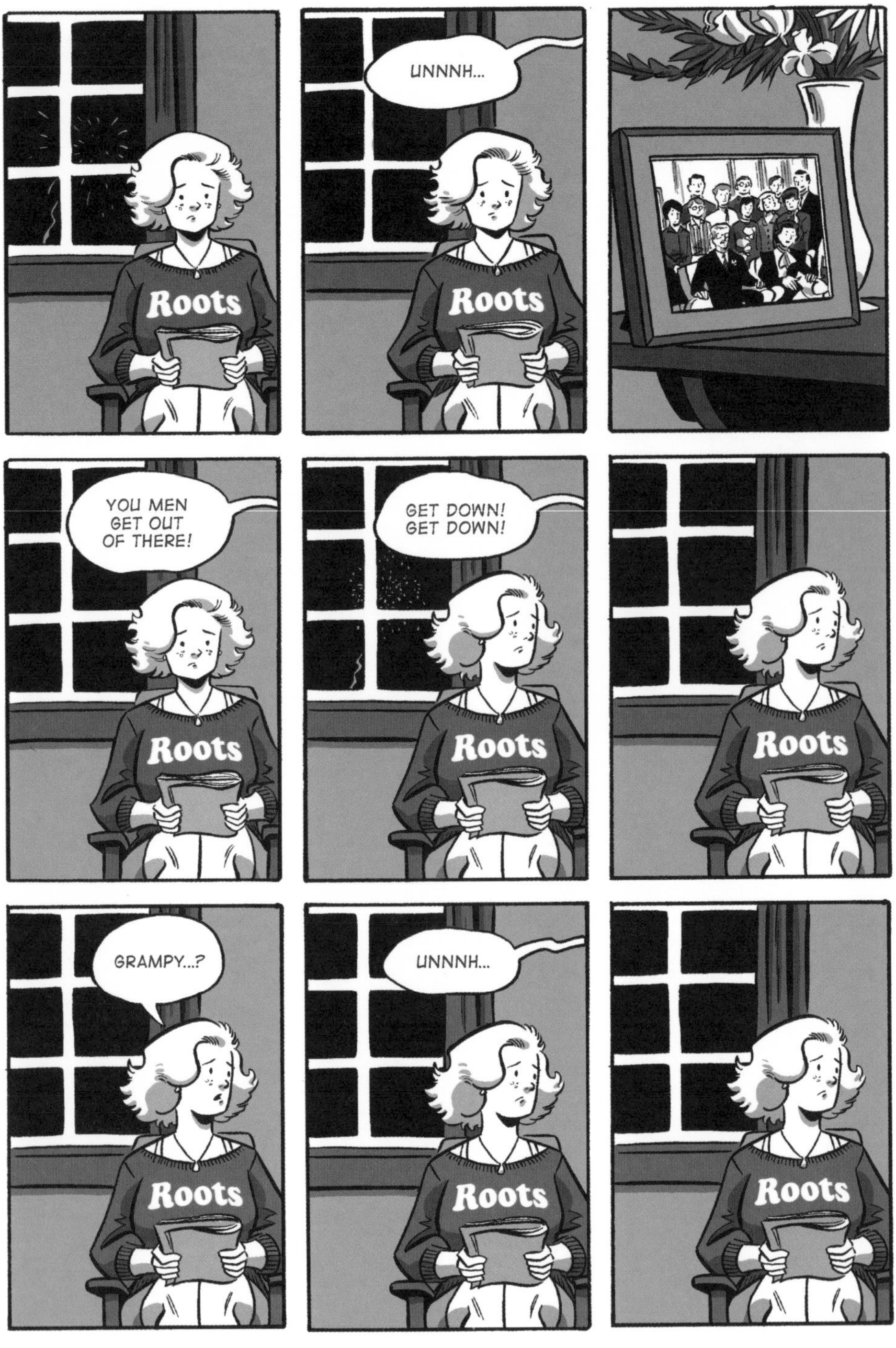
Roots
UNNNH...
YOU MEN GET OUT OF THERE!
GET DOWN! GET DOWN!
GRAMPY...?
UNNNH...

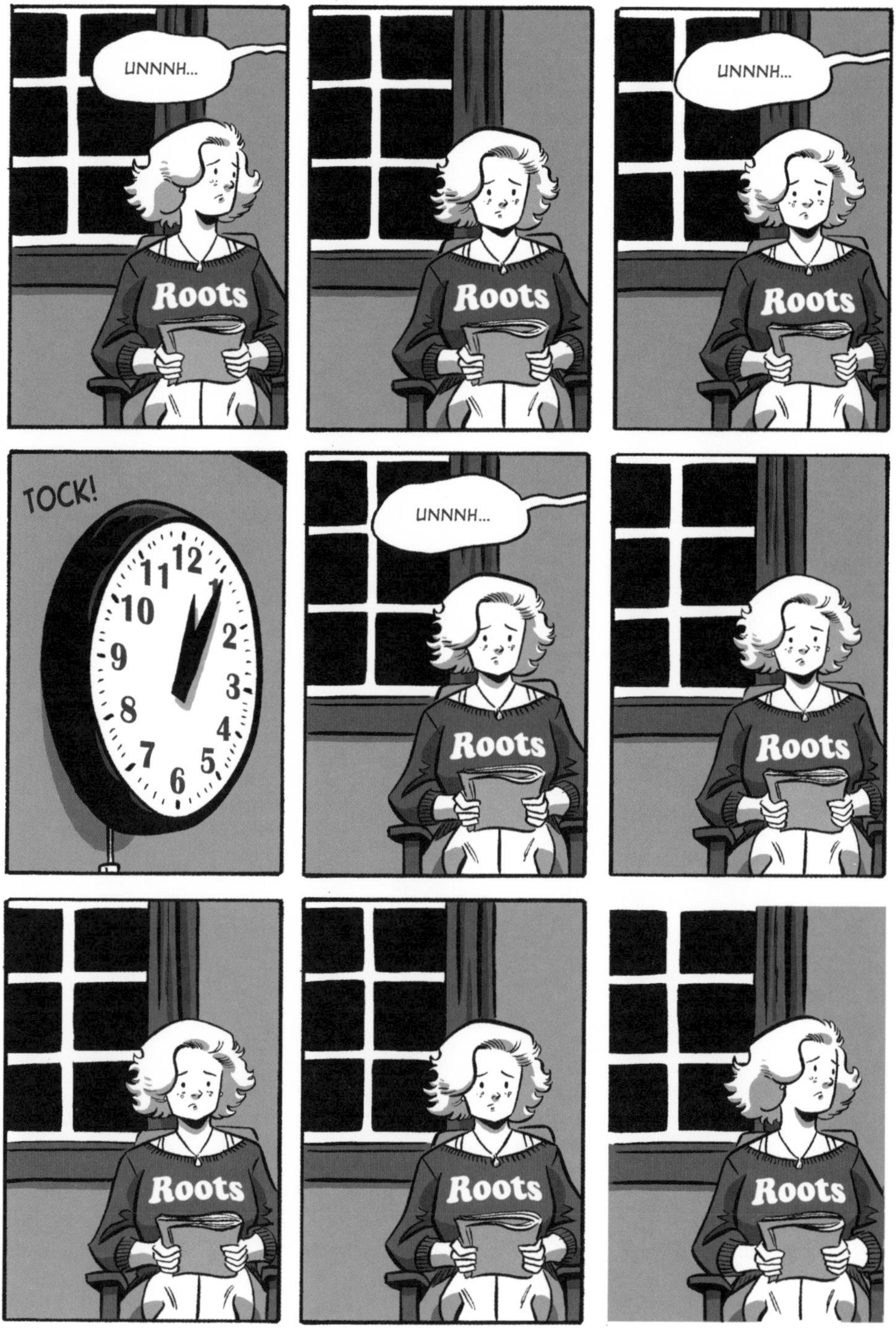
UNNNH...
UNNNH...
TOCK!
UNNNH...
Roots

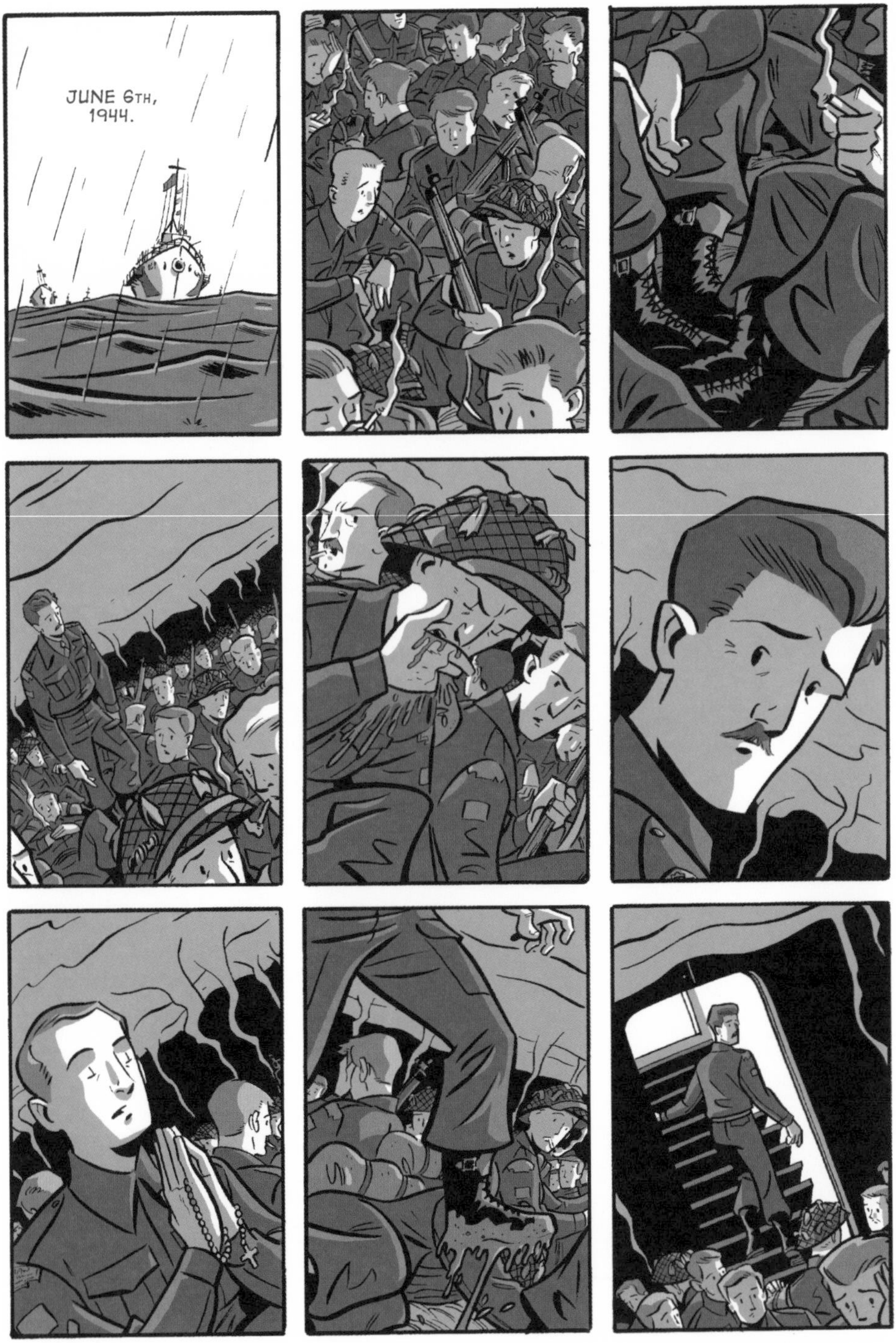
JUNE 6TH,
1944.

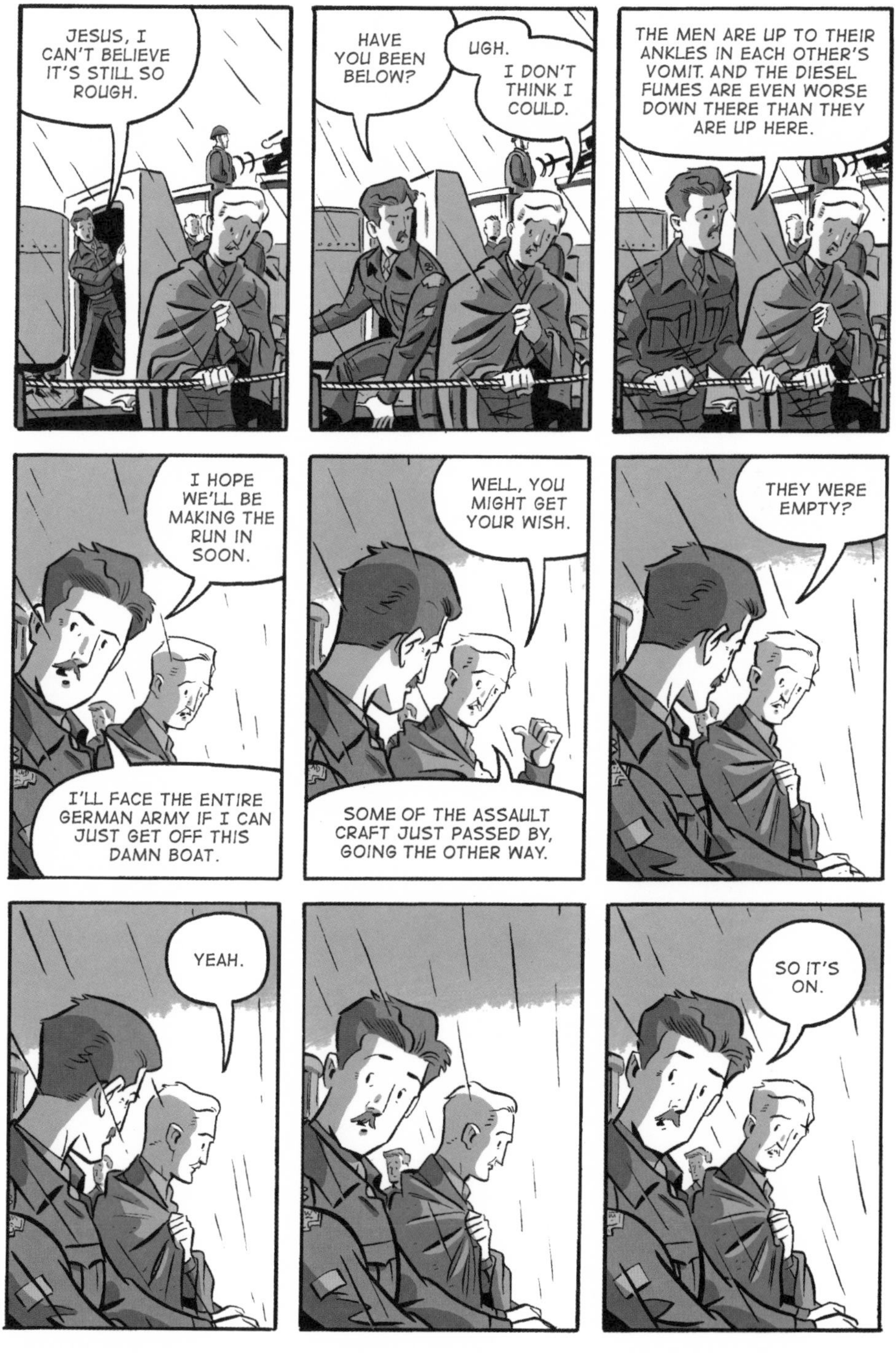
JESUS, I CAN'T BELIEVE IT'S STILL SO ROUGH.
HAVE YOU BEEN BELOW?
UGH.
I DON'T THINK I COULD.
THE MEN ARE UP TO THEIR ANKLES IN EACH OTHER'S VOMIT. AND THE DIESEL FUMES ARE EVEN WORSE DOWN THERE THAN THEY ARE UP HERE.
I HOPE WE'LL BE MAKING THE RUN IN SOON.
I'LL FACE THE ENTIRE GERMAN ARMY IF I CAN JUST GET OFF THIS DAMN BOAT.
WELL, YOU MIGHT GET YOUR WISH.
SOME OF THE ASSAULT CRAFT JUST PASSED BY, GOING THE OTHER WAY.
THEY WERE EMPTY?
YEAH.
SO IT'S ON.

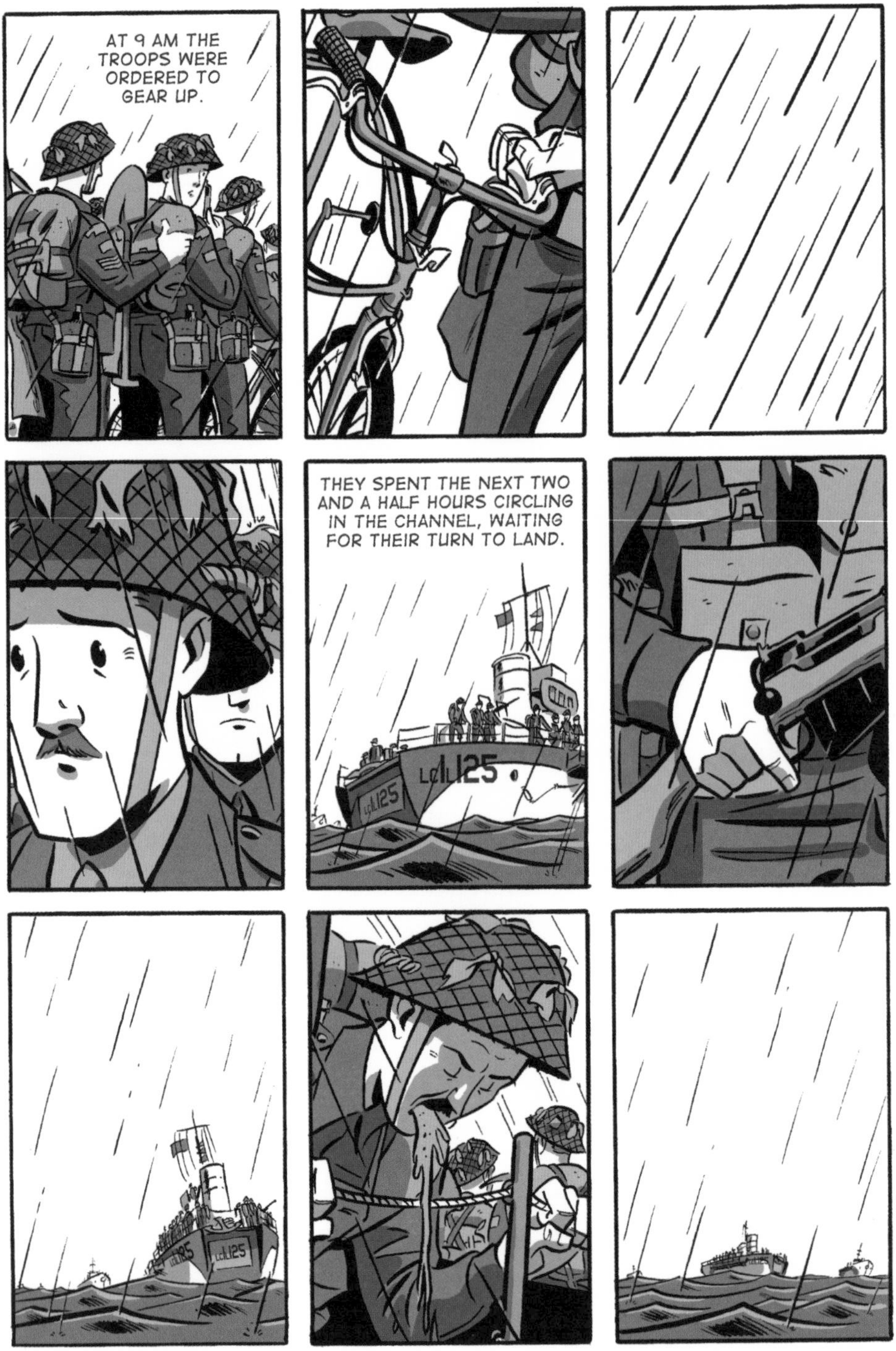
AT 9 AM THE TROOPS WERE ORDERED TO GEAR UP.
THEY SPENT THE NEXT TWO AND A HALF HOURS CIRCLING IN THE CHANNEL, WAITING FOR THEIR TURN TO LAND.
LCIL125

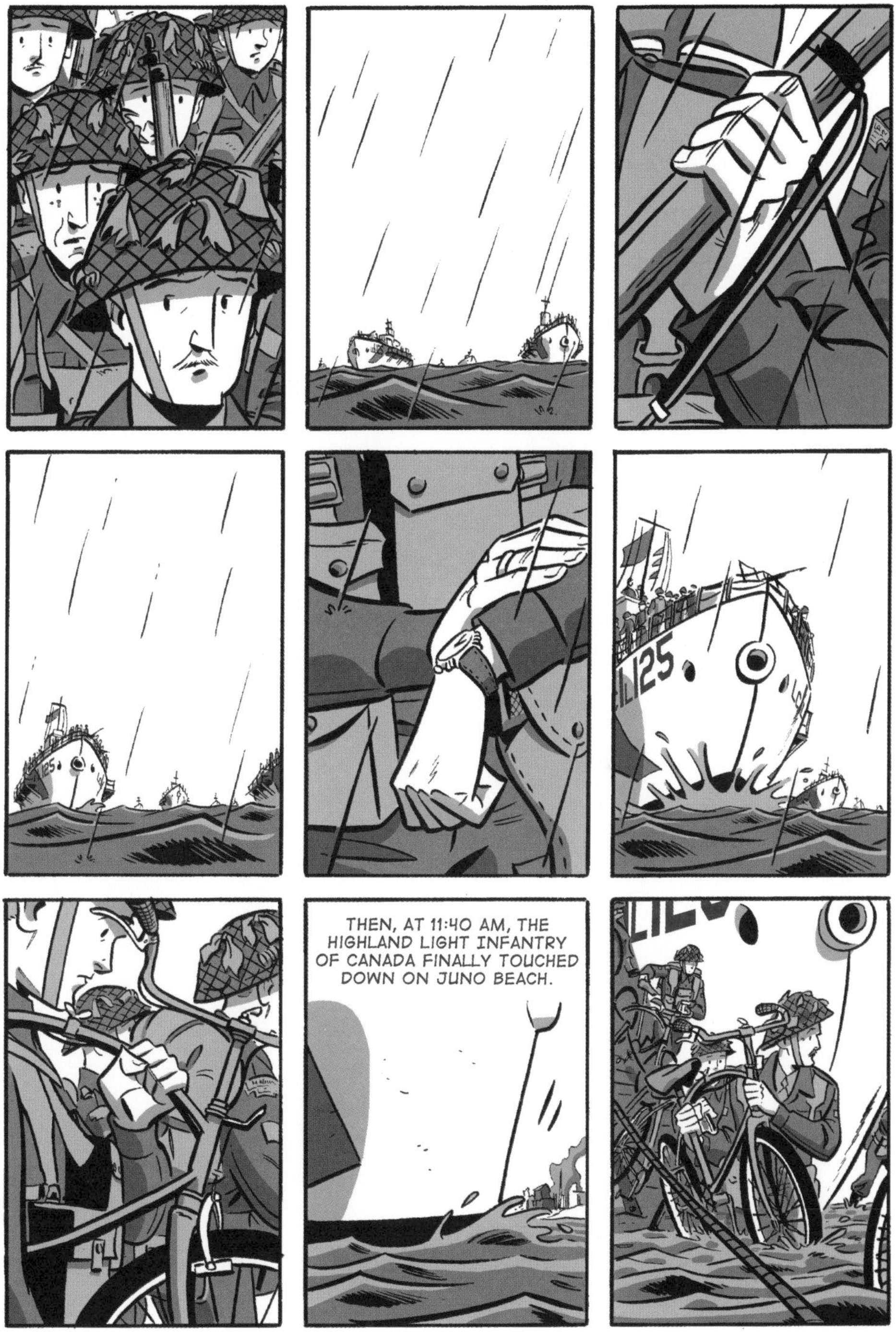
THEN, AT 11:40 AM, THE HIGHLAND LIGHT INFANTRY OF CANADA FINALLY TOUCHED DOWN ON JUNO BEACH.

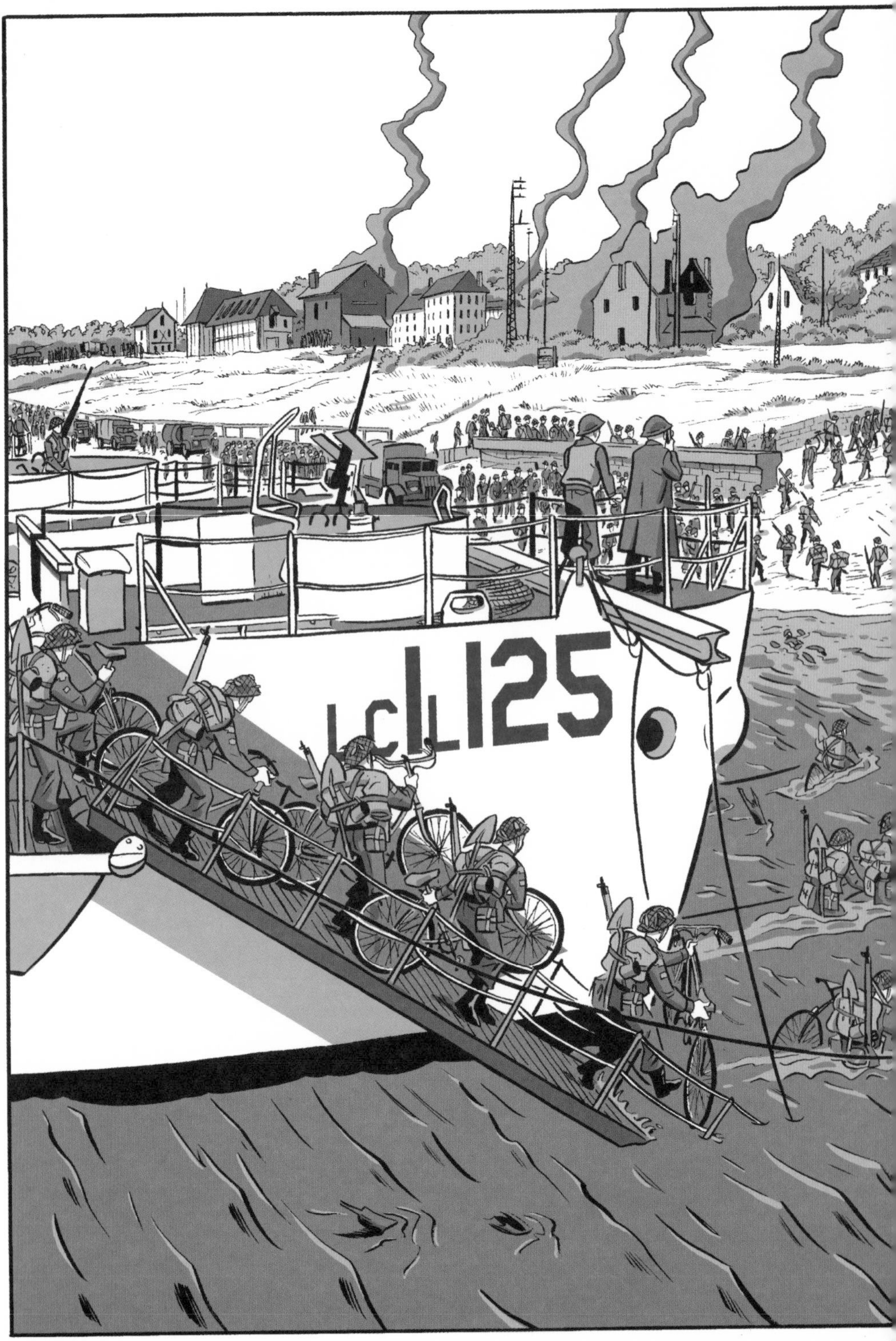
LCIL 125

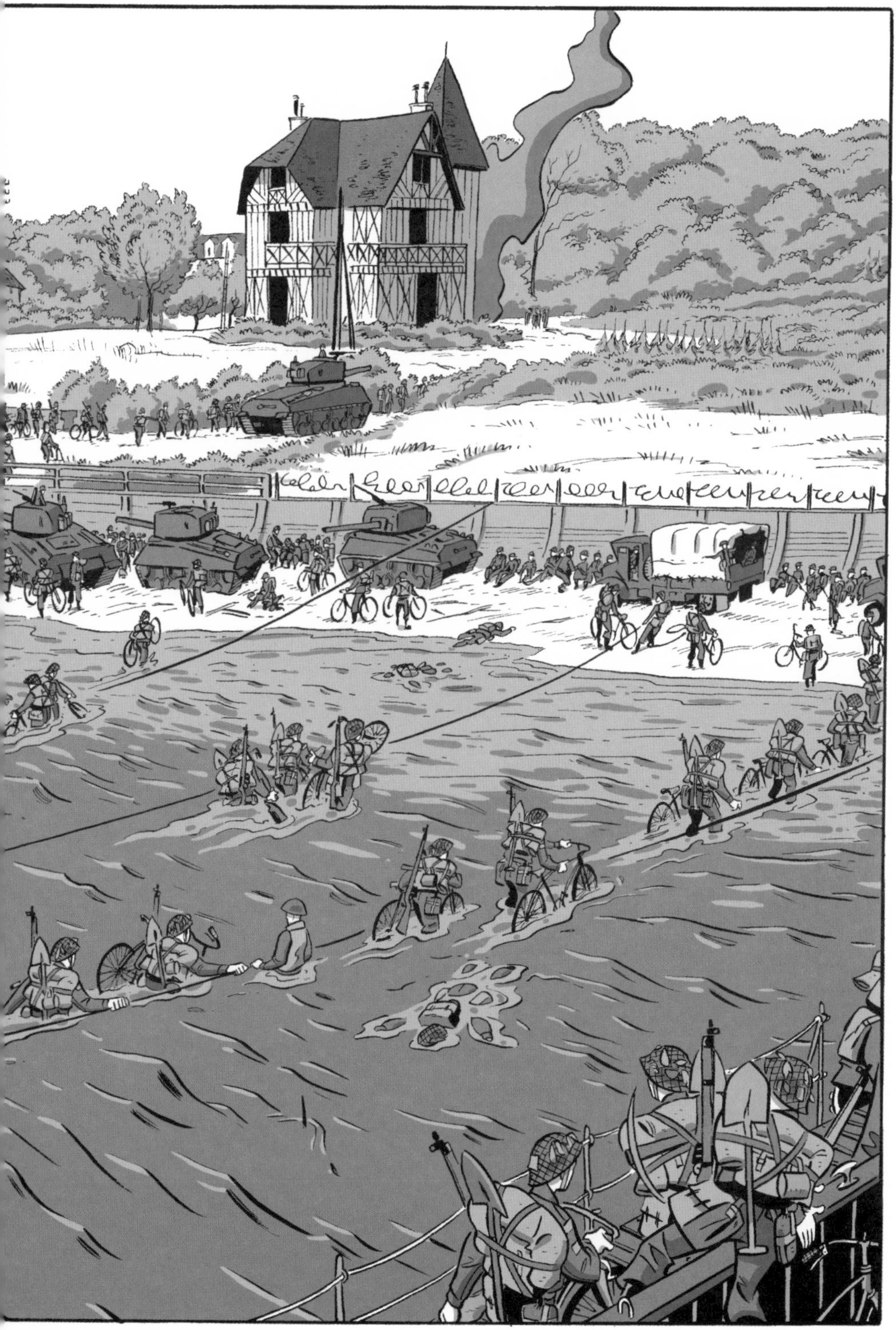

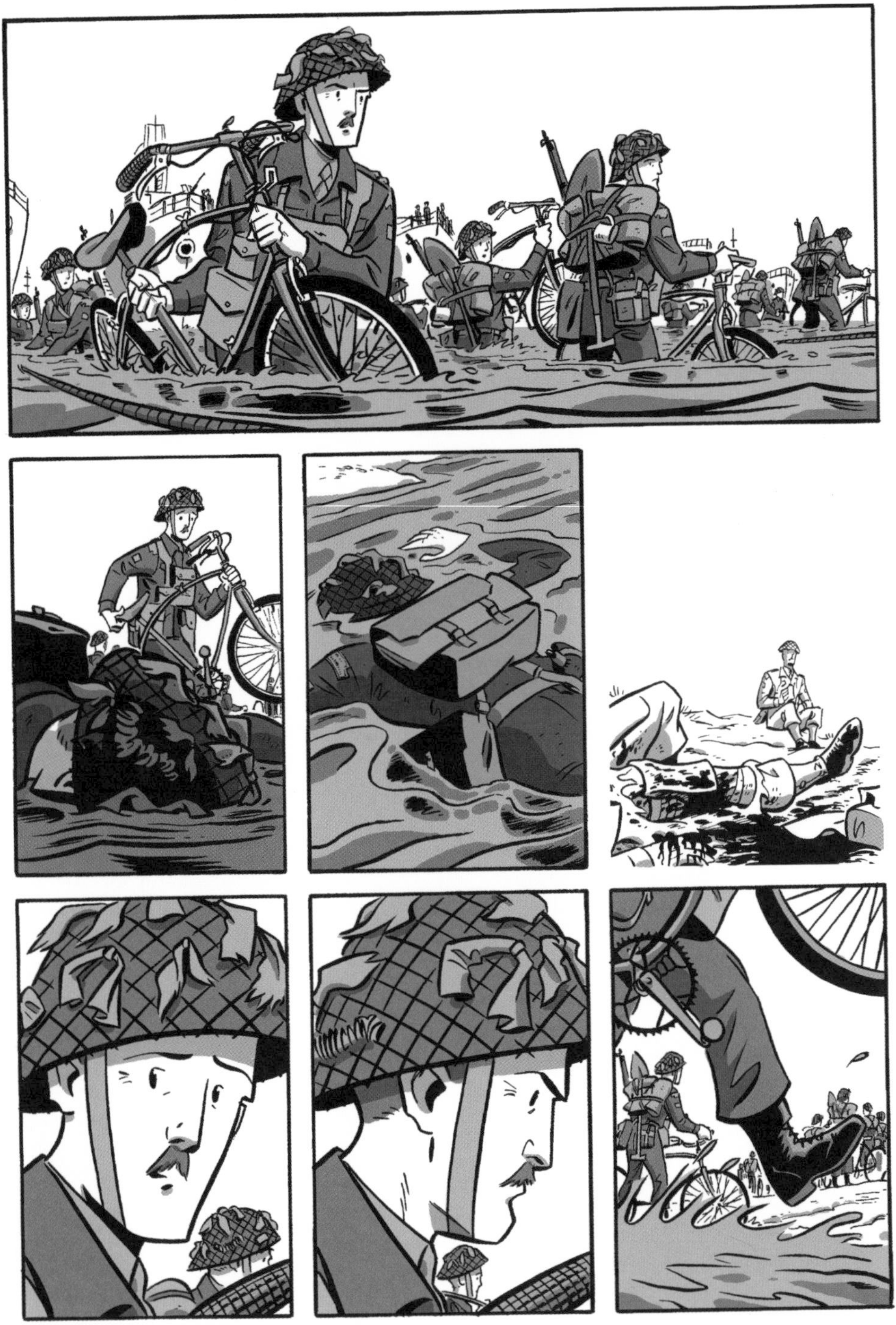

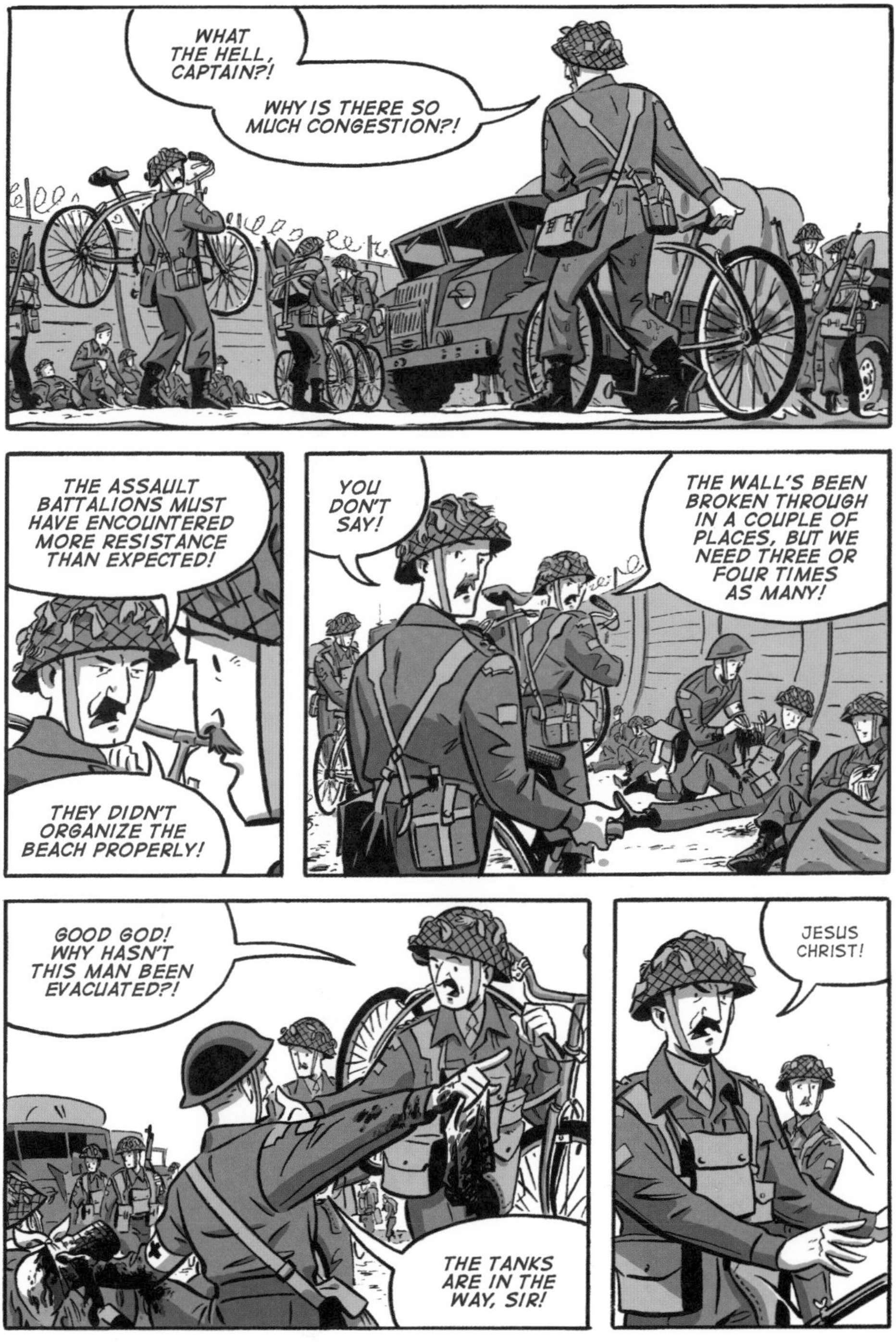

WHAT THE HELL, CAPTAIN?!
WHY IS THERE SO MUCH CONGESTION?!
THE ASSAULT BATTALIONS MUST HAVE ENCOUNTERED MORE RESISTANCE THAN EXPECTED!
THEY DIDN'T ORGANIZE THE BEACH PROPERLY!
YOU DON'T SAY!
THE WALL'S BEEN BROKEN THROUGH IN A COUPLE OF PLACES, BUT WE NEED THREE OR FOUR TIMES AS MANY!
GOOD GOD! WHY HASN'T THIS MAN BEEN EVACUATED?!
THE TANKS ARE IN THE WAY, SIR!
JESUS CHRIST!

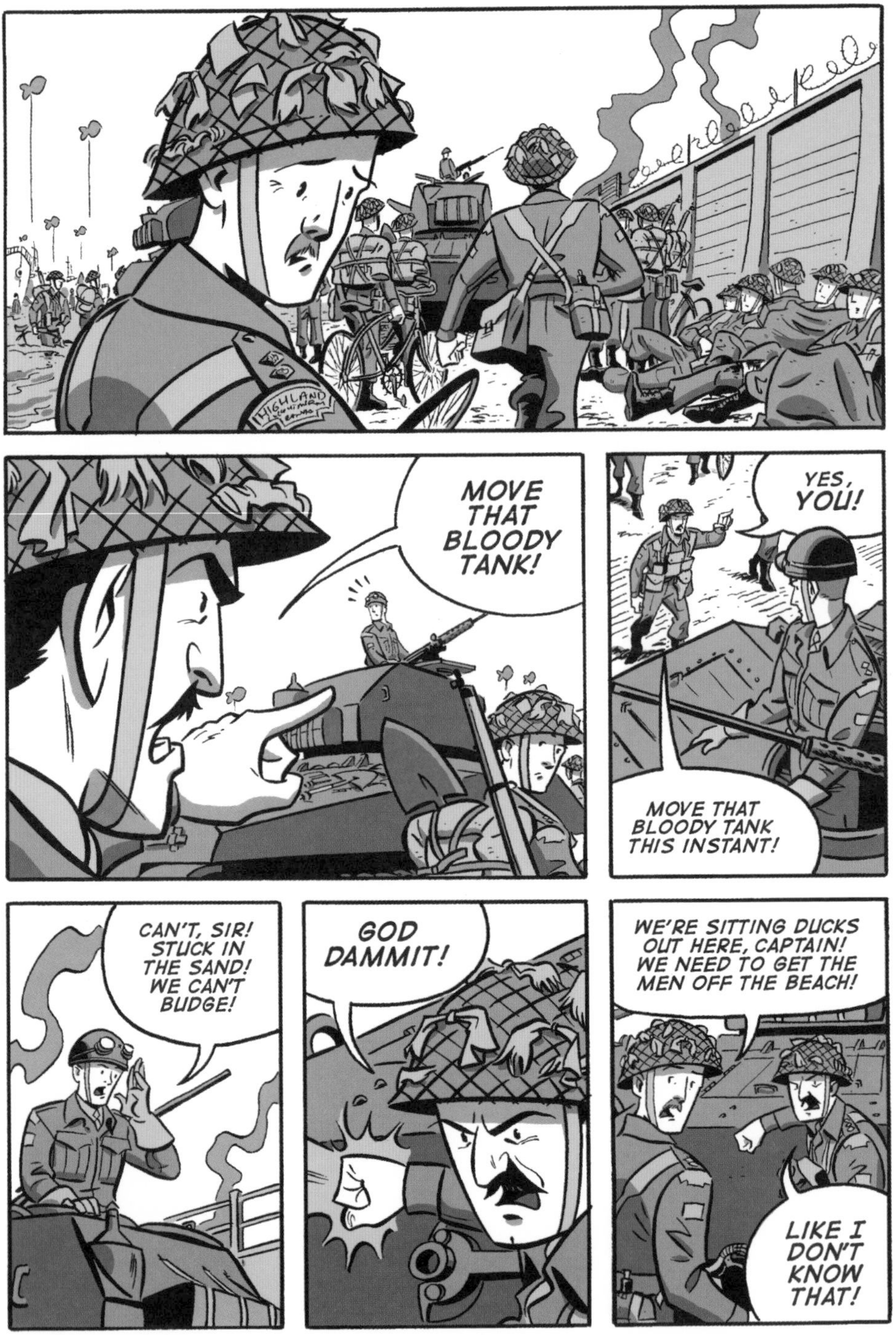
HIGHLAND
MOVE THAT BLOODY TANK!
YES, YOU!
MOVE THAT BLOODY TANK THIS INSTANT!
CAN'T, SIR! STUCK IN THE SAND! WE CAN'T BUDGE!
GOD DAMMIT!
WE'RE SITTING DUCKS OUT HERE, CAPTAIN! WE NEED TO GET THE MEN OFF THE BEACH!
LIKE I DON'T KNOW THAT!

FORTUNATELY, AIR COVER WAS STRONG AND THE BEACH HAD BEEN CLEARED OF SNIPERS.

BEYOND THE WALL IT WAS A DIFFERENT STORY.

THE BATTALIONS THAT HAD STORMED THE BEACH WERE STILL FIGHTING THERE.

SO THE REGIMENT WAITED THINGS OUT BEHIND A CHURCH, AFRAID OF BEING FIRED AT ON THE ROAD.

ONCE IN THE CLEAR, THEY FINALLY MOUNTED THEIR BICYCLES.

GERMAN GUNNERS SPOTTED THEM IMMEDIATELY.

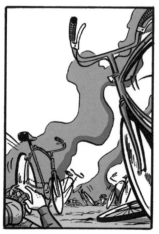

HA!

IN TRUE MILITARY FASHION, ONLY ONE PATCHING KIT PER PLATOON HAD BEEN ISSUED.

SO WHEN THEIR TIRES WENT FLAT, THEY SIMPLY RODE ON THE RIMS.

FASTER, SERGEANT!

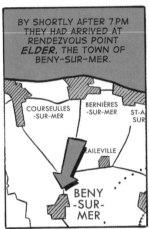

BY SHORTLY AFTER 7 PM THEY HAD ARRIVED AT RENDEZVOUS POINT *ELDER*, THE TOWN OF BENY-SUR-MER.

COURSEULLES -SUR-MER

BERNIÈRES -SUR-MER

ST-A SUR

RAILEVILLE

BENY -SUR- MER

THERE THEY REGROUPED, AND PREPARED TO MOVE ON TO THEIR OBJECTIVE.

759/1

BUT ONCE AGAIN, THE ROAD AHEAD WAS BLOCKED BY UNITS THAT HAD COME ASHORE AHEAD OF THEM.

CAEN

THEY PASSED THE TIME BY ENTERTAINING THE EXCITED AND GRATEFUL FRENCH VILLAGERS.

MONTREZ-MOI ...LA CARTE... DES VINS.

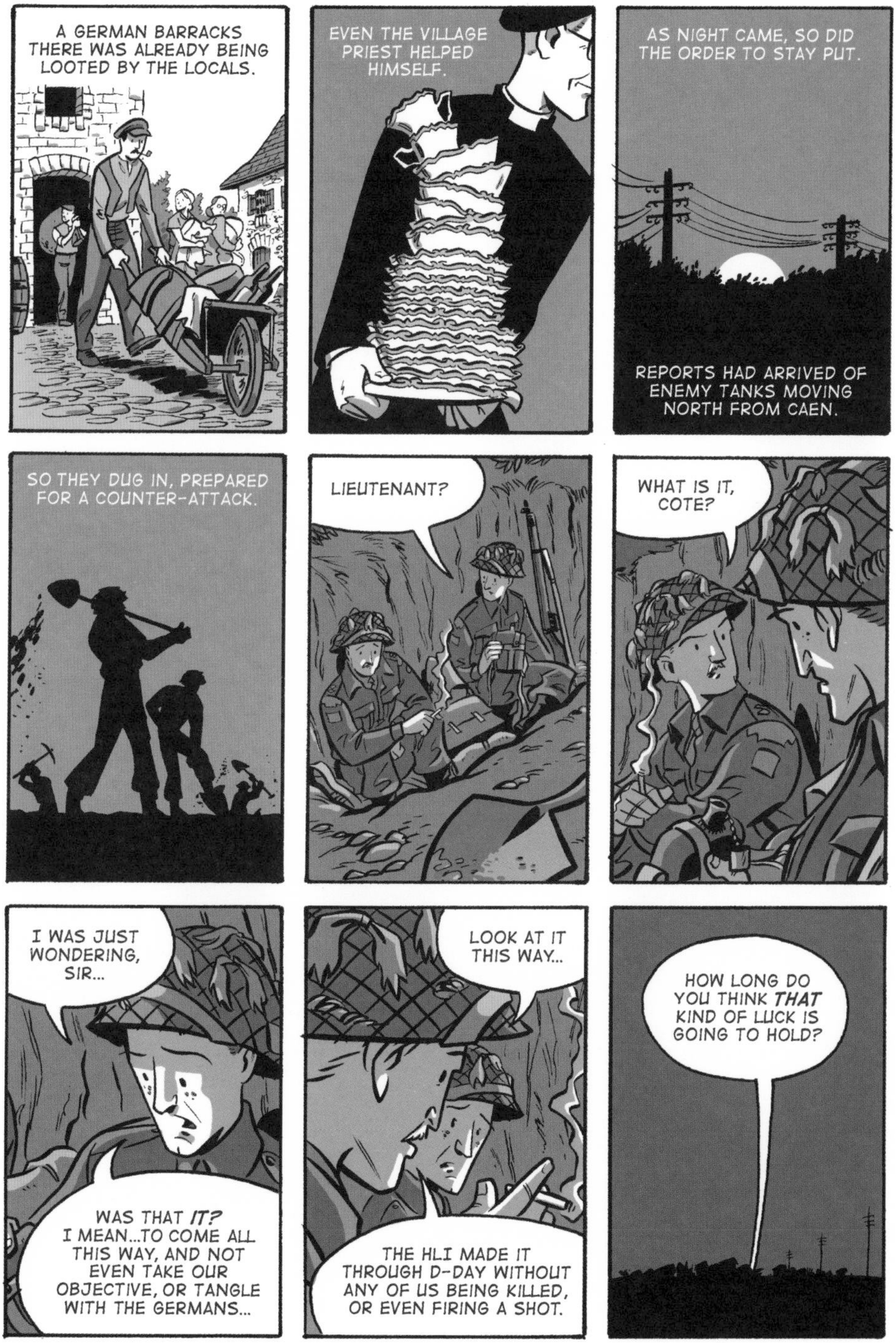
A GERMAN BARRACKS THERE WAS ALREADY BEING LOOTED BY THE LOCALS.
EVEN THE VILLAGE PRIEST HELPED HIMSELF.
AS NIGHT CAME, SO DID THE ORDER TO STAY PUT.
REPORTS HAD ARRIVED OF ENEMY TANKS MOVING NORTH FROM CAEN.
SO THEY DUG IN, PREPARED FOR A COUNTER-ATTACK.
LIEUTENANT?
WHAT IS IT, COTE?
I WAS JUST WONDERING, SIR...
WAS THAT *IT?* I MEAN...TO COME ALL THIS WAY, AND NOT EVEN TAKE OUR OBJECTIVE, OR TANGLE WITH THE GERMANS...
LOOK AT IT THIS WAY...
THE HLI MADE IT THROUGH D-DAY WITHOUT ANY OF US BEING KILLED, OR EVEN FIRING A SHOT.
HOW LONG DO YOU THINK ***THAT*** KIND OF LUCK IS GOING TO HOLD?

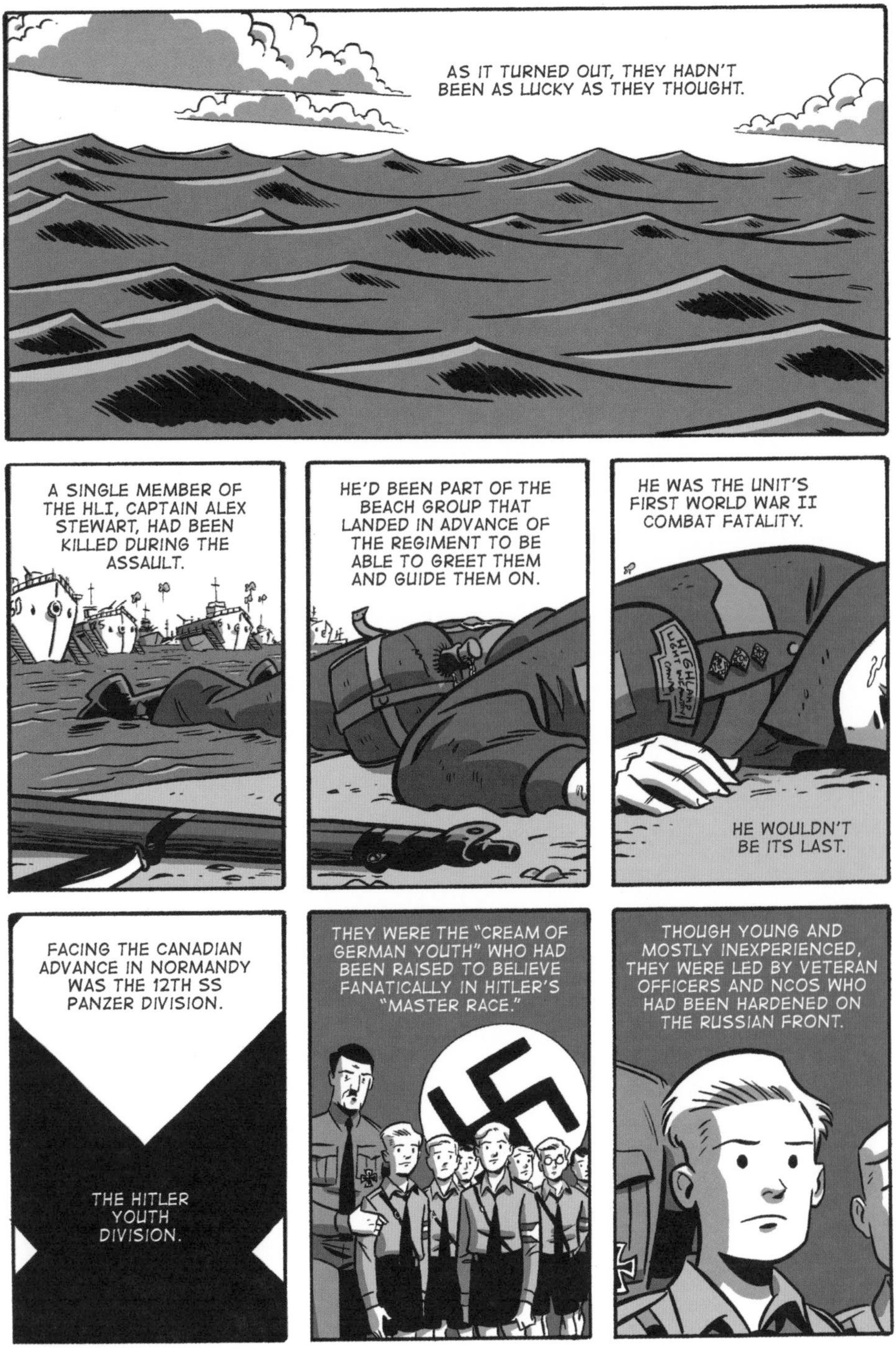
AS IT TURNED OUT, THEY HADN'T BEEN AS LUCKY AS THEY THOUGHT.
A SINGLE MEMBER OF THE HLI, CAPTAIN ALEX STEWART, HAD BEEN KILLED DURING THE ASSAULT.
HE'D BEEN PART OF THE BEACH GROUP THAT LANDED IN ADVANCE OF THE REGIMENT TO BE ABLE TO GREET THEM AND GUIDE THEM ON.
HE WAS THE UNIT'S FIRST WORLD WAR II COMBAT FATALITY.
HE WOULDN'T BE ITS LAST.
FACING THE CANADIAN ADVANCE IN NORMANDY WAS THE 12TH SS PANZER DIVISION.
THE HITLER YOUTH DIVISION.
THEY WERE THE "CREAM OF GERMAN YOUTH" WHO HAD BEEN RAISED TO BELIEVE FANATICALLY IN HITLER'S "MASTER RACE."
THOUGH YOUNG AND MOSTLY INEXPERIENCED, THEY WERE LED BY VETERAN OFFICERS AND NCOS WHO HAD BEEN HARDENED ON THE RUSSIAN FRONT.

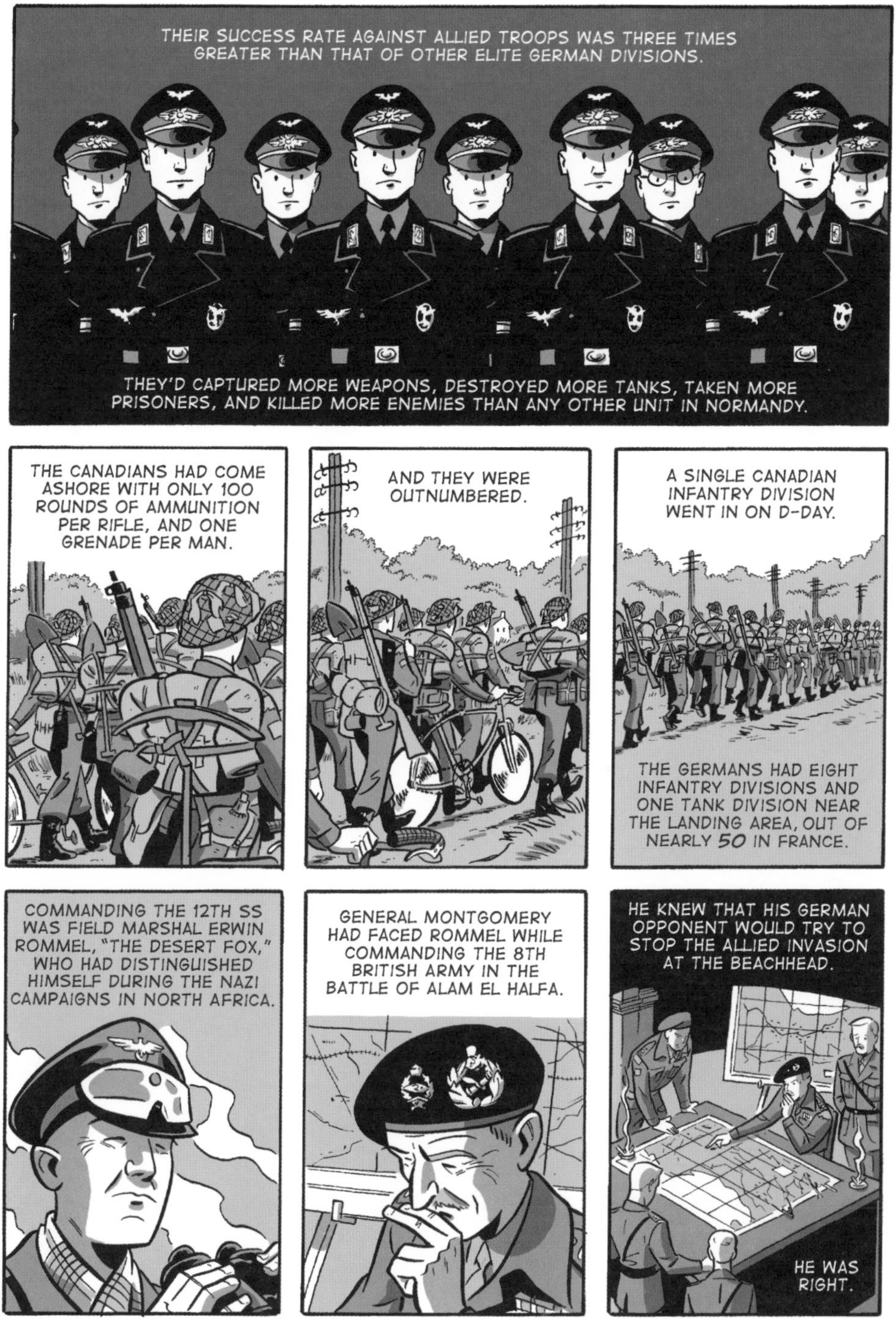
THEIR SUCCESS RATE AGAINST ALLIED TROOPS WAS THREE TIMES GREATER THAN THAT OF OTHER ELITE GERMAN DIVISIONS.
THEY'D CAPTURED MORE WEAPONS, DESTROYED MORE TANKS, TAKEN MORE PRISONERS, AND KILLED MORE ENEMIES THAN ANY OTHER UNIT IN NORMANDY.
THE CANADIANS HAD COME ASHORE WITH ONLY 100 ROUNDS OF AMMUNITION PER RIFLE, AND ONE GRENADE PER MAN.
AND THEY WERE OUTNUMBERED.
A SINGLE CANADIAN INFANTRY DIVISION WENT IN ON D-DAY.
THE GERMANS HAD EIGHT INFANTRY DIVISIONS AND ONE TANK DIVISION NEAR THE LANDING AREA, OUT OF NEARLY 50 IN FRANCE.
COMMANDING THE 12TH SS WAS FIELD MARSHAL ERWIN ROMMEL, "THE DESERT FOX," WHO HAD DISTINGUISHED HIMSELF DURING THE NAZI CAMPAIGNS IN NORTH AFRICA.
GENERAL MONTGOMERY HAD FACED ROMMEL WHILE COMMANDING THE 8TH BRITISH ARMY IN THE BATTLE OF ALAM EL HALFA.
HE KNEW THAT HIS GERMAN OPPONENT WOULD TRY TO STOP THE ALLIED INVASION AT THE BEACHHEAD.
HE WAS RIGHT.

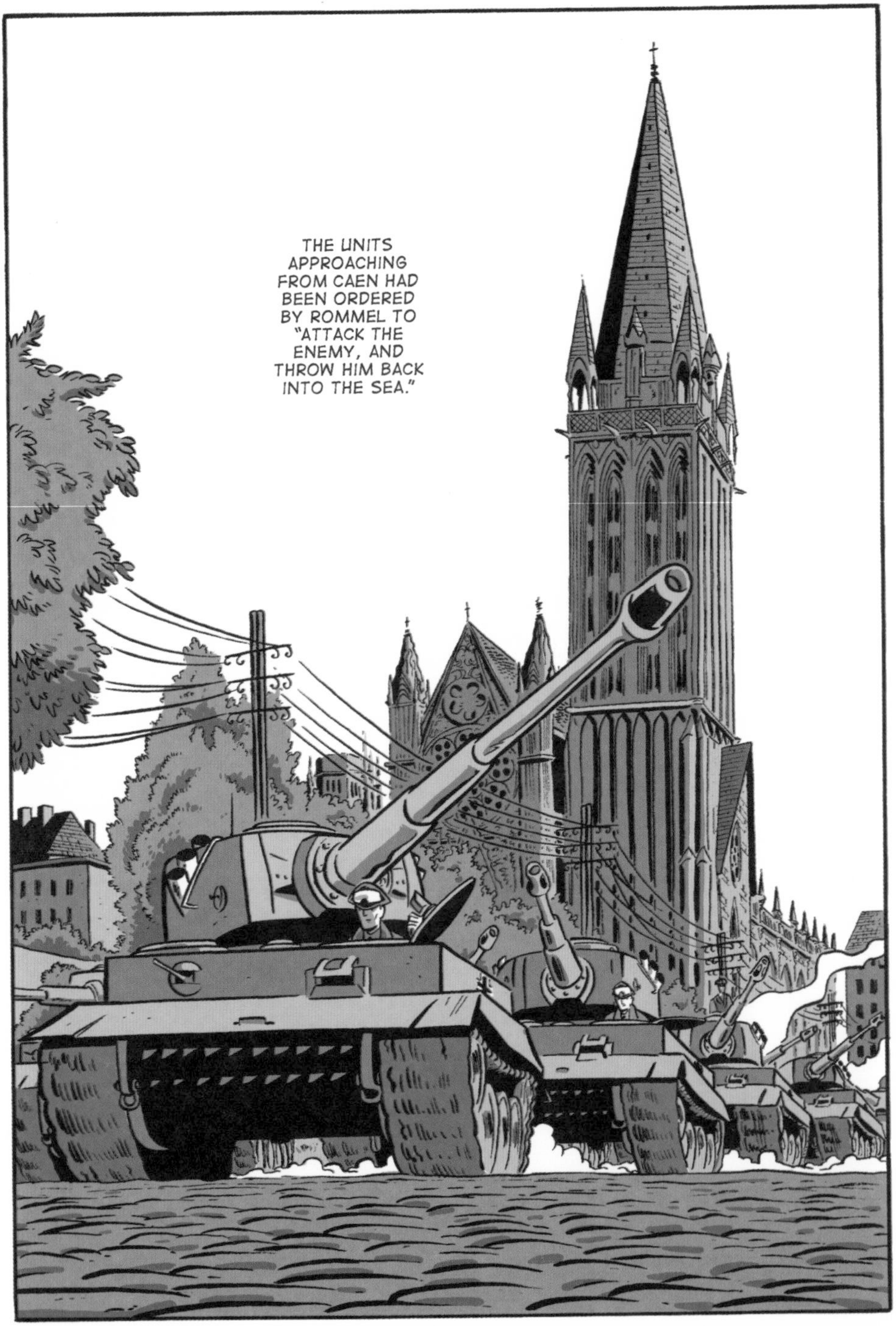
THE UNITS APPROACHING FROM CAEN HAD BEEN ORDERED BY ROMMEL TO "ATTACK THE ENEMY, AND THROW HIM BACK INTO THE SEA."

ON JUNE 7TH, ANOTHER CANADIAN REGIMENT, THE NORTH NOVA SCOTIA HIGHLANDERS, TOOK THE TOWN OF BURON, JUST FOUR MILES NORTHWEST OF CAEN.

THEY WERE THE FIRST TO BEAR THE BRUNT OF THE GERMAN COUNTER-ATTACK.

THE NAZIS USED AN ENGLISH-SPEAKING OFFICER TO BROADCAST FALSE ORDERS OVER THE CANADIANS' WIRELESS RADIOS.

DON'T STAND DOWN IN THE TRENCHES!

GET UP AND ADVANCE!

ENTIRE COMPANIES OF THE NNS WERE KILLED IN THIS MANNER.

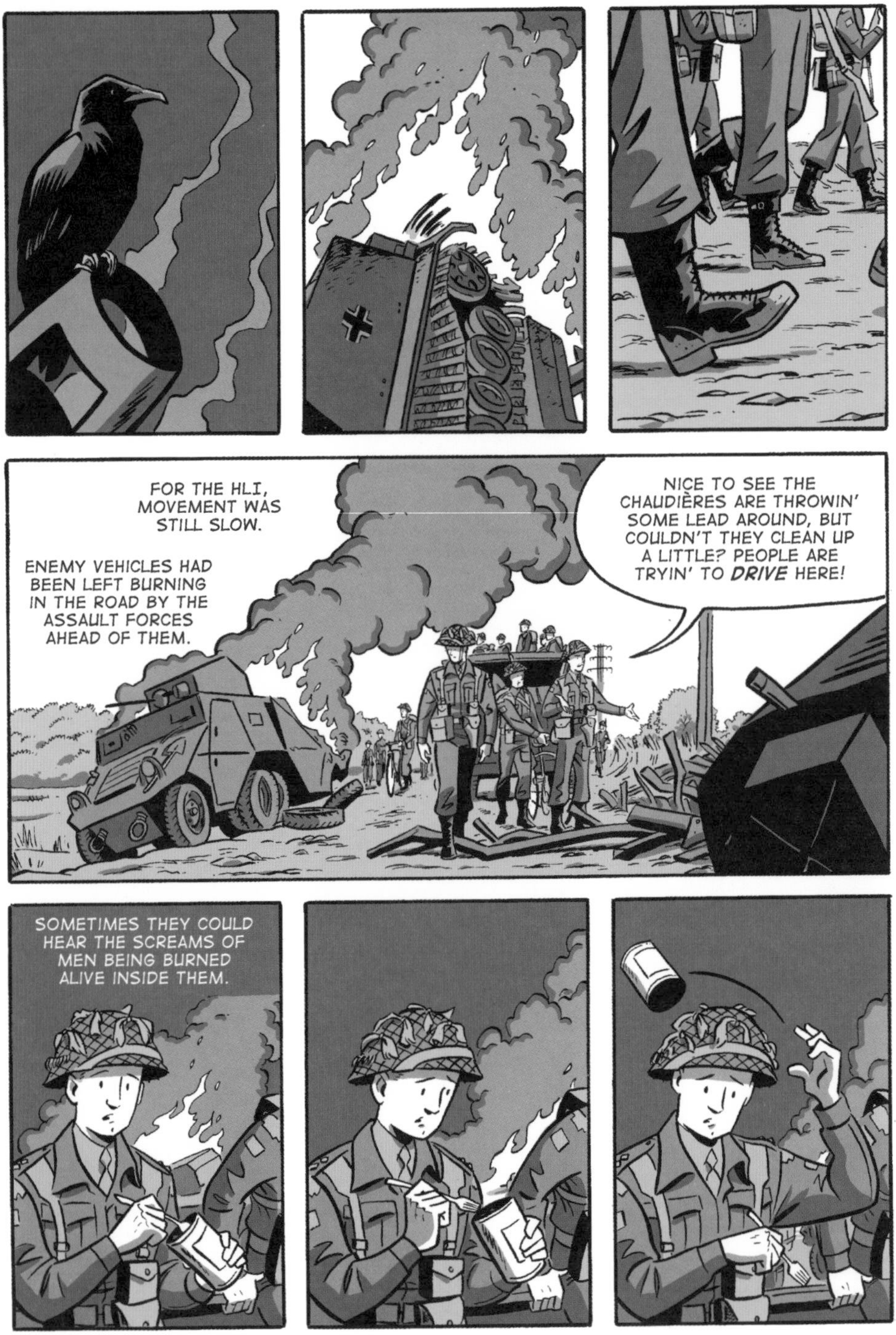
FOR THE HLI, MOVEMENT WAS STILL SLOW.
ENEMY VEHICLES HAD BEEN LEFT BURNING IN THE ROAD BY THE ASSAULT FORCES AHEAD OF THEM.
NICE TO SEE THE CHAUDIÈRES ARE THROWIN' SOME LEAD AROUND, BUT COULDN'T THEY CLEAN UP A LITTLE? PEOPLE ARE TRYIN' TO *DRIVE* HERE!
SOMETIMES THEY COULD HEAR THE SCREAMS OF MEN BEING BURNED ALIVE INSIDE THEM.

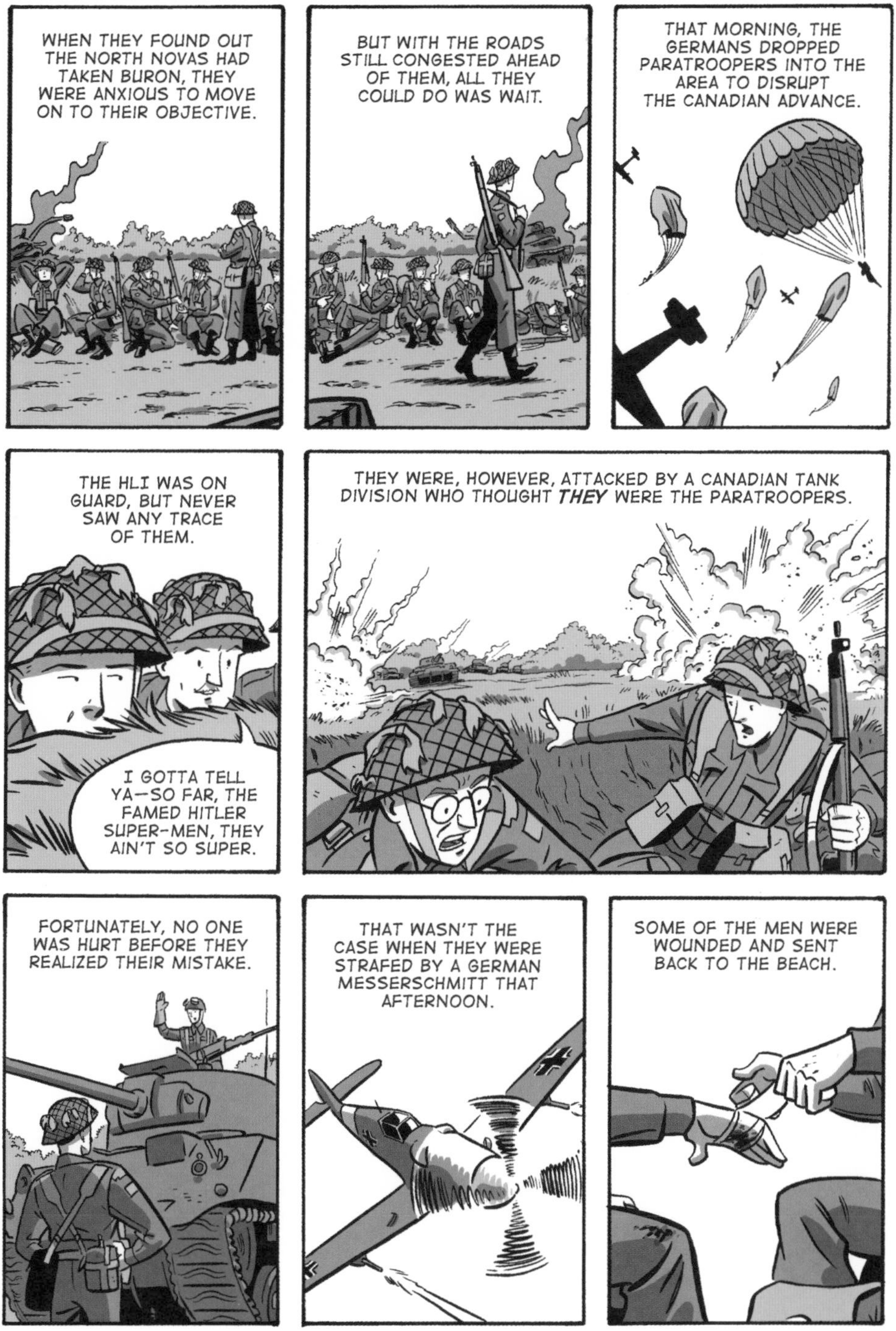
WHEN THEY FOUND OUT THE NORTH NOVAS HAD TAKEN BURON, THEY WERE ANXIOUS TO MOVE ON TO THEIR OBJECTIVE.
BUT WITH THE ROADS STILL CONGESTED AHEAD OF THEM, ALL THEY COULD DO WAS WAIT.
THAT MORNING, THE GERMANS DROPPED PARATROOPERS INTO THE AREA TO DISRUPT THE CANADIAN ADVANCE.
THE HLI WAS ON GUARD, BUT NEVER SAW ANY TRACE OF THEM.
I GOTTA TELL YA—SO FAR, THE FAMED HITLER SUPER-MEN, THEY AIN'T SO SUPER.
THEY WERE, HOWEVER, ATTACKED BY A CANADIAN TANK DIVISION WHO THOUGHT *THEY* WERE THE PARATROOPERS.
FORTUNATELY, NO ONE WAS HURT BEFORE THEY REALIZED THEIR MISTAKE.
THAT WASN'T THE CASE WHEN THEY WERE STRAFED BY A GERMAN MESSERSCHMITT THAT AFTERNOON.
SOME OF THE MEN WERE WOUNDED AND SENT BACK TO THE BEACH.

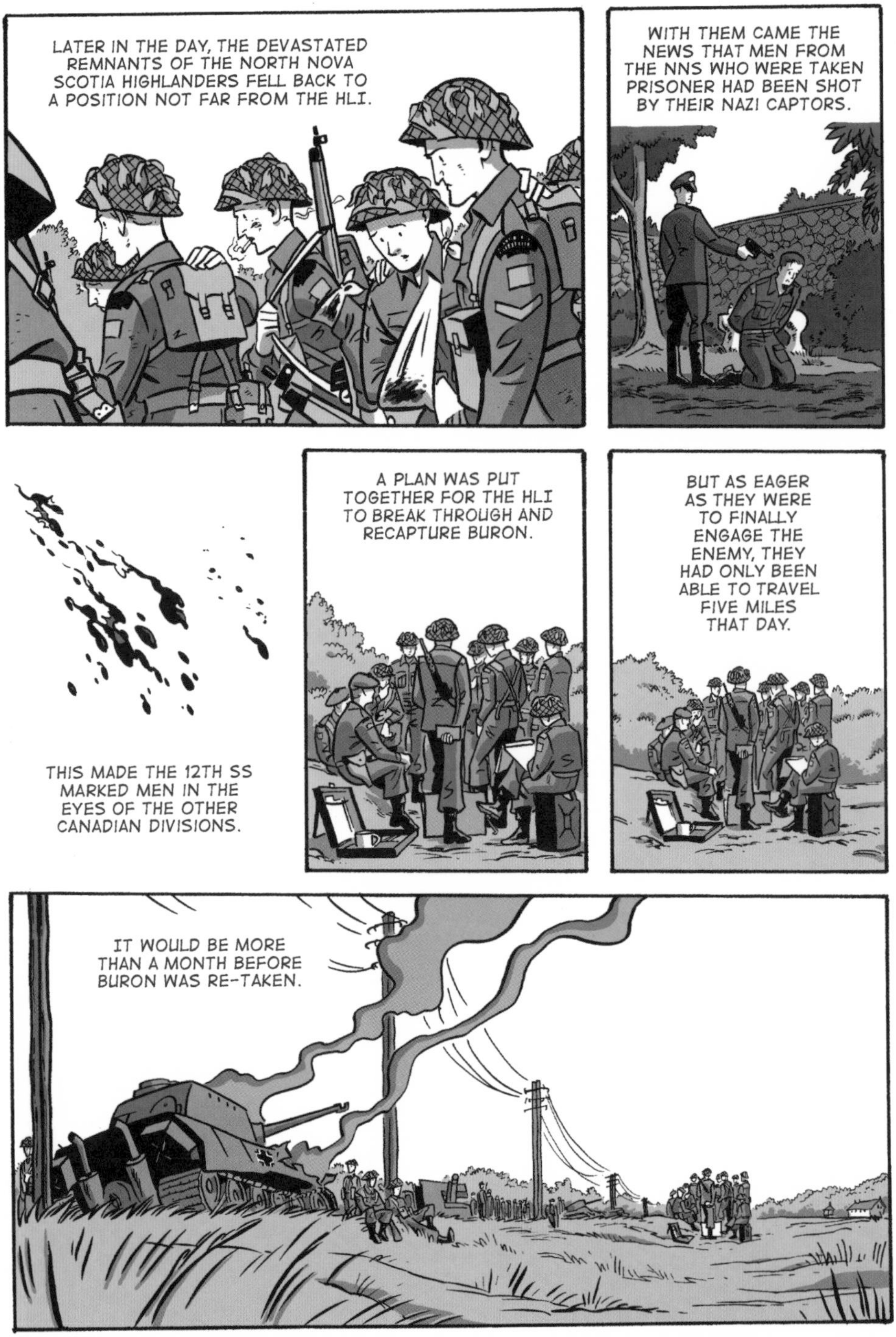
LATER IN THE DAY, THE DEVASTATED REMNANTS OF THE NORTH NOVA SCOTIA HIGHLANDERS FELL BACK TO A POSITION NOT FAR FROM THE HLI.
WITH THEM CAME THE NEWS THAT MEN FROM THE NNS WHO WERE TAKEN PRISONER HAD BEEN SHOT BY THEIR NAZI CAPTORS.
THIS MADE THE 12TH SS MARKED MEN IN THE EYES OF THE OTHER CANADIAN DIVISIONS.
A PLAN WAS PUT TOGETHER FOR THE HLI TO BREAK THROUGH AND RECAPTURE BURON.
BUT AS EAGER AS THEY WERE TO FINALLY ENGAGE THE ENEMY, THEY HAD ONLY BEEN ABLE TO TRAVEL FIVE MILES THAT DAY.
IT WOULD BE MORE THAN A MONTH BEFORE BURON WAS RE-TAKEN.

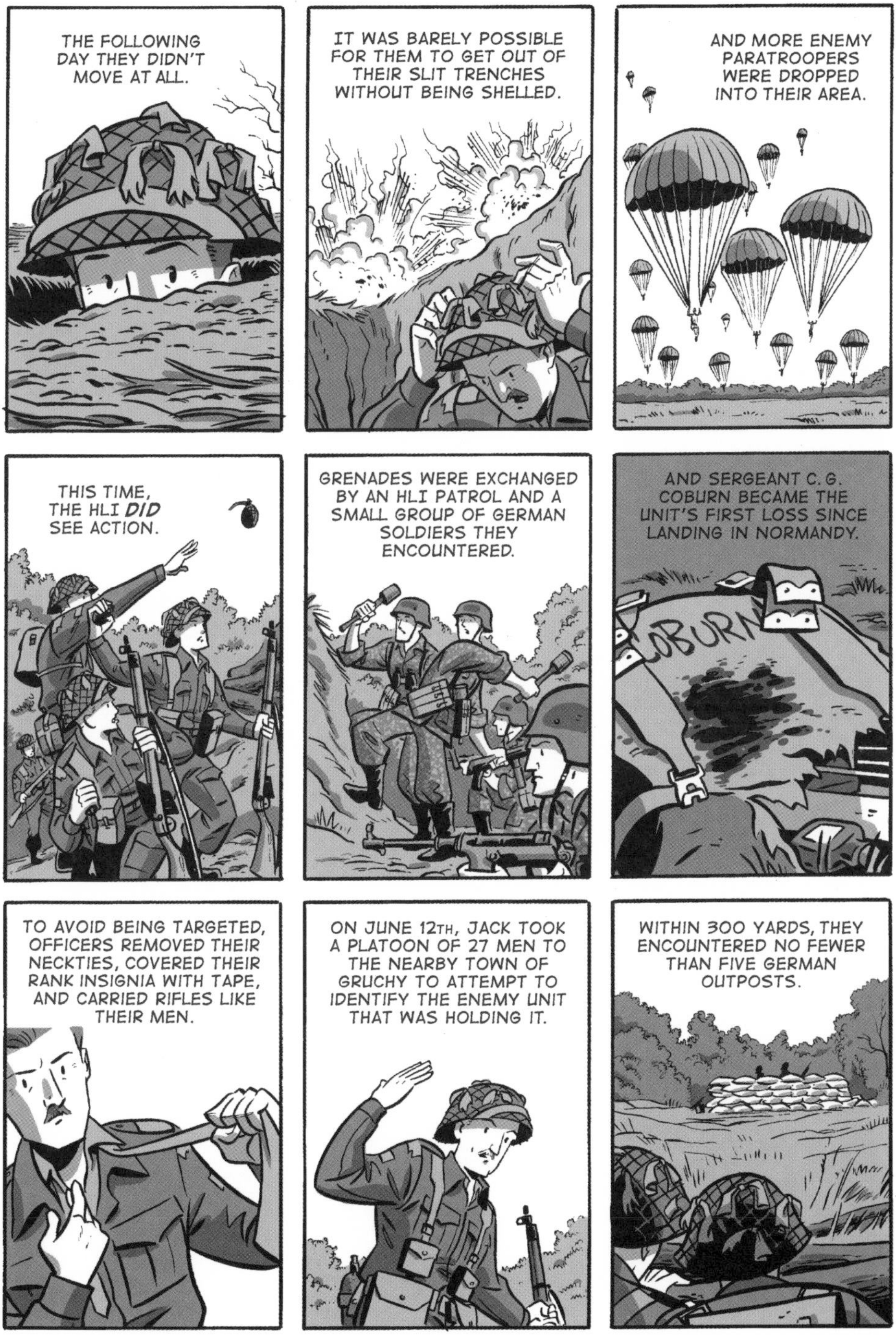
THE FOLLOWING DAY THEY DIDN'T MOVE AT ALL.
IT WAS BARELY POSSIBLE FOR THEM TO GET OUT OF THEIR SLIT TRENCHES WITHOUT BEING SHELLED.
AND MORE ENEMY PARATROOPERS WERE DROPPED INTO THEIR AREA.
THIS TIME, THE HLI *DID* SEE ACTION.
GRENADES WERE EXCHANGED BY AN HLI PATROL AND A SMALL GROUP OF GERMAN SOLDIERS THEY ENCOUNTERED.
AND SERGEANT C.G. COBURN BECAME THE UNIT'S FIRST LOSS SINCE LANDING IN NORMANDY.
TO AVOID BEING TARGETED, OFFICERS REMOVED THEIR NECKTIES, COVERED THEIR RANK INSIGNIA WITH TAPE, AND CARRIED RIFLES LIKE THEIR MEN.
ON JUNE 12TH, JACK TOOK A PLATOON OF 27 MEN TO THE NEARBY TOWN OF GRUCHY TO ATTEMPT TO IDENTIFY THE ENEMY UNIT THAT WAS HOLDING IT.
WITHIN 300 YARDS, THEY ENCOUNTERED NO FEWER THAN FIVE GERMAN OUTPOSTS.

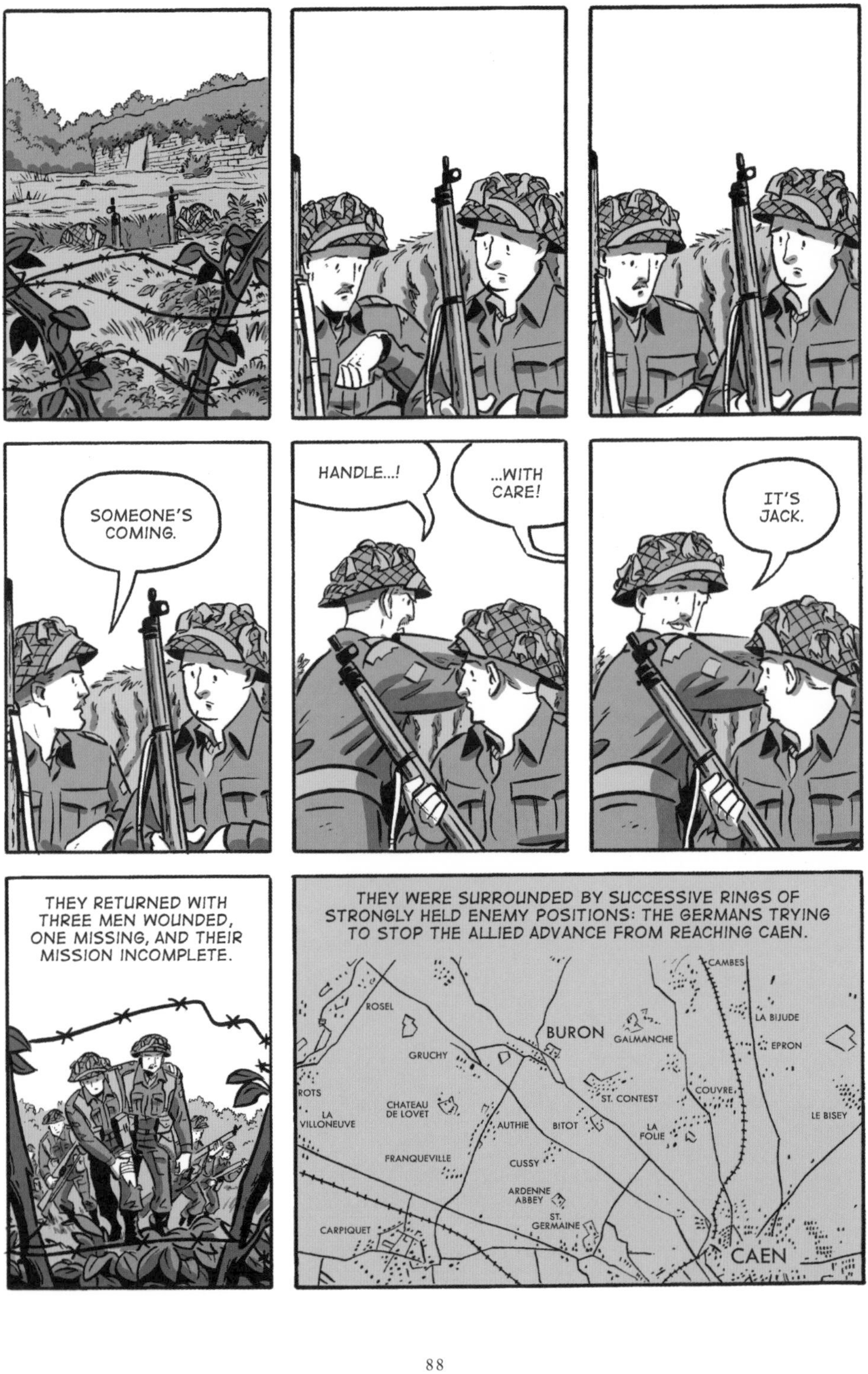
SOMEONE'S COMING.
HANDLE...!
...WITH CARE!
IT'S JACK.
THEY RETURNED WITH THREE MEN WOUNDED, ONE MISSING, AND THEIR MISSION INCOMPLETE.
THEY WERE SURROUNDED BY SUCCESSIVE RINGS OF STRONGLY HELD ENEMY POSITIONS: THE GERMANS TRYING TO STOP THE ALLIED ADVANCE FROM REACHING CAEN.
CAMBES
ROSEL
LA BIJUDE
BURON
GALMANCHE
EPRON
GRUCHY
ROTS
COUVRE
ST. CONTEST
CHATEAU DE LOVET
LA VILLONEUVE
LE BISEY
AUTHIE
BITOT
LA FOLIE
FRANQUEVILLE
CUSSY
ARDENNE ABBEY
ST. GERMAINE
CARPIQUET
CAEN

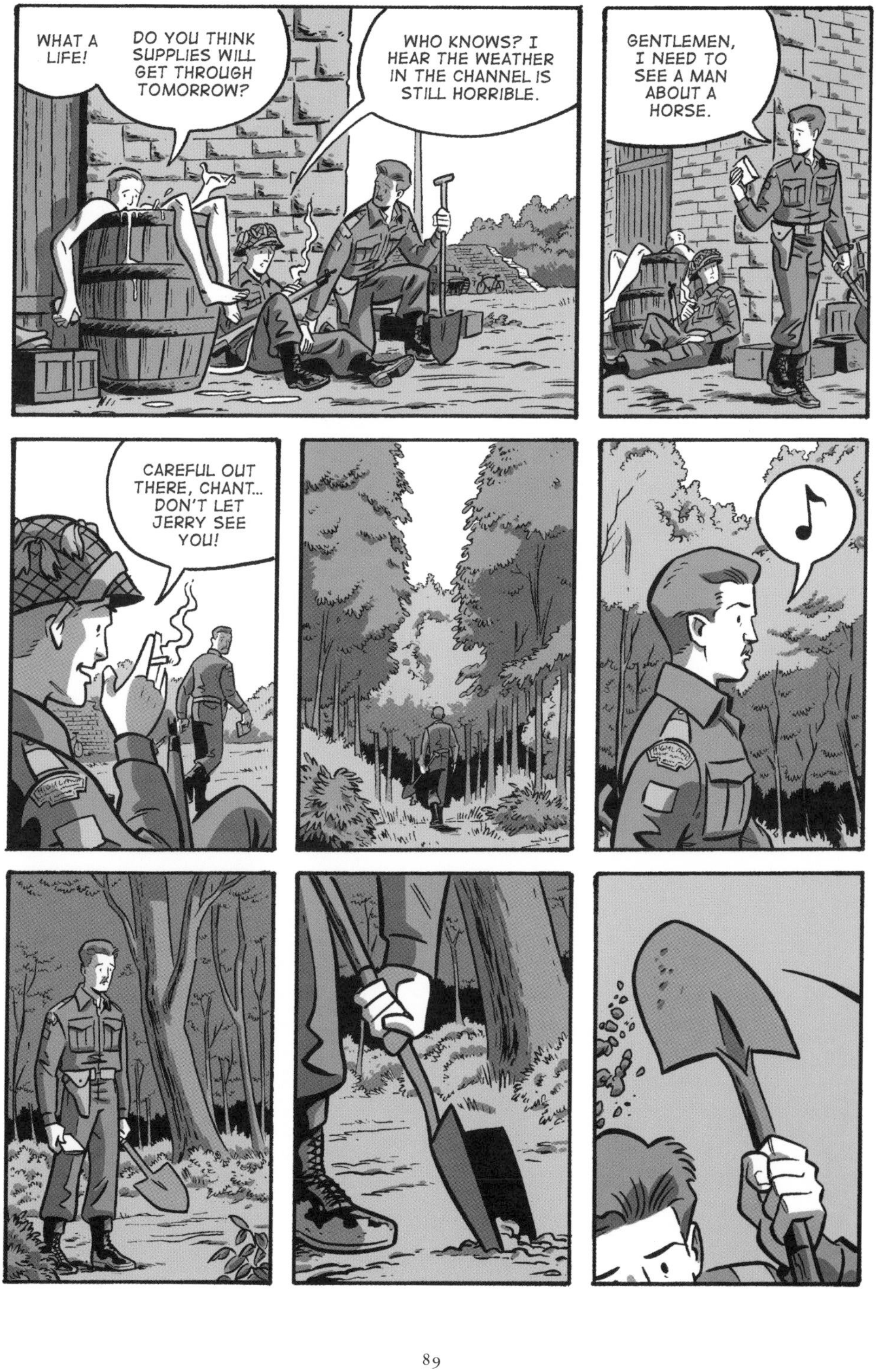
WHAT A LIFE!
DO YOU THINK SUPPLIES WILL GET THROUGH TOMORROW?
WHO KNOWS? I HEAR THE WEATHER IN THE CHANNEL IS STILL HORRIBLE.
GENTLEMEN, I NEED TO SEE A MAN ABOUT A HORSE.
CAREFUL OUT THERE, CHANT... DON'T LET JERRY SEE YOU!
♪

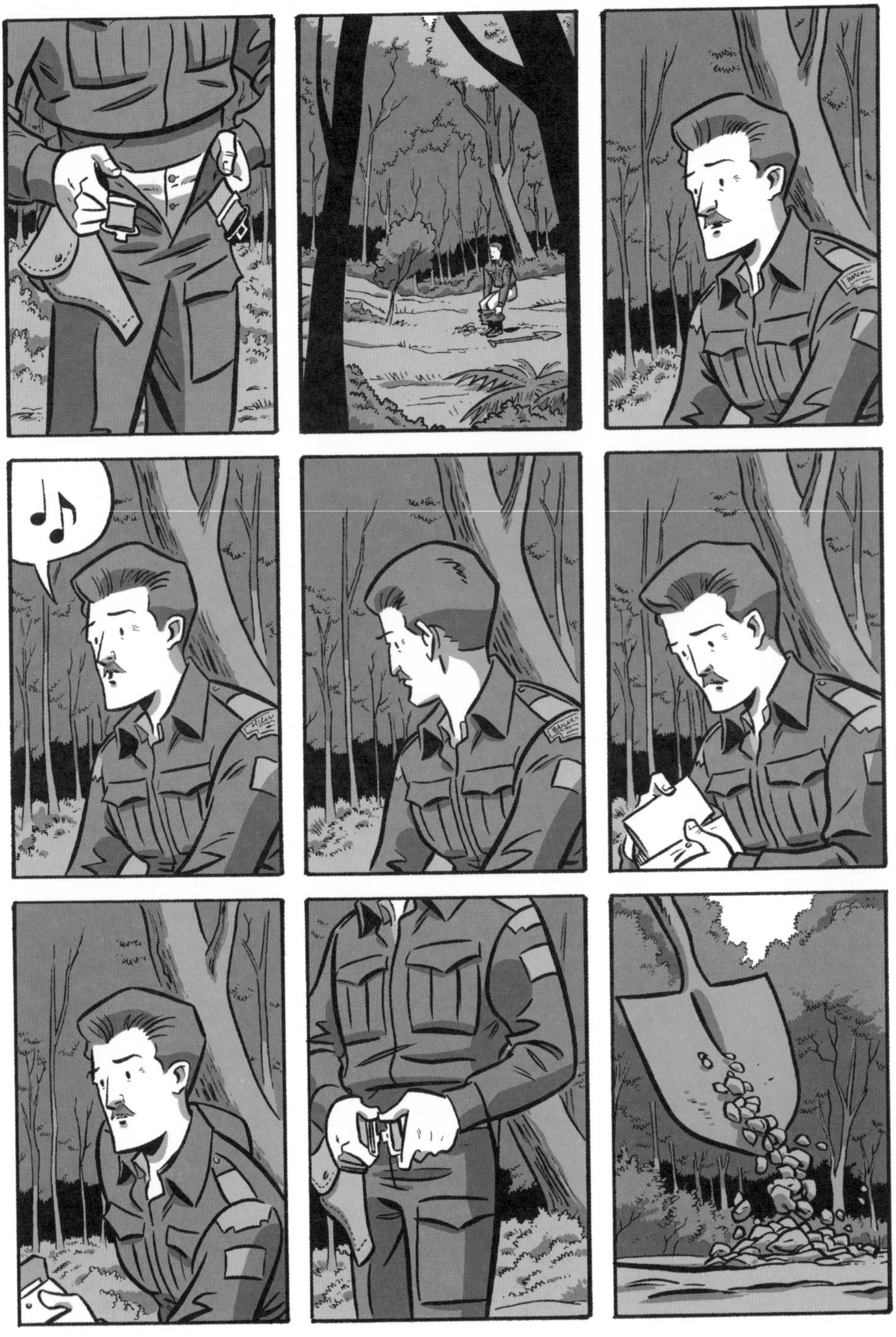

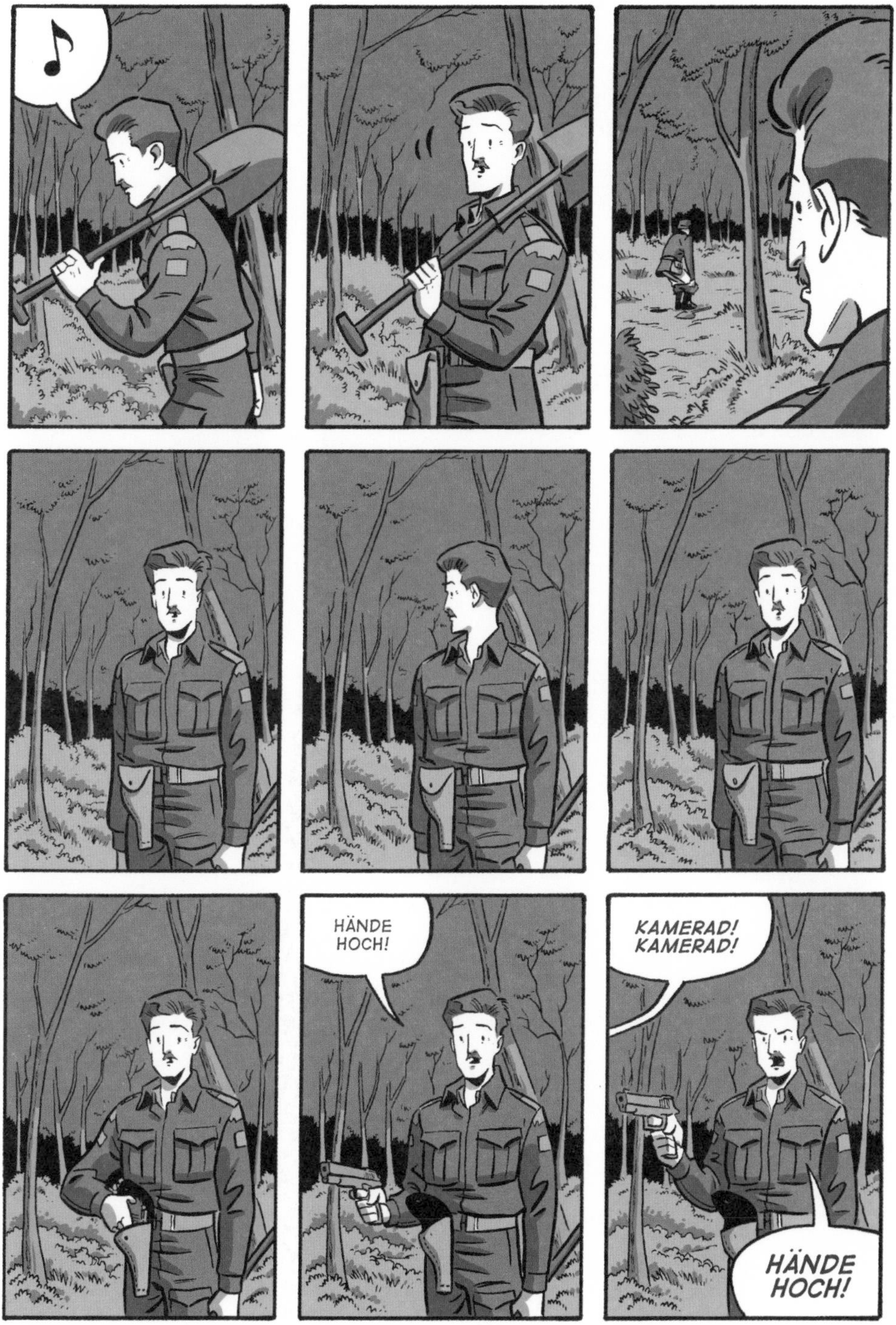
♪
HÄNDE HOCH!
KAMERAD! KAMERAD!
HÄNDE HOCH!

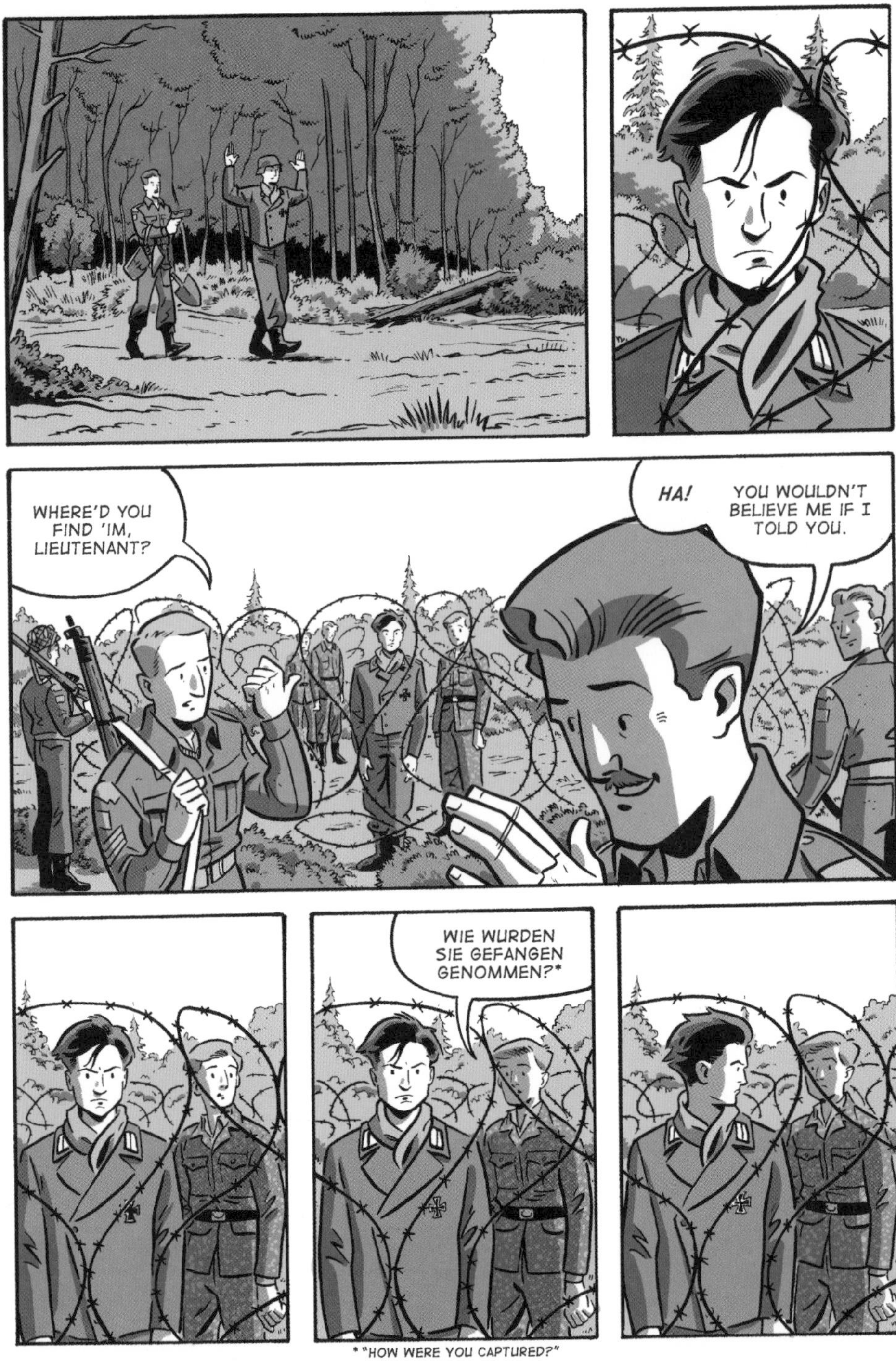
WHERE'D YOU FIND 'IM, LIEUTENANT?
HA!
YOU WOULDN'T BELIEVE ME IF I TOLD YOU.
WIE WURDEN SIE GEFANGEN GENOMMEN?*

* "HOW WERE YOU CAPTURED?"

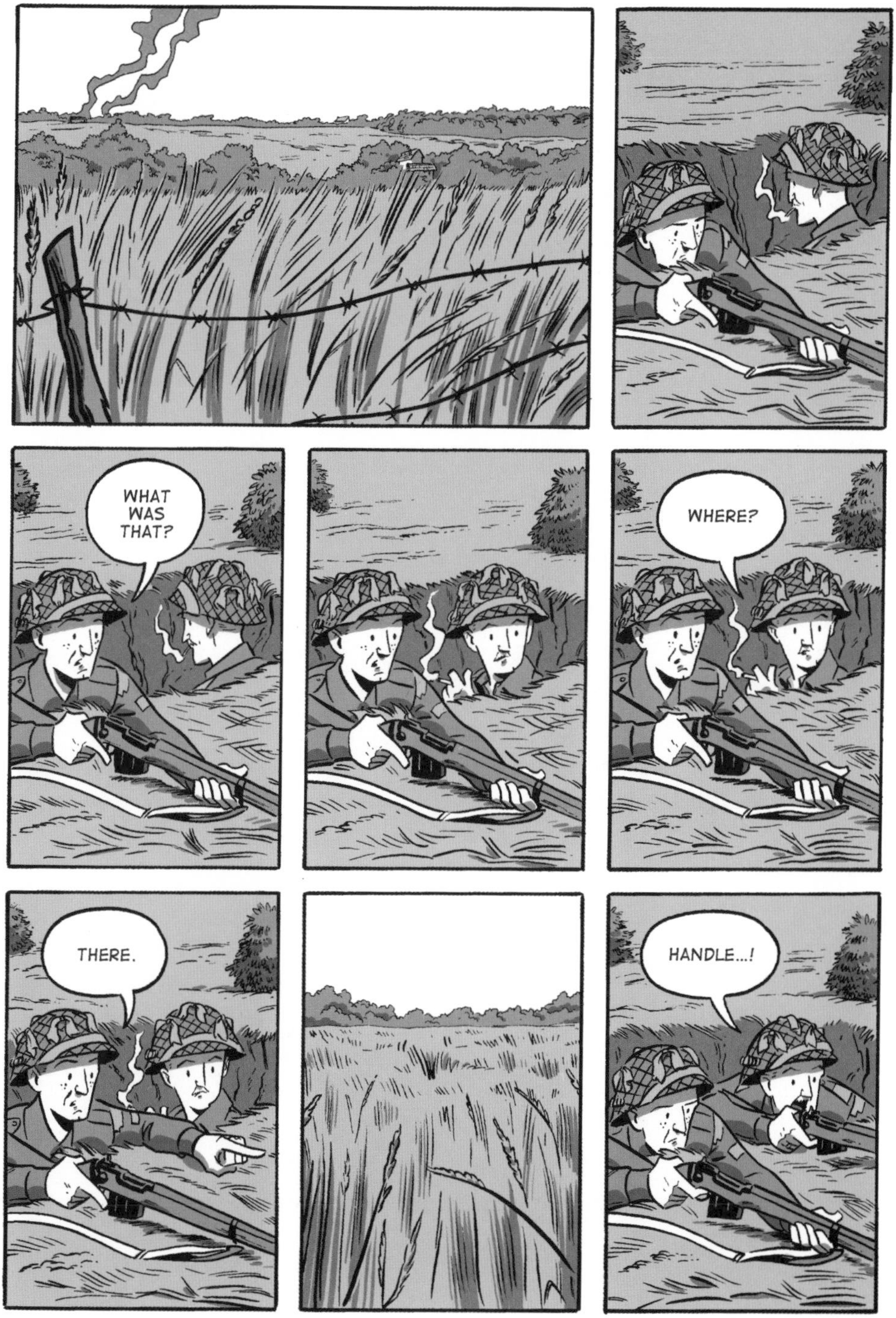
WHAT WAS THAT?
WHERE?
THERE.
HANDLE...!

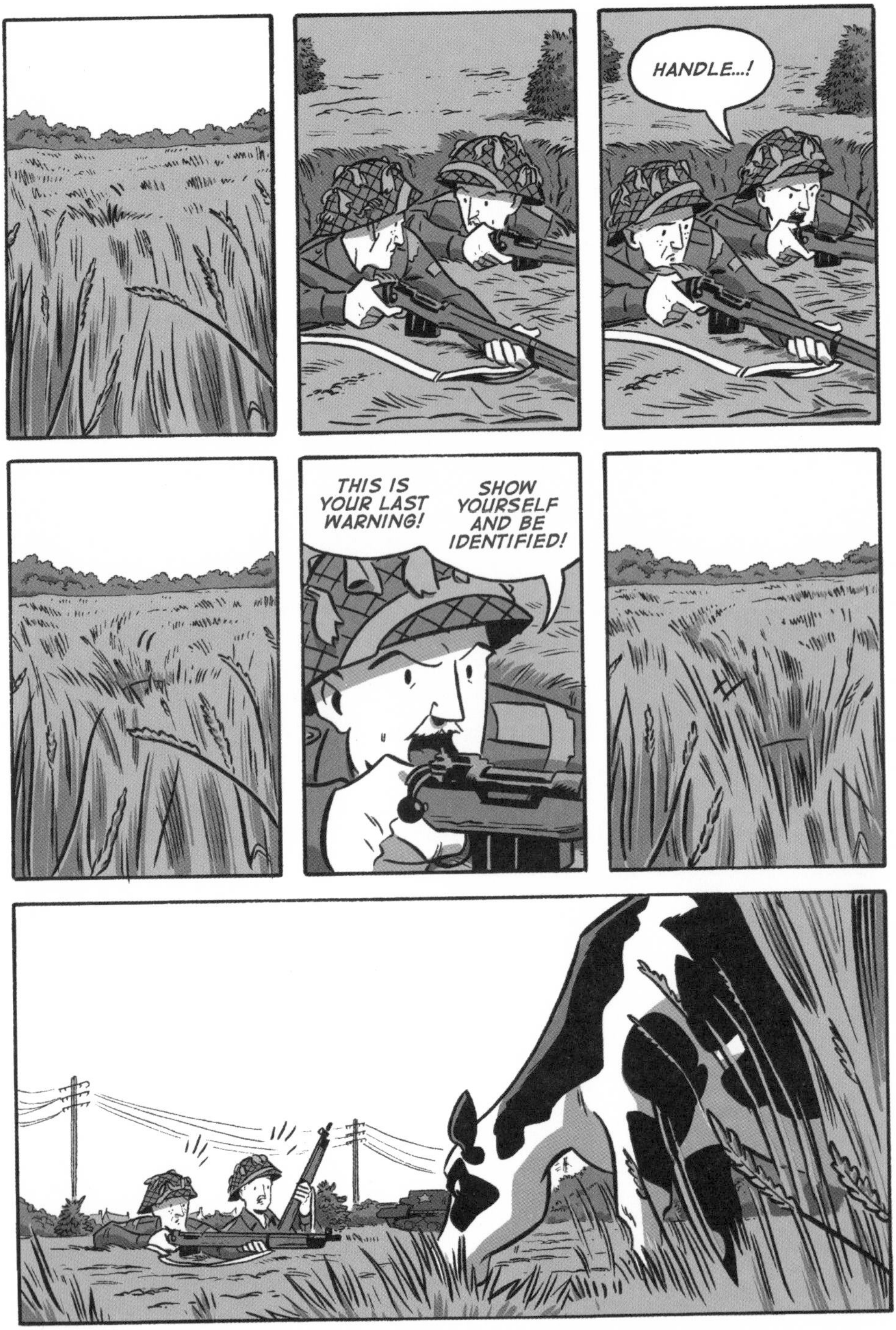
HANDLE...!
THIS IS YOUR LAST WARNING!
SHOW YOURSELF AND BE IDENTIFIED!

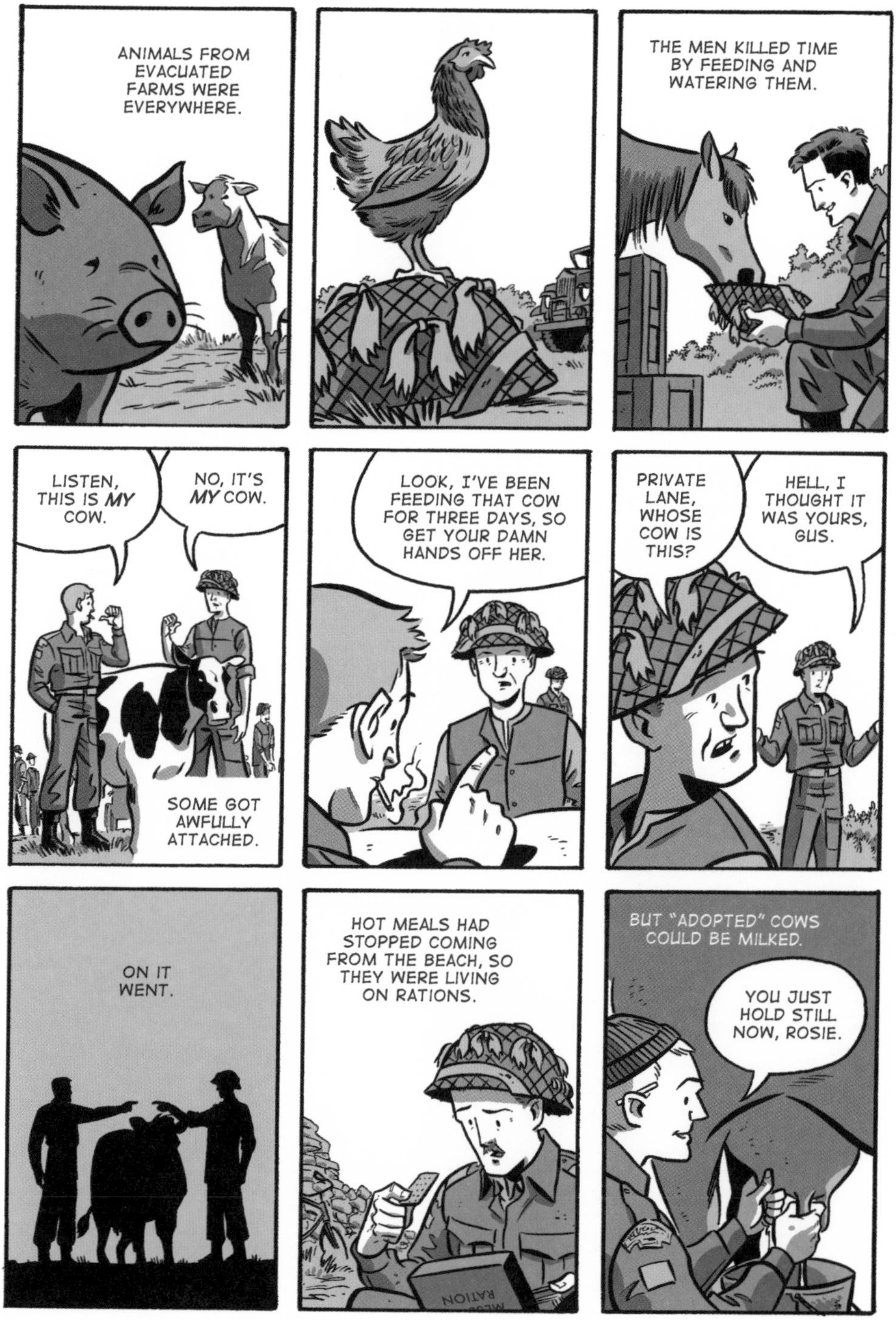
ANIMALS FROM EVACUATED FARMS WERE EVERYWHERE.
THE MEN KILLED TIME BY FEEDING AND WATERING THEM.
LISTEN, THIS IS MY COW.
NO, IT'S MY COW.
SOME GOT AWFULLY ATTACHED.
LOOK, I'VE BEEN FEEDING THAT COW FOR THREE DAYS, SO GET YOUR DAMN HANDS OFF HER.
PRIVATE LANE, WHOSE COW IS THIS?
HELL, I THOUGHT IT WAS YOURS, GUS.
ON IT WENT.
HOT MEALS HAD STOPPED COMING FROM THE BEACH, SO THEY WERE LIVING ON RATIONS.
BUT "ADOPTED" COWS COULD BE MILKED.
YOU JUST HOLD STILL NOW, ROSIE.

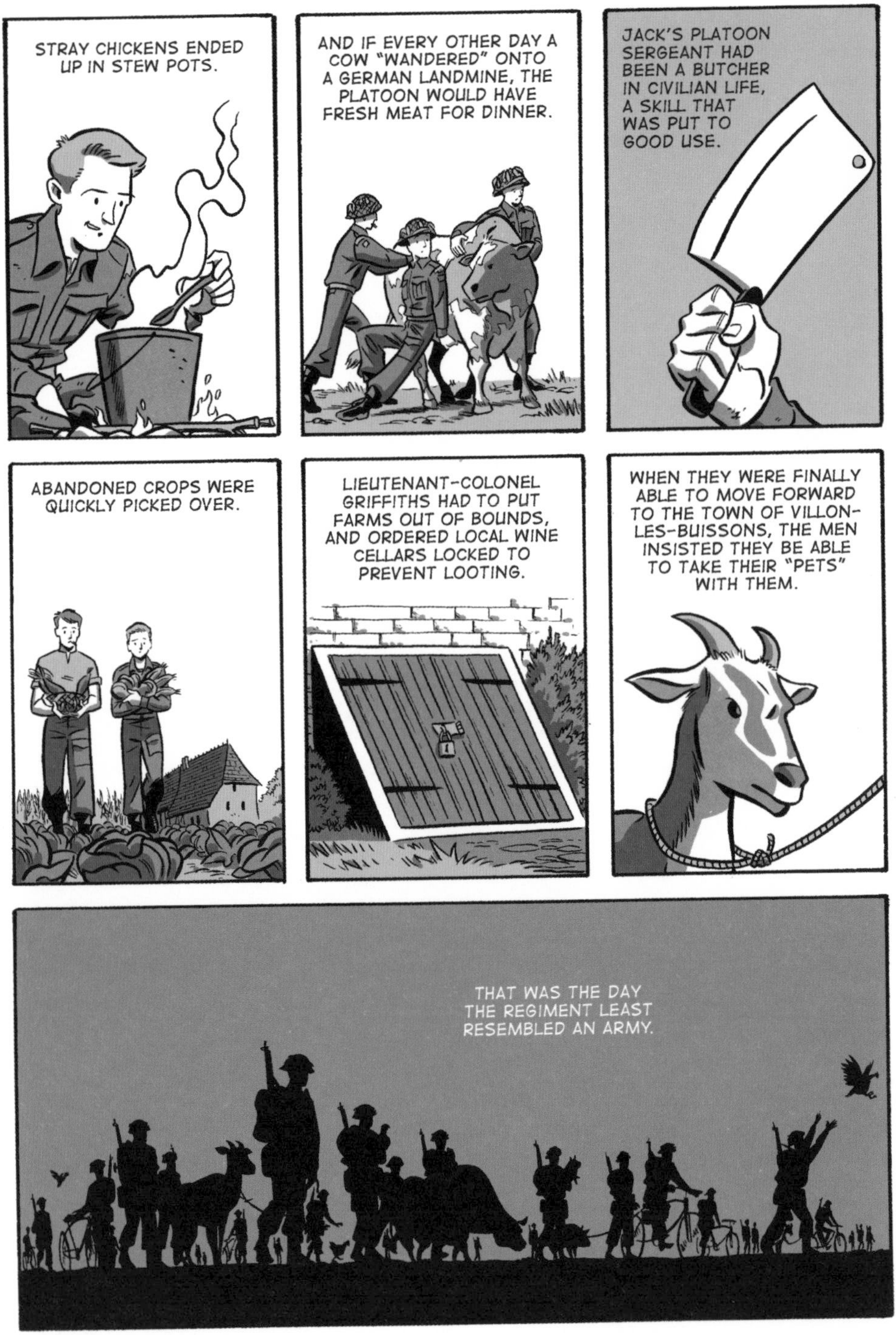
STRAY CHICKENS ENDED UP IN STEW POTS.
AND IF EVERY OTHER DAY A COW "WANDERED" ONTO A GERMAN LANDMINE, THE PLATOON WOULD HAVE FRESH MEAT FOR DINNER.
JACK'S PLATOON SERGEANT HAD BEEN A BUTCHER IN CIVILIAN LIFE, A SKILL THAT WAS PUT TO GOOD USE.
ABANDONED CROPS WERE QUICKLY PICKED OVER.
LIEUTENANT-COLONEL GRIFFITHS HAD TO PUT FARMS OUT OF BOUNDS, AND ORDERED LOCAL WINE CELLARS LOCKED TO PREVENT LOOTING.
WHEN THEY WERE FINALLY ABLE TO MOVE FORWARD TO THE TOWN OF VILLON-LES-BUISSONS, THE MEN INSISTED THEY BE ABLE TO TAKE THEIR "PETS" WITH THEM.
THAT WAS THE DAY THE REGIMENT LEAST RESEMBLED AN ARMY.

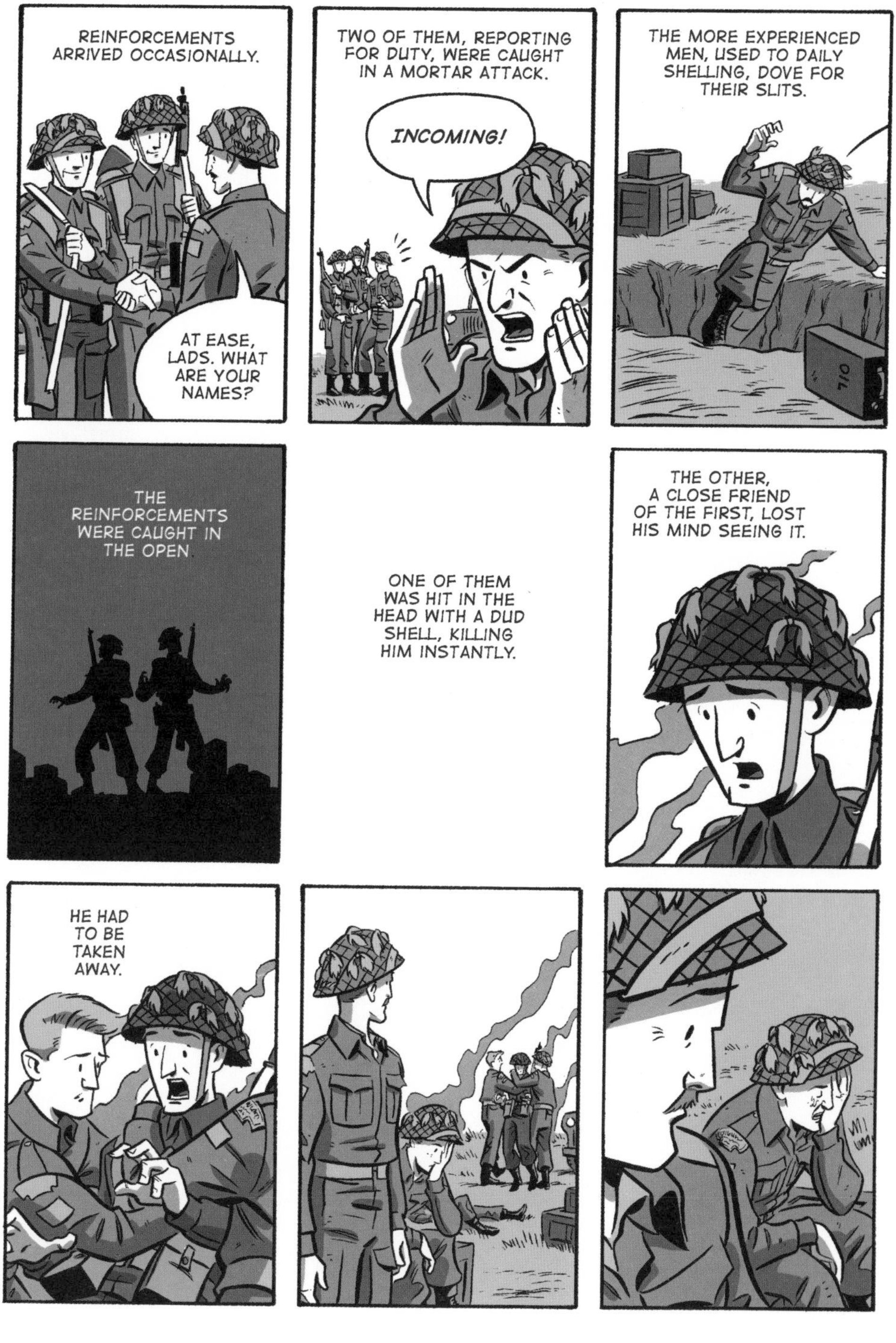
REINFORCEMENTS ARRIVED OCCASIONALLY.
AT EASE, LADS. WHAT ARE YOUR NAMES?
TWO OF THEM, REPORTING FOR DUTY, WERE CAUGHT IN A MORTAR ATTACK.
INCOMING!
THE MORE EXPERIENCED MEN, USED TO DAILY SHELLING, DOVE FOR THEIR SLITS.
THE REINFORCEMENTS WERE CAUGHT IN THE OPEN.
ONE OF THEM WAS HIT IN THE HEAD WITH A DUD SHELL, KILLING HIM INSTANTLY.
THE OTHER, A CLOSE FRIEND OF THE FIRST, LOST HIS MIND SEEING IT.
HE HAD TO BE TAKEN AWAY.

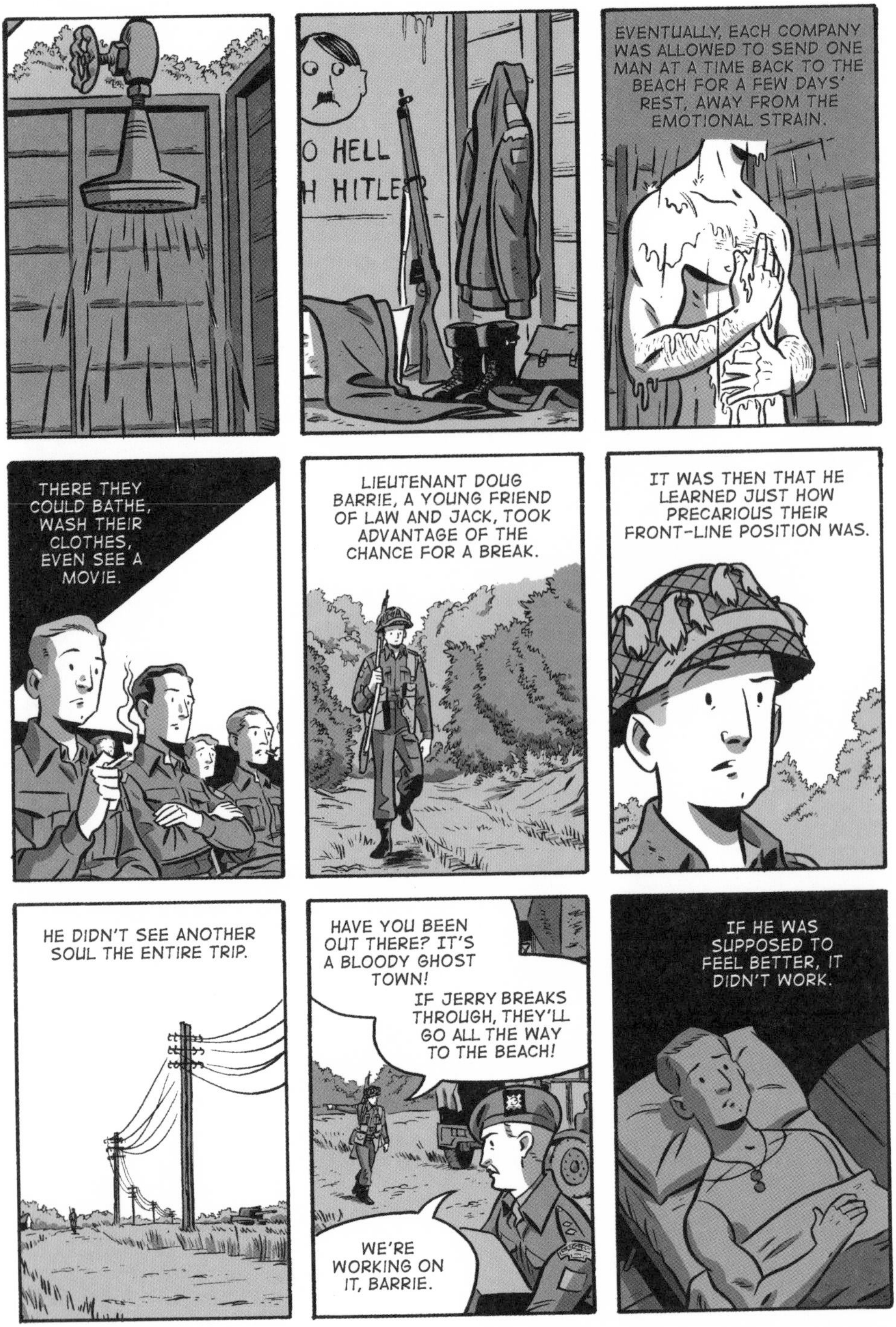
O HELL
H HITLE
EVENTUALLY, EACH COMPANY WAS ALLOWED TO SEND ONE MAN AT A TIME BACK TO THE BEACH FOR A FEW DAYS' REST, AWAY FROM THE EMOTIONAL STRAIN.
THERE THEY COULD BATHE, WASH THEIR CLOTHES, EVEN SEE A MOVIE.
LIEUTENANT DOUG BARRIE, A YOUNG FRIEND OF LAW AND JACK, TOOK ADVANTAGE OF THE CHANCE FOR A BREAK.
IT WAS THEN THAT HE LEARNED JUST HOW PRECARIOUS THEIR FRONT-LINE POSITION WAS.
HE DIDN'T SEE ANOTHER SOUL THE ENTIRE TRIP.
HAVE YOU BEEN OUT THERE? IT'S A BLOODY GHOST TOWN!
IF JERRY BREAKS THROUGH, THEY'LL GO ALL THE WAY TO THE BEACH!
WE'RE WORKING ON IT, BARRIE.
IF HE WAS SUPPOSED TO FEEL BETTER, IT DIDN'T WORK.

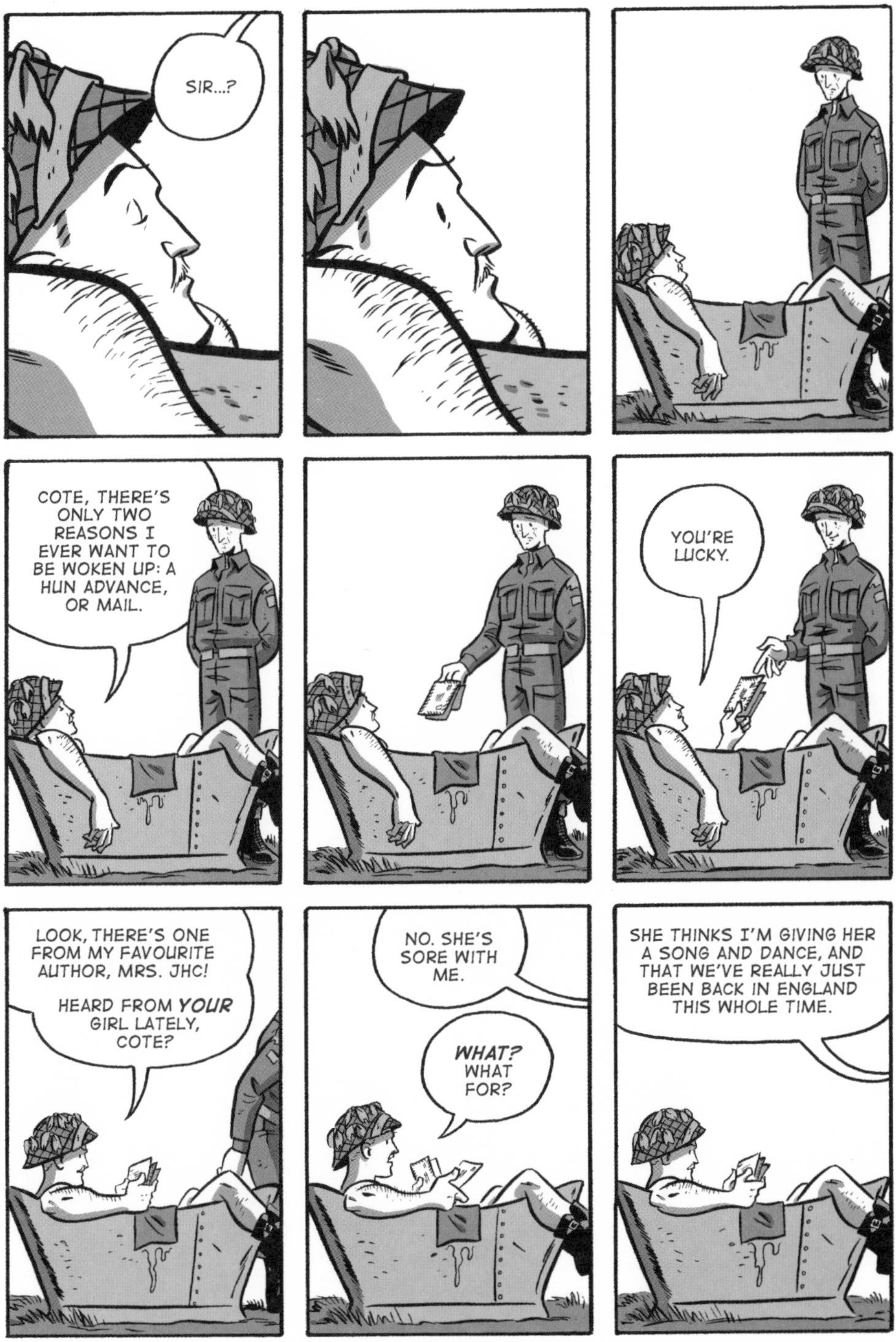
SIR...?
COTE, THERE'S ONLY TWO REASONS I EVER WANT TO BE WOKEN UP: A HUN ADVANCE, OR MAIL.
YOU'RE LUCKY.
LOOK, THERE'S ONE FROM MY FAVOURITE AUTHOR, MRS. JHC!
HEARD FROM **YOUR** GIRL LATELY, COTE?
NO. SHE'S SORE WITH ME.
**WHAT?** WHAT FOR?
SHE THINKS I'M GIVING HER A SONG AND DANCE, AND THAT WE'VE REALLY JUST BEEN BACK IN ENGLAND THIS WHOLE TIME.

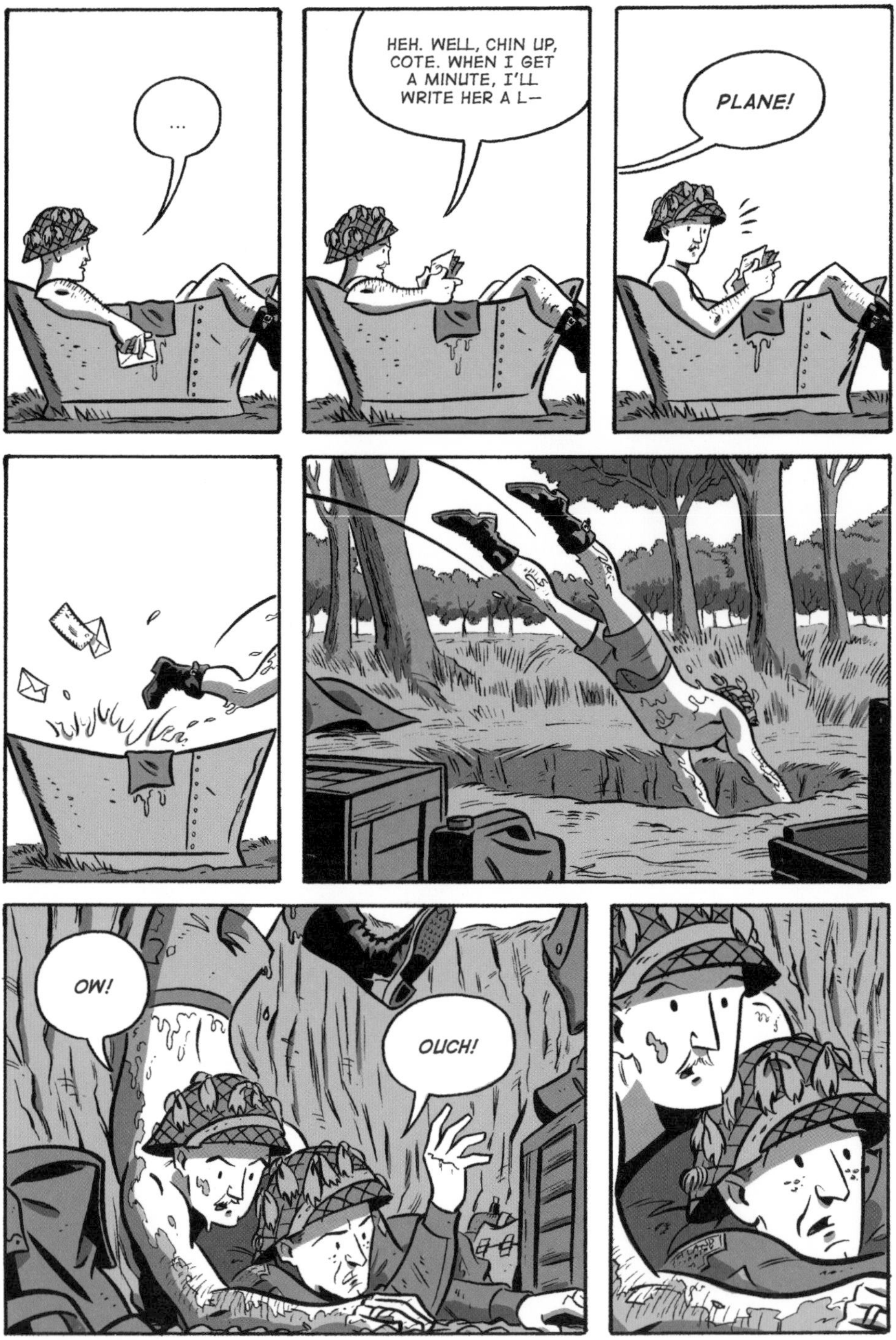
...
HEH. WELL, CHIN UP, COTE. WHEN I GET A MINUTE, I'LL WRITE HER A L—
PLANE!
OW!
OUCH!

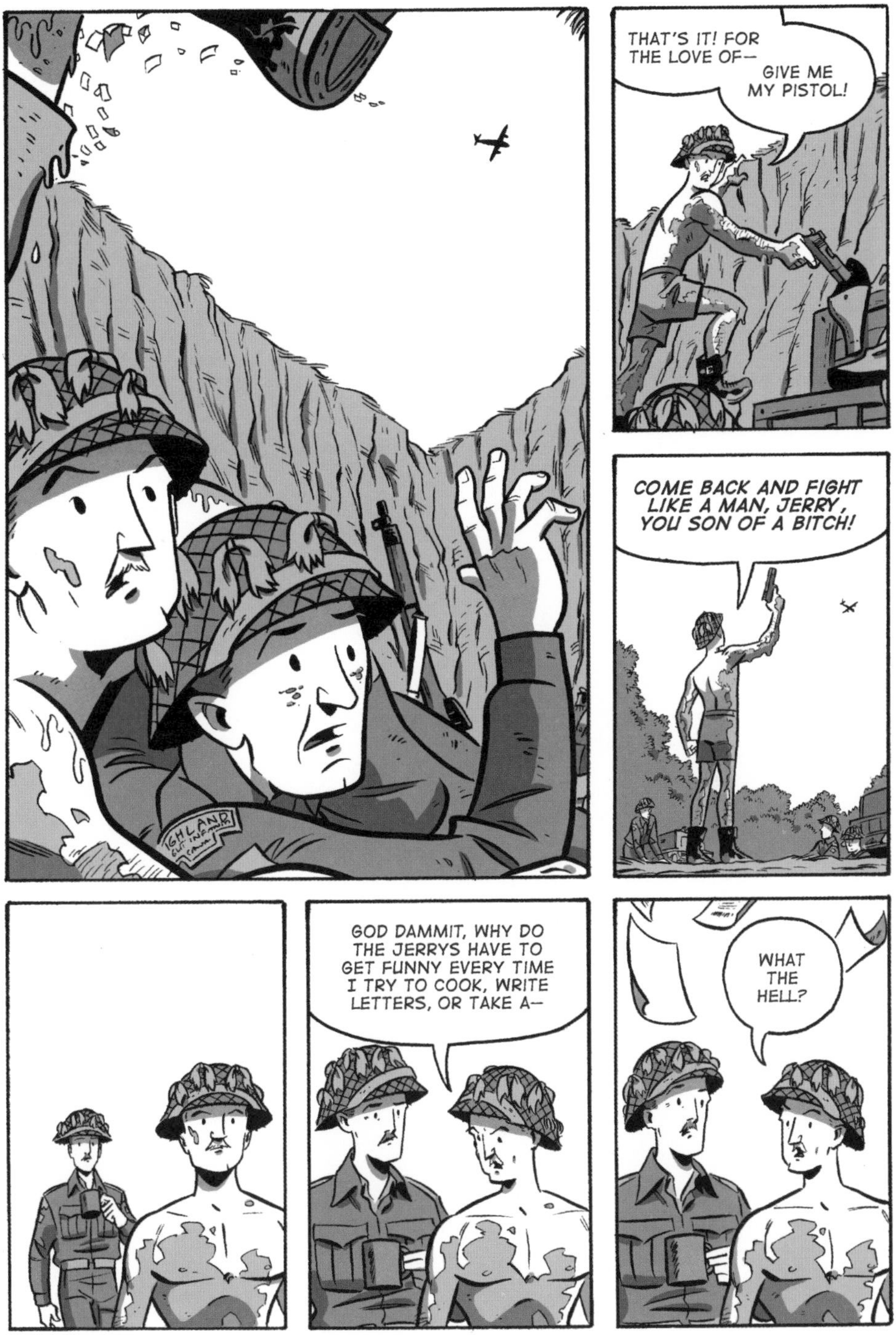
THAT'S IT! FOR THE LOVE OF—
GIVE ME MY PISTOL!
COME BACK AND FIGHT LIKE A MAN, JERRY, YOU SON OF A BITCH!
GOD DAMMIT, WHY DO THE JERRYS HAVE TO GET FUNNY EVERY TIME I TRY TO COOK, WRITE LETTERS, OR TAKE A—
WHAT THE HELL?

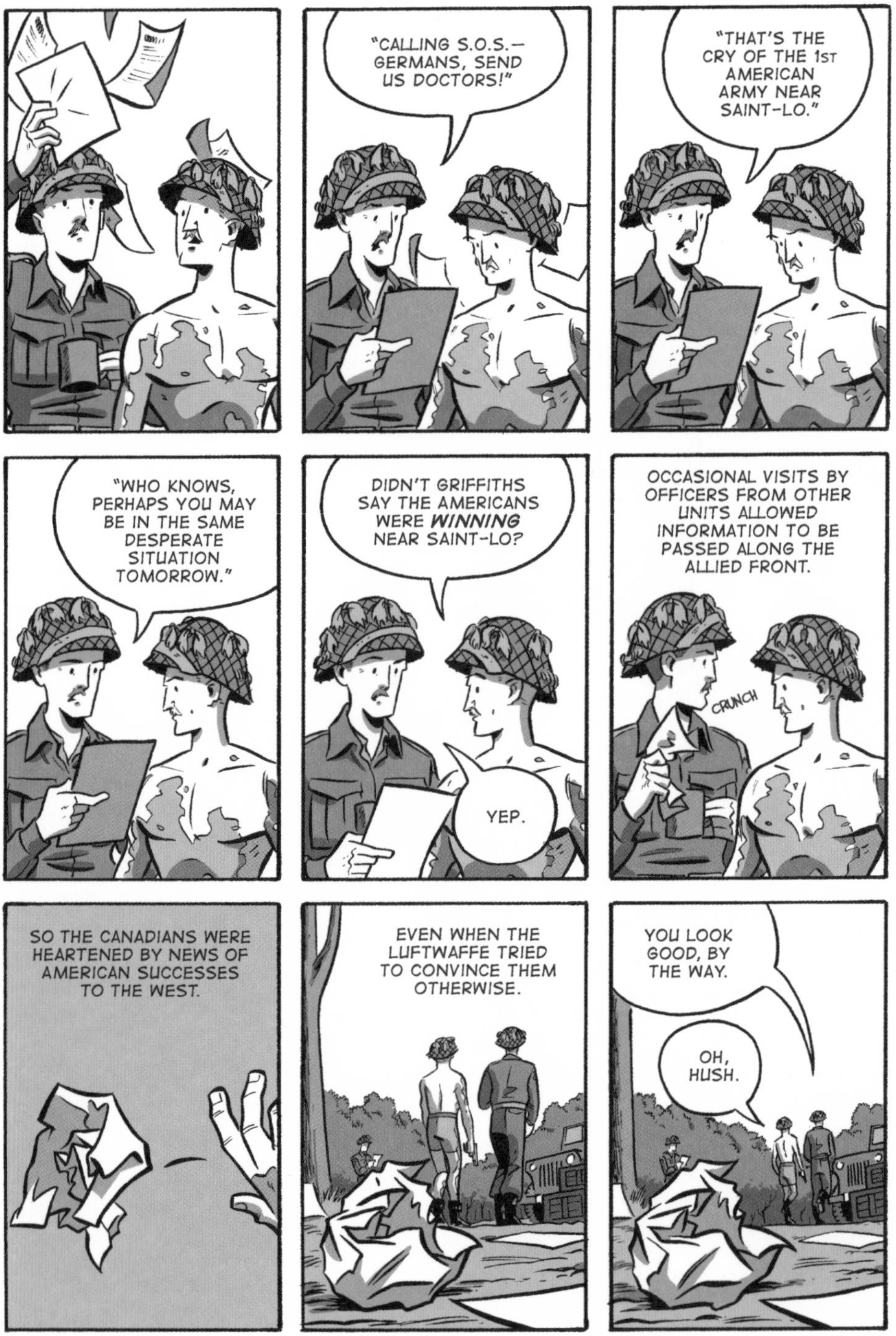
"CALLING S.O.S.— GERMANS, SEND US DOCTORS!"
"THAT'S THE CRY OF THE 1ST AMERICAN ARMY NEAR SAINT-LO."
"WHO KNOWS, PERHAPS YOU MAY BE IN THE SAME DESPERATE SITUATION TOMORROW."
DIDN'T GRIFFITHS SAY THE AMERICANS WERE *WINNING* NEAR SAINT-LO?
YEP.
OCCASIONAL VISITS BY OFFICERS FROM OTHER UNITS ALLOWED INFORMATION TO BE PASSED ALONG THE ALLIED FRONT.
CRUNCH
SO THE CANADIANS WERE HEARTENED BY NEWS OF AMERICAN SUCCESSES TO THE WEST.
EVEN WHEN THE LUFTWAFFE TRIED TO CONVINCE THEM OTHERWISE.
YOU LOOK GOOD, BY THE WAY.
OH, HUSH.

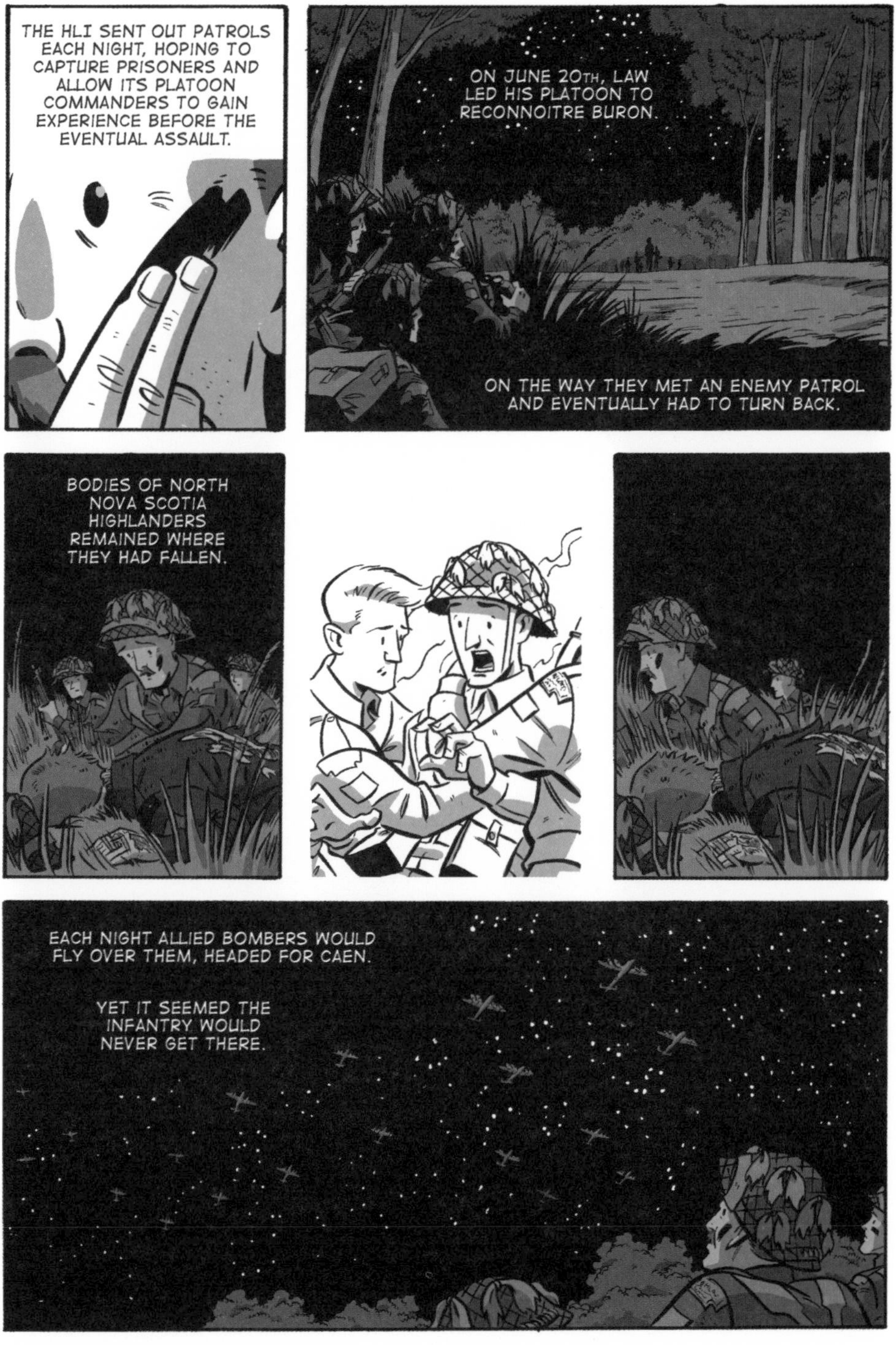
THE HLI SENT OUT PATROLS EACH NIGHT, HOPING TO CAPTURE PRISONERS AND ALLOW ITS PLATOON COMMANDERS TO GAIN EXPERIENCE BEFORE THE EVENTUAL ASSAULT.
ON JUNE 20TH, LAW LED HIS PLATOON TO RECONNOITRE BURON.
ON THE WAY THEY MET AN ENEMY PATROL AND EVENTUALLY HAD TO TURN BACK.
BODIES OF NORTH NOVA SCOTIA HIGHLANDERS REMAINED WHERE THEY HAD FALLEN.
EACH NIGHT ALLIED BOMBERS WOULD FLY OVER THEM, HEADED FOR CAEN.
YET IT SEEMED THE INFANTRY WOULD NEVER GET THERE.

ON JUNE 28TH THEY PREPARED TO ATTACK BURON IN OPERATION ABERLOUR.

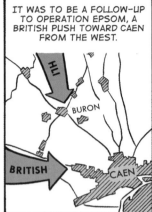

IT WAS TO BE A FOLLOW-UP TO OPERATION EPSOM, A BRITISH PUSH TOWARD CAEN FROM THE WEST.

HLI

BURON

BRITISH

CAEN

THE MEN ARE READY, SIR. WHAT ARE YOUR ORDERS?

I HATE TO SAY IT...

...BUT THE ORDER IS "STAND DOWN."

ABERLOUR HAS BEEN CANCELLED.

OPERATION EPSOM FAILED TO CAPTURE ITS OBJECTIVES TO THE WEST.

AS IT TURNS OUT, JERRY'S DUG IN HARDER THAN WE THOUGHT.

AND WITHOUT THE BRITS CROSSING THE RIVER, THERE'S NO REASON FOR US TO GO CHARGING INTO BURON JUST TO STAND THERE WITH OUR DICKS FLAPPING IN THE BREEZE.

WE'LL CONTINUE HOLDING THE LINE UNTIL ORDERED OTHERWISE.

FOUR TIMES THROUGHOUT THE MONTH PLANS WERE MADE FOR AN ASSAULT.

EACH TIME, IT WAS CALLED OFF.

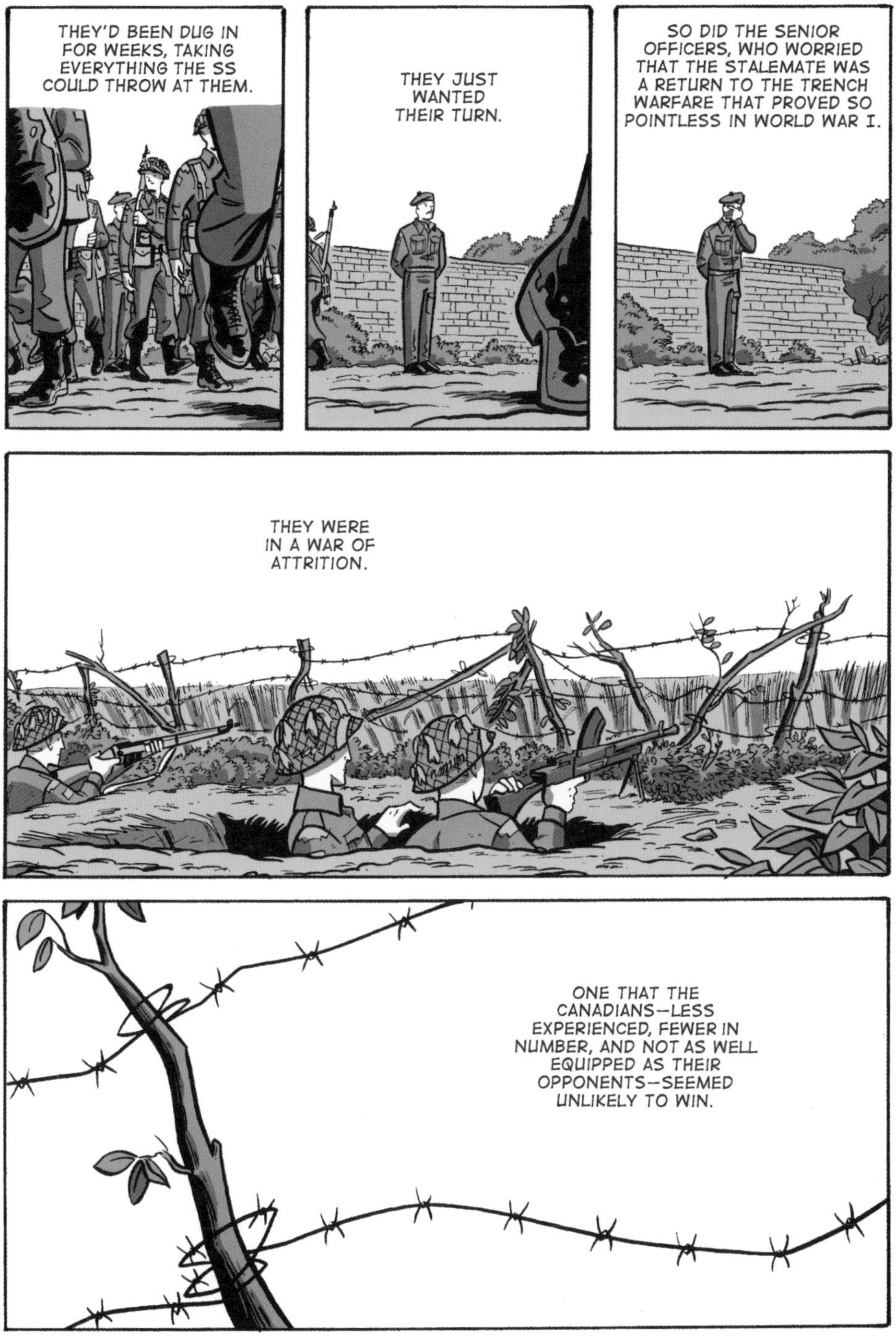
THEY'D BEEN DUG IN FOR WEEKS, TAKING EVERYTHING THE SS COULD THROW AT THEM.
THEY JUST WANTED THEIR TURN.
SO DID THE SENIOR OFFICERS, WHO WORRIED THAT THE STALEMATE WAS A RETURN TO THE TRENCH WARFARE THAT PROVED SO POINTLESS IN WORLD WAR I.
THEY WERE IN A WAR OF ATTRITION.
ONE THAT THE CANADIANS—LESS EXPERIENCED, FEWER IN NUMBER, AND NOT AS WELL EQUIPPED AS THEIR OPPONENTS—SEEMED UNLIKELY TO WIN.

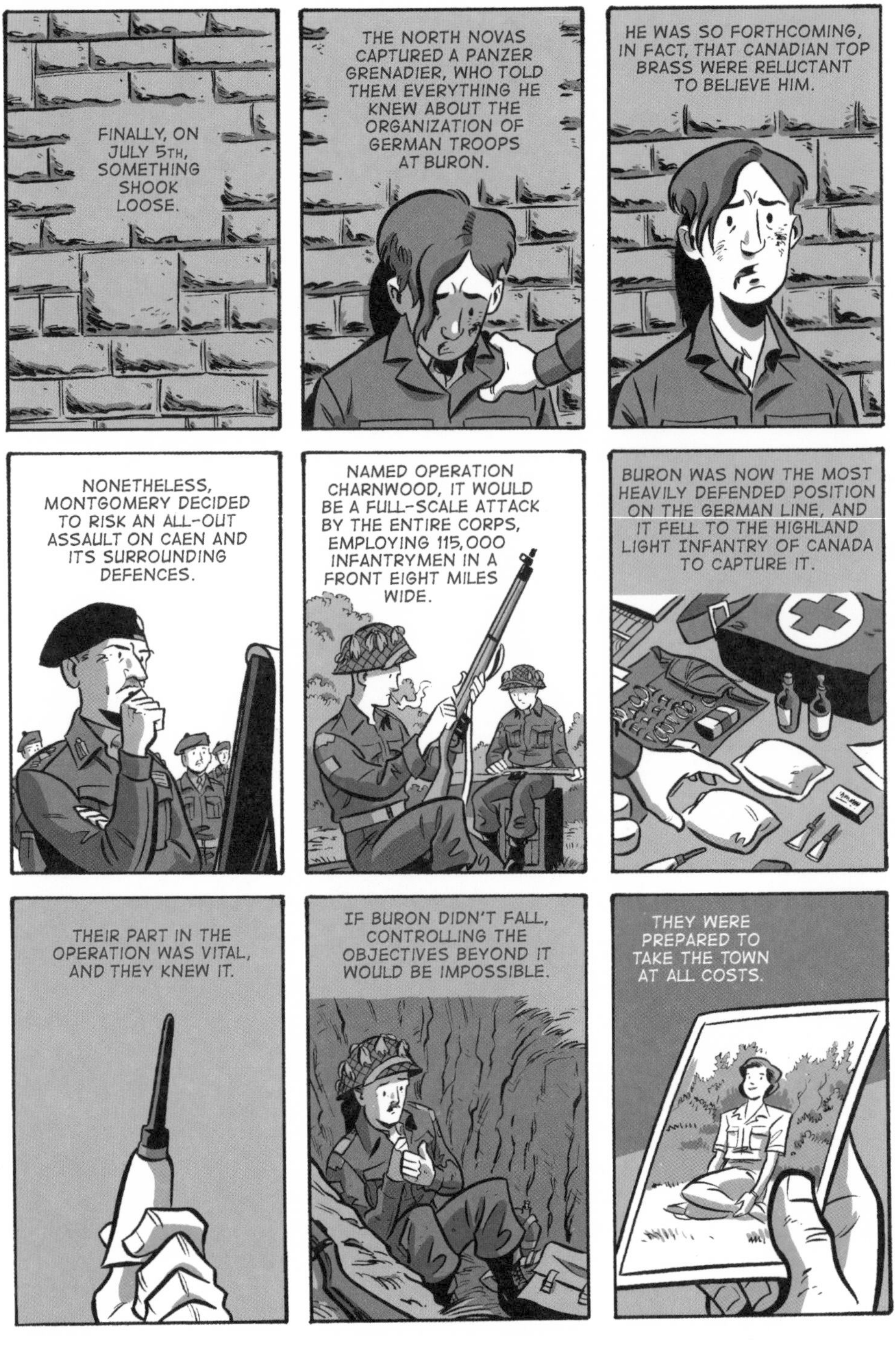
FINALLY, ON JULY 5TH, SOMETHING SHOOK LOOSE.
THE NORTH NOVAS CAPTURED A PANZER GRENADIER, WHO TOLD THEM EVERYTHING HE KNEW ABOUT THE ORGANIZATION OF GERMAN TROOPS AT BURON.
HE WAS SO FORTHCOMING, IN FACT, THAT CANADIAN TOP BRASS WERE RELUCTANT TO BELIEVE HIM.
NONETHELESS, MONTGOMERY DECIDED TO RISK AN ALL-OUT ASSAULT ON CAEN AND ITS SURROUNDING DEFENCES.
NAMED OPERATION CHARNWOOD, IT WOULD BE A FULL-SCALE ATTACK BY THE ENTIRE CORPS, EMPLOYING 115,000 INFANTRYMEN IN A FRONT EIGHT MILES WIDE.
BURON WAS NOW THE MOST HEAVILY DEFENDED POSITION ON THE GERMAN LINE, AND IT FELL TO THE HIGHLAND LIGHT INFANTRY OF CANADA TO CAPTURE IT.
THEIR PART IN THE OPERATION WAS VITAL, AND THEY KNEW IT.
IF BURON DIDN'T FALL, CONTROLLING THE OBJECTIVES BEYOND IT WOULD BE IMPOSSIBLE.
THEY WERE PREPARED TO TAKE THE TOWN AT ALL COSTS.

ON JULY 7TH, FIVE HUNDRED ALLIED PLANES TOOK PART IN THE BOMBING OF CAEN.

THE HLI WAR DIARY CALLS IT "A GRAND SHOW."

THAT NIGHT, THE REGIMENT FINALLY MOVED ON FROM WHERE THEY'D DUG IN A MONTH BEFORE.

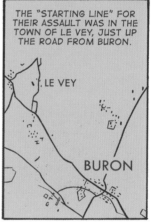

THE "STARTING LINE" FOR THEIR ASSAULT WAS IN THE TOWN OF LE VEY, JUST UP THE ROAD FROM BURON.

LE VEY

BURON

AFTER A SLEEPLESS NIGHT, THEY FORMED UP AT 7:30 AM.

"B" COMPANY, WITH LAW LEADING ONE OF THREE PLATOONS, WAS ON THE LEFT FLANK OF THE ASSAULT.

"A" COMPANY, WITH JACK LEADING HIS PLATOON, WAS IN BEHIND.

ONCE THE OTHER COMPANIES HAD TAKEN BURON, THEY WERE TO PUSH THROUGH TO THE HIGH GROUND SOUTH OF TOWN.

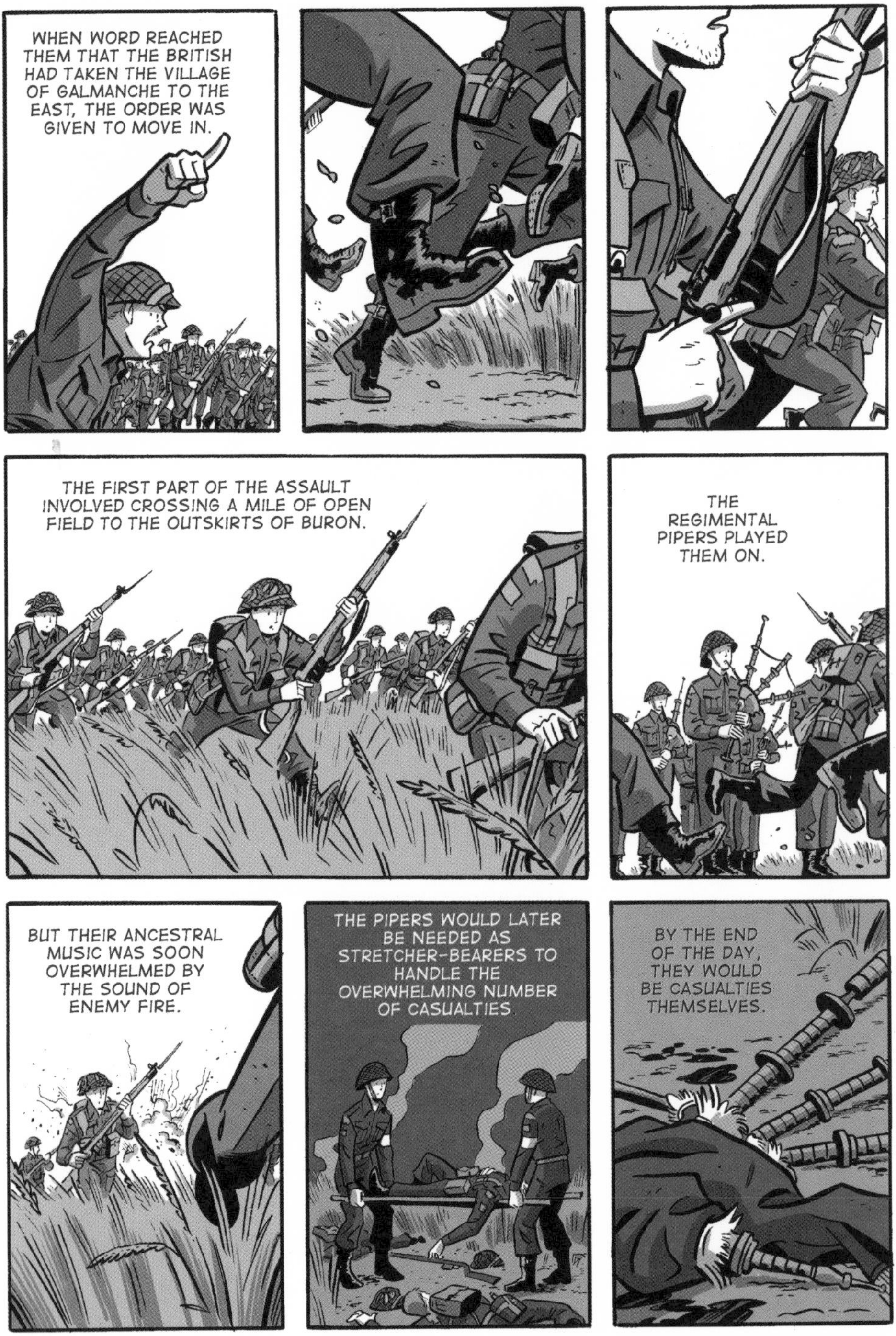
WHEN WORD REACHED THEM THAT THE BRITISH HAD TAKEN THE VILLAGE OF GALMANCHE TO THE EAST, THE ORDER WAS GIVEN TO MOVE IN.
THE FIRST PART OF THE ASSAULT INVOLVED CROSSING A MILE OF OPEN FIELD TO THE OUTSKIRTS OF BURON.
THE REGIMENTAL PIPERS PLAYED THEM ON.
BUT THEIR ANCESTRAL MUSIC WAS SOON OVERWHELMED BY THE SOUND OF ENEMY FIRE.
THE PIPERS WOULD LATER BE NEEDED AS STRETCHER-BEARERS TO HANDLE THE OVERWHELMING NUMBER OF CASUALTIES.
BY THE END OF THE DAY, THEY WOULD BE CASUALTIES THEMSELVES.

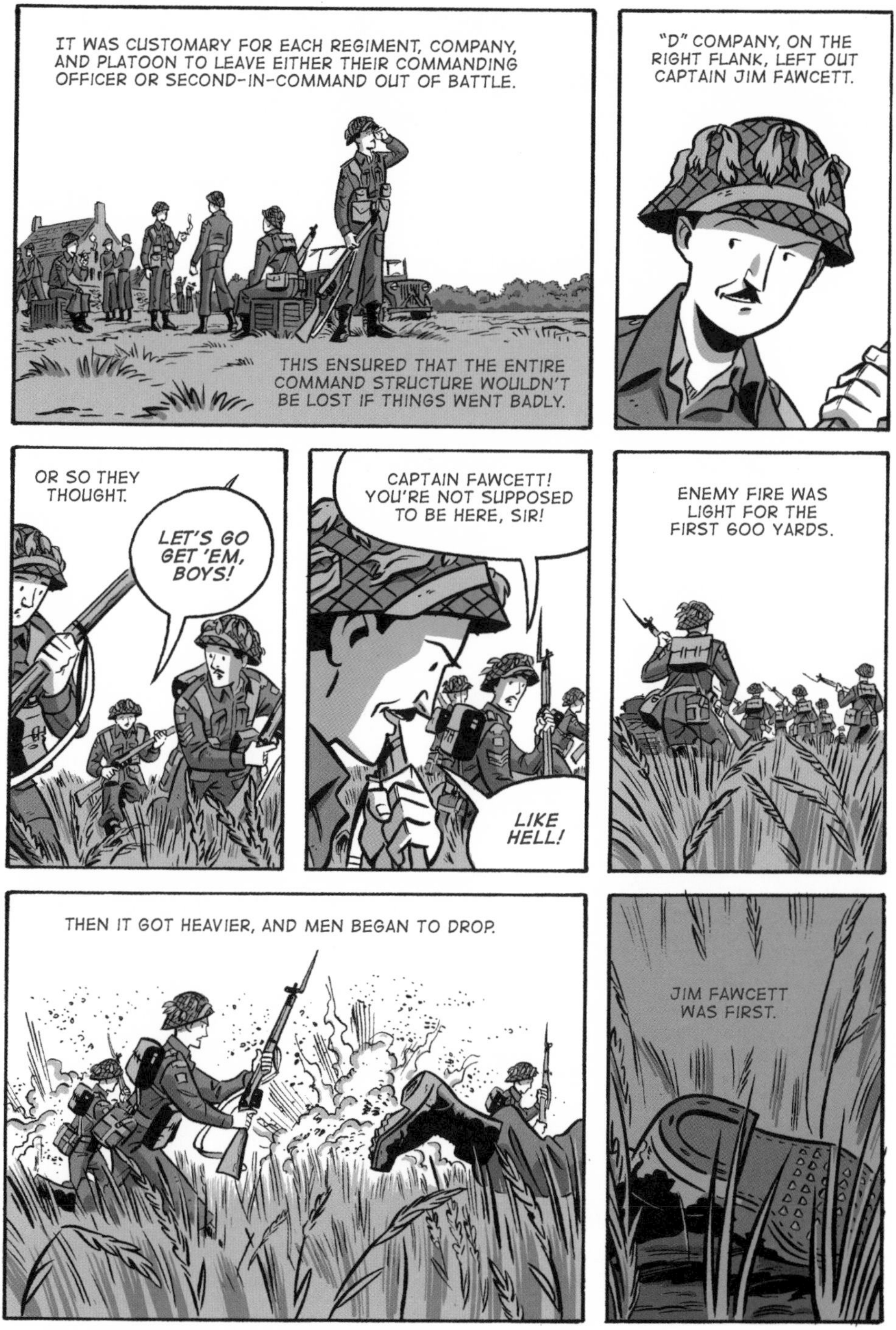
IT WAS CUSTOMARY FOR EACH REGIMENT, COMPANY, AND PLATOON TO LEAVE EITHER THEIR COMMANDING OFFICER OR SECOND-IN-COMMAND OUT OF BATTLE.
THIS ENSURED THAT THE ENTIRE COMMAND STRUCTURE WOULDN'T BE LOST IF THINGS WENT BADLY.
"D" COMPANY, ON THE RIGHT FLANK, LEFT OUT CAPTAIN JIM FAWCETT.
OR SO THEY THOUGHT.
LET'S GO GET 'EM, BOYS!
CAPTAIN FAWCETT! YOU'RE NOT SUPPOSED TO BE HERE, SIR!
LIKE HELL!
ENEMY FIRE WAS LIGHT FOR THE FIRST 600 YARDS.
THEN IT GOT HEAVIER, AND MEN BEGAN TO DROP.
JIM FAWCETT WAS FIRST.

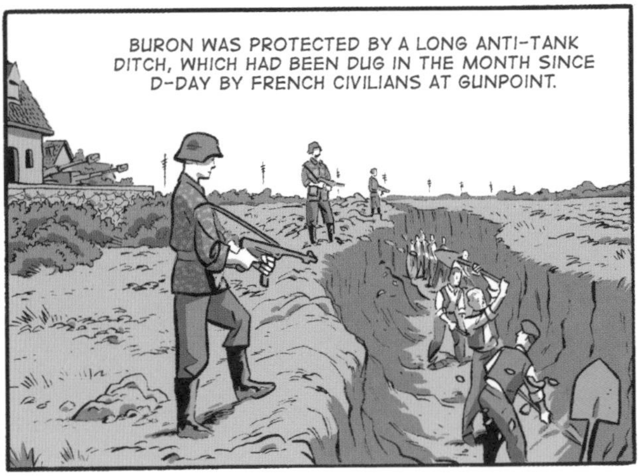
BURON WAS PROTECTED BY A LONG ANTI-TANK DITCH, WHICH HAD BEEN DUG IN THE MONTH SINCE D-DAY BY FRENCH CIVILIANS AT GUNPOINT.

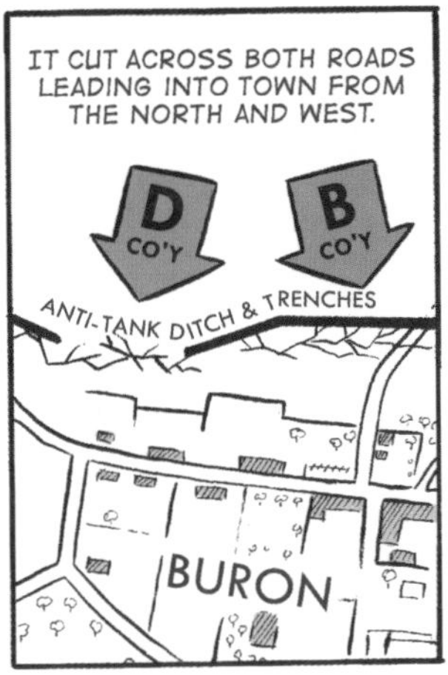
IT CUT ACROSS BOTH ROADS LEADING INTO TOWN FROM THE NORTH AND WEST.
D CO'Y
B CO'Y
ANTI-TANK DITCH & TRENCHES
BURON

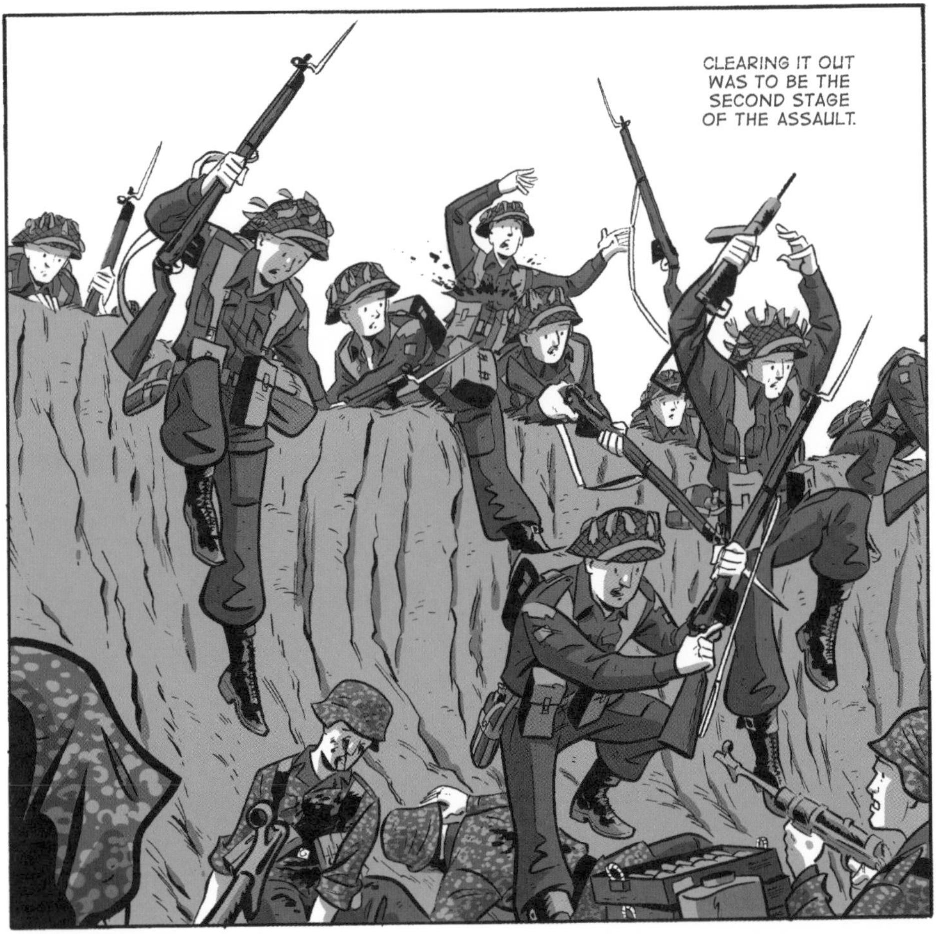
CLEARING IT OUT WAS TO BE THE SECOND STAGE OF THE ASSAULT.

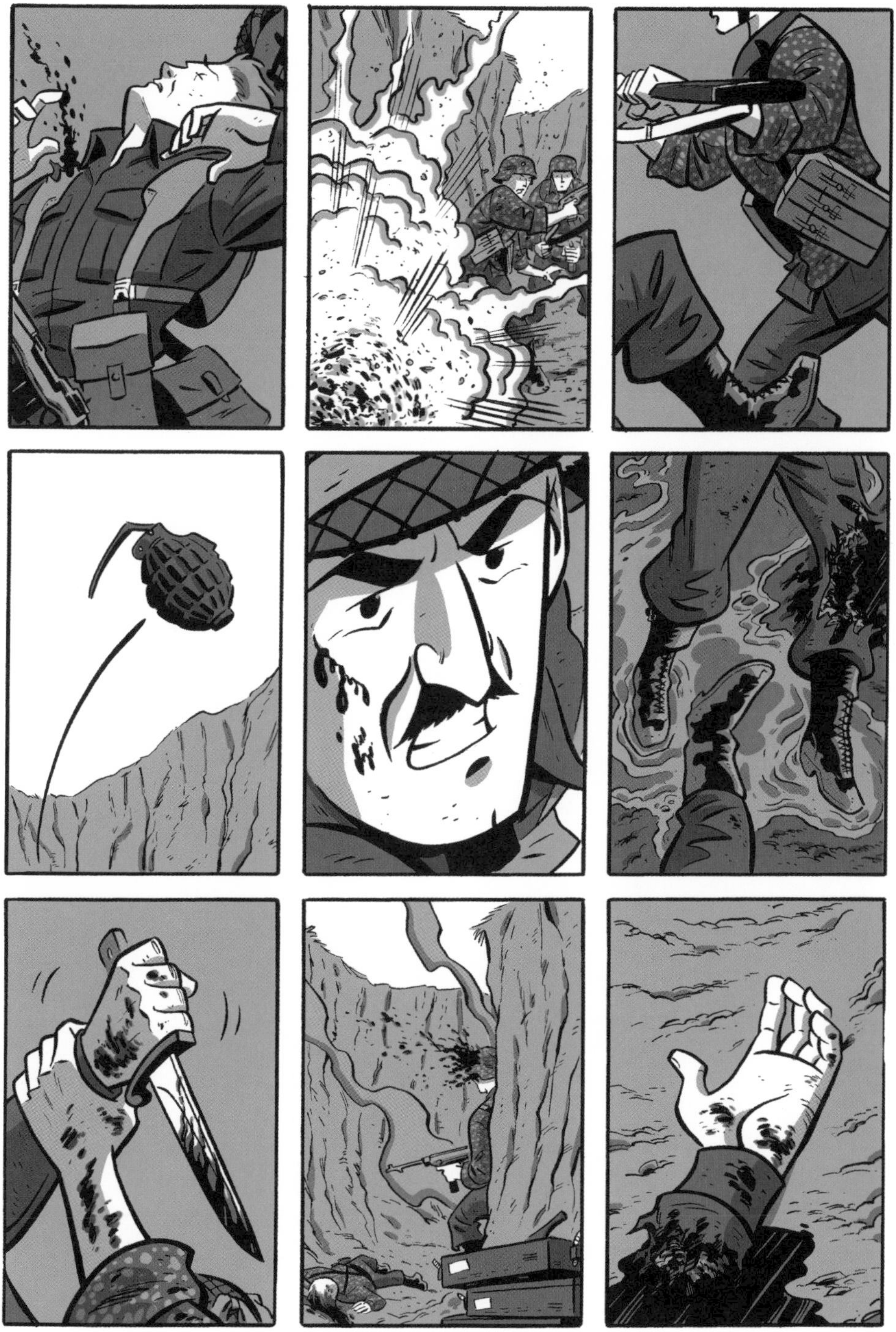

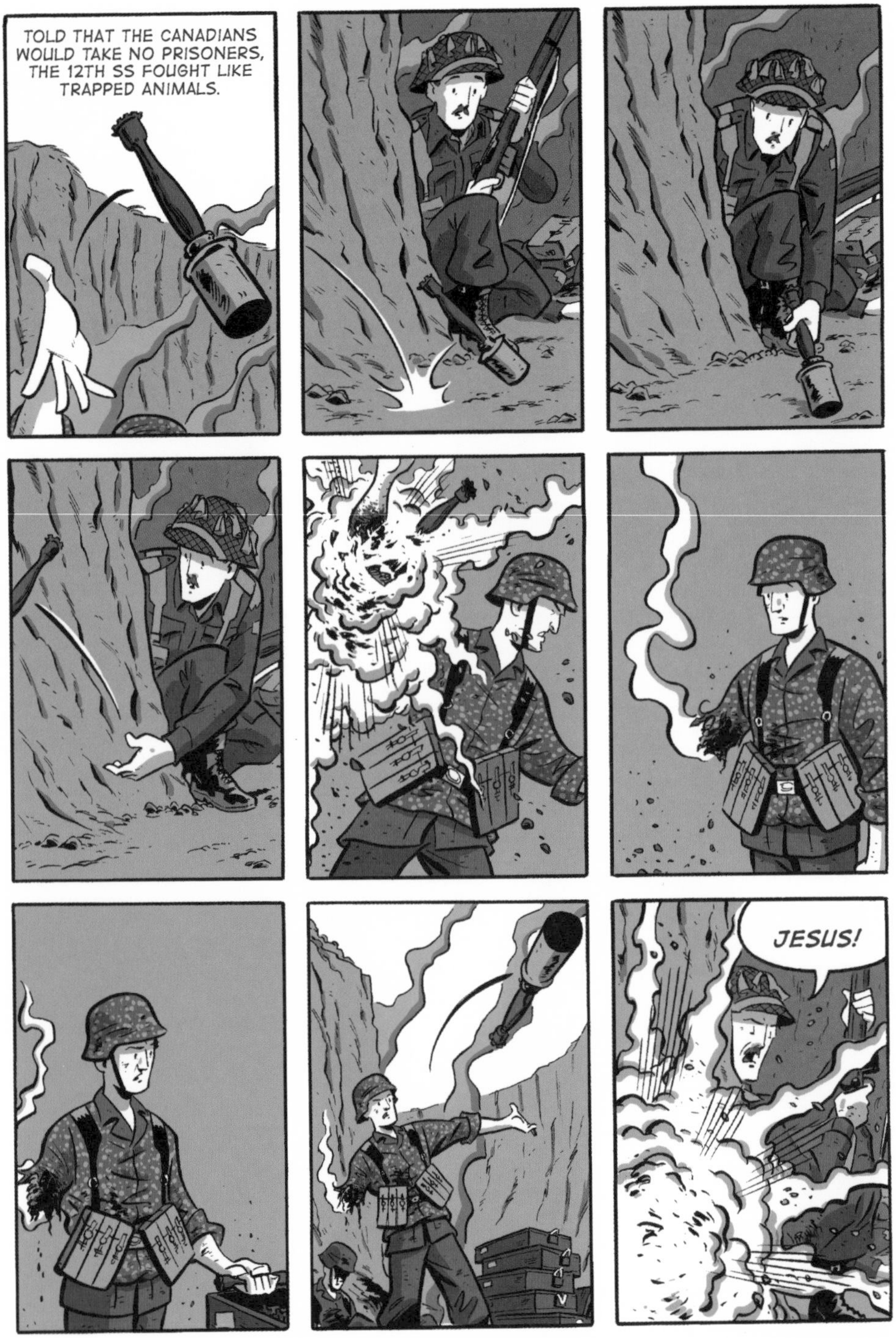
TOLD THAT THE CANADIANS WOULD TAKE NO PRISONERS, THE 12TH SS FOUGHT LIKE TRAPPED ANIMALS.
JESUS!

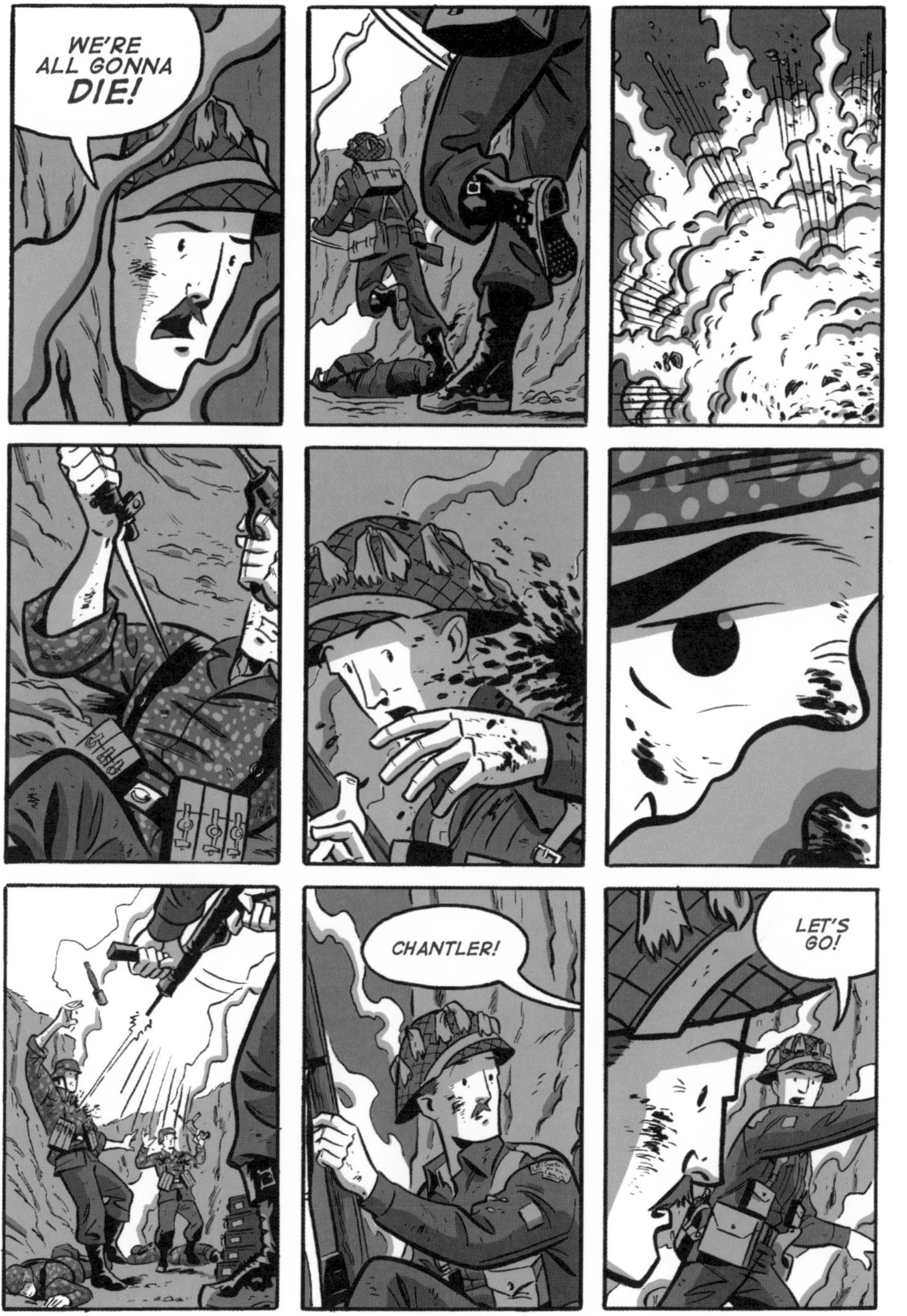
WE'RE ALL GONNA DIE!
CHANTLER!
LET'S GO!

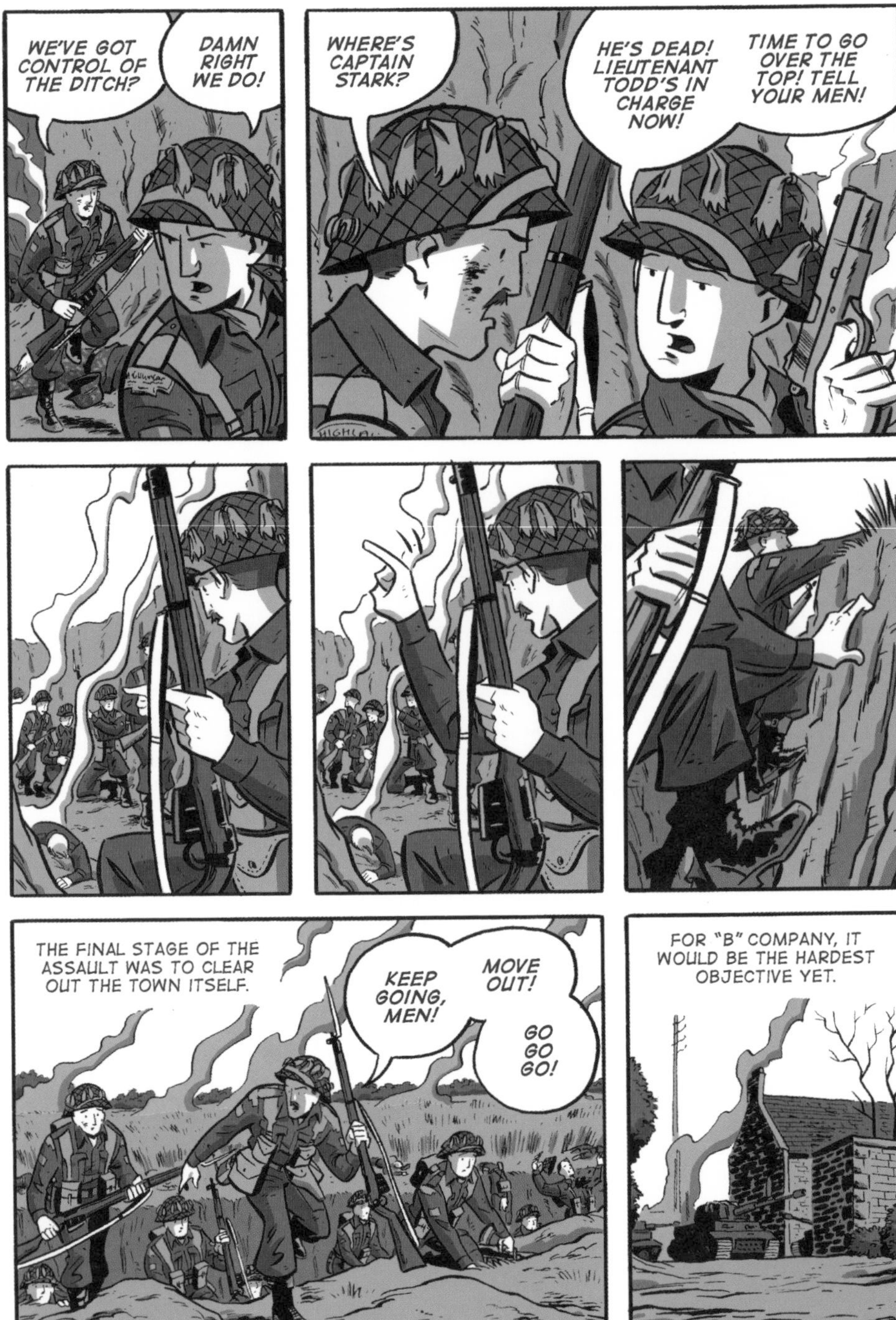
WE'VE GOT CONTROL OF THE DITCH?
DAMN RIGHT WE DO!
WHERE'S CAPTAIN STARK?
HE'S DEAD! LIEUTENANT TODD'S IN CHARGE NOW!
TIME TO GO OVER THE TOP! TELL YOUR MEN!
THE FINAL STAGE OF THE ASSAULT WAS TO CLEAR OUT THE TOWN ITSELF.
KEEP GOING, MEN!
MOVE OUT!
GO GO GO!
FOR "B" COMPANY, IT WOULD BE THE HARDEST OBJECTIVE YET.

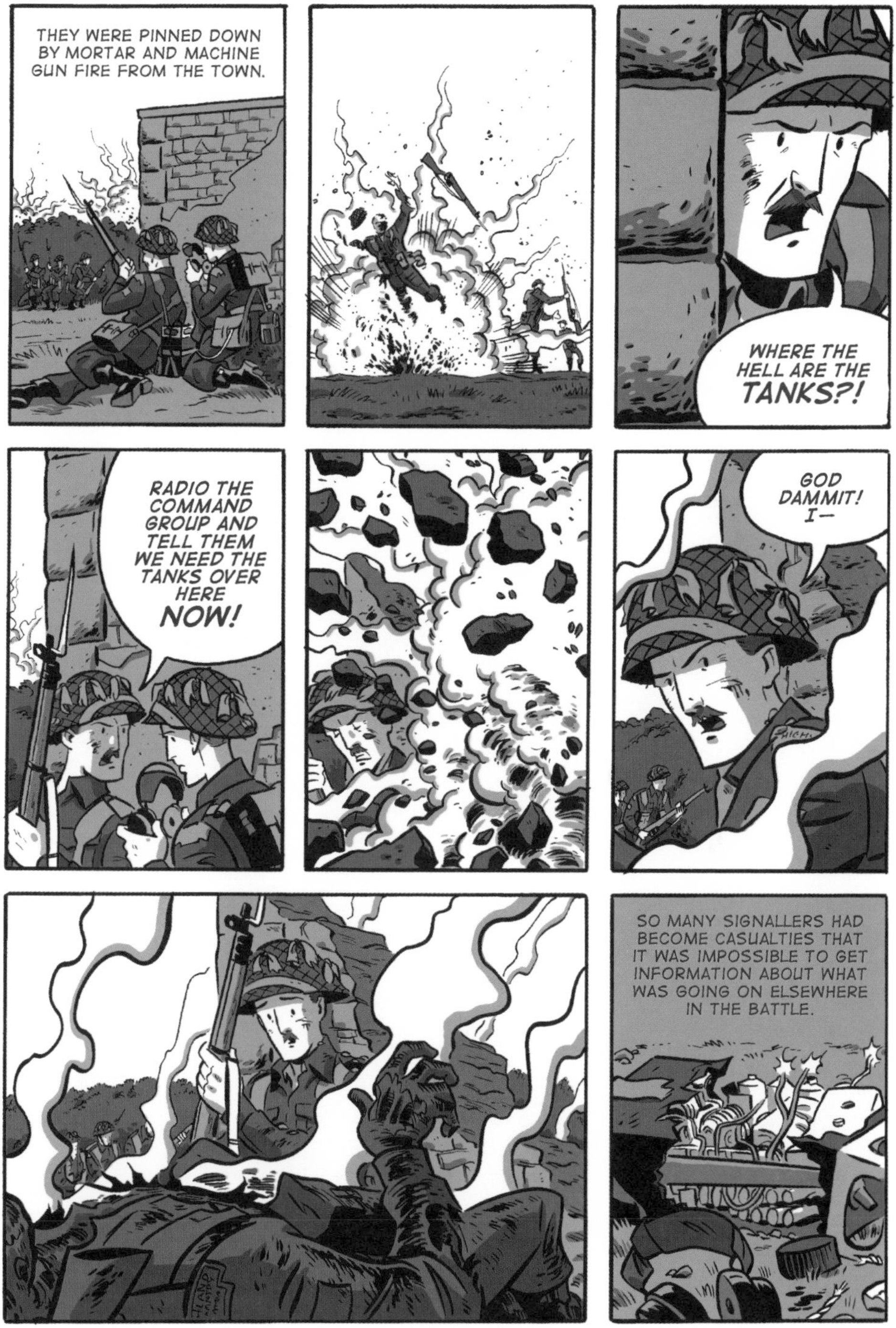
THEY WERE PINNED DOWN BY MORTAR AND MACHINE GUN FIRE FROM THE TOWN.
WHERE THE HELL ARE THE TANKS?!
RADIO THE COMMAND GROUP AND TELL THEM WE NEED THE TANKS OVER HERE NOW!
GOD DAMMIT! I—
SO MANY SIGNALLERS HAD BECOME CASUALTIES THAT IT WAS IMPOSSIBLE TO GET INFORMATION ABOUT WHAT WAS GOING ON ELSEWHERE IN THE BATTLE.

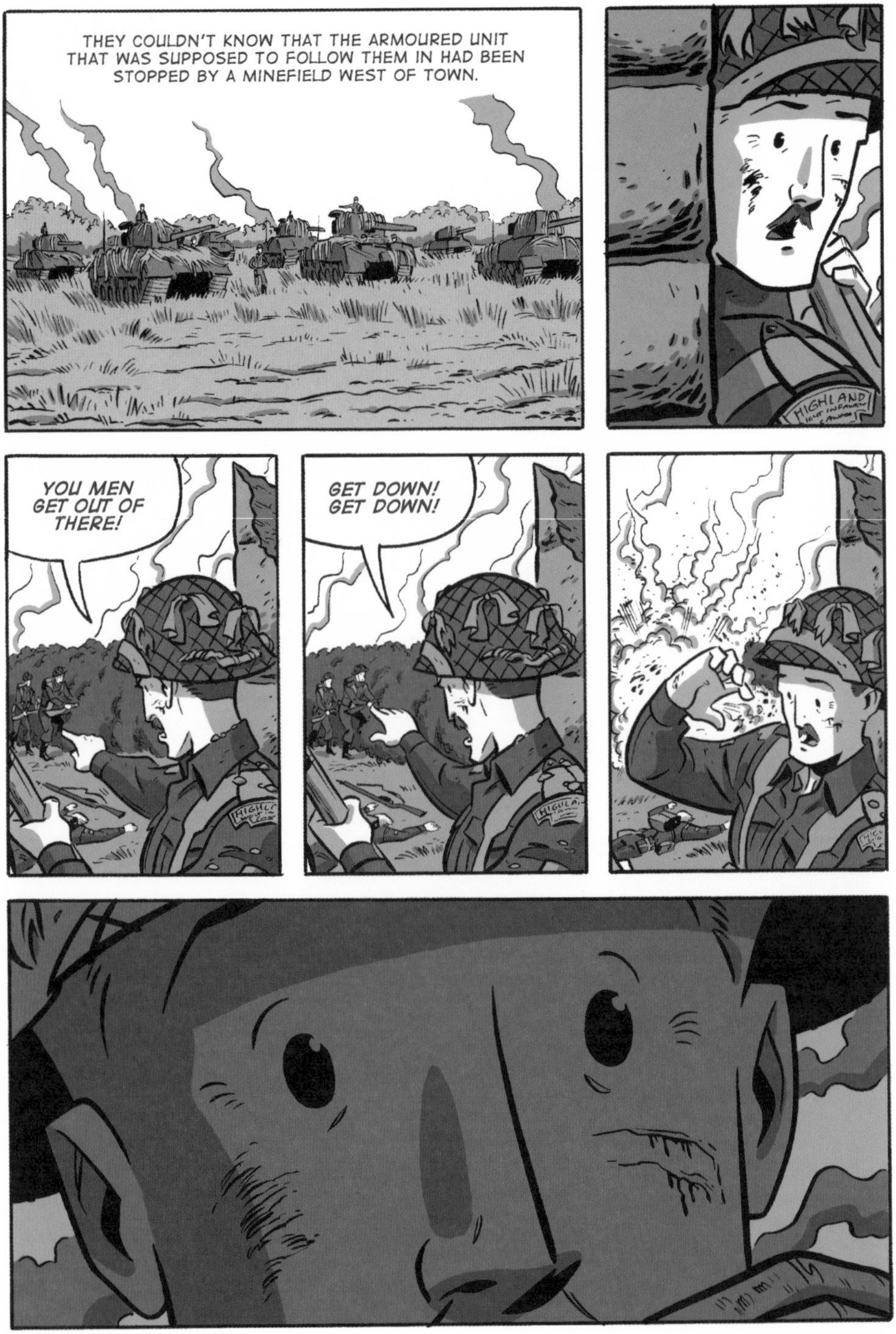
THEY COULDN'T KNOW THAT THE ARMOURED UNIT THAT WAS SUPPOSED TO FOLLOW THEM IN HAD BEEN STOPPED BY A MINEFIELD WEST OF TOWN.
HIGHLAND
YOU MEN GET OUT OF THERE!
GET DOWN! GET DOWN!

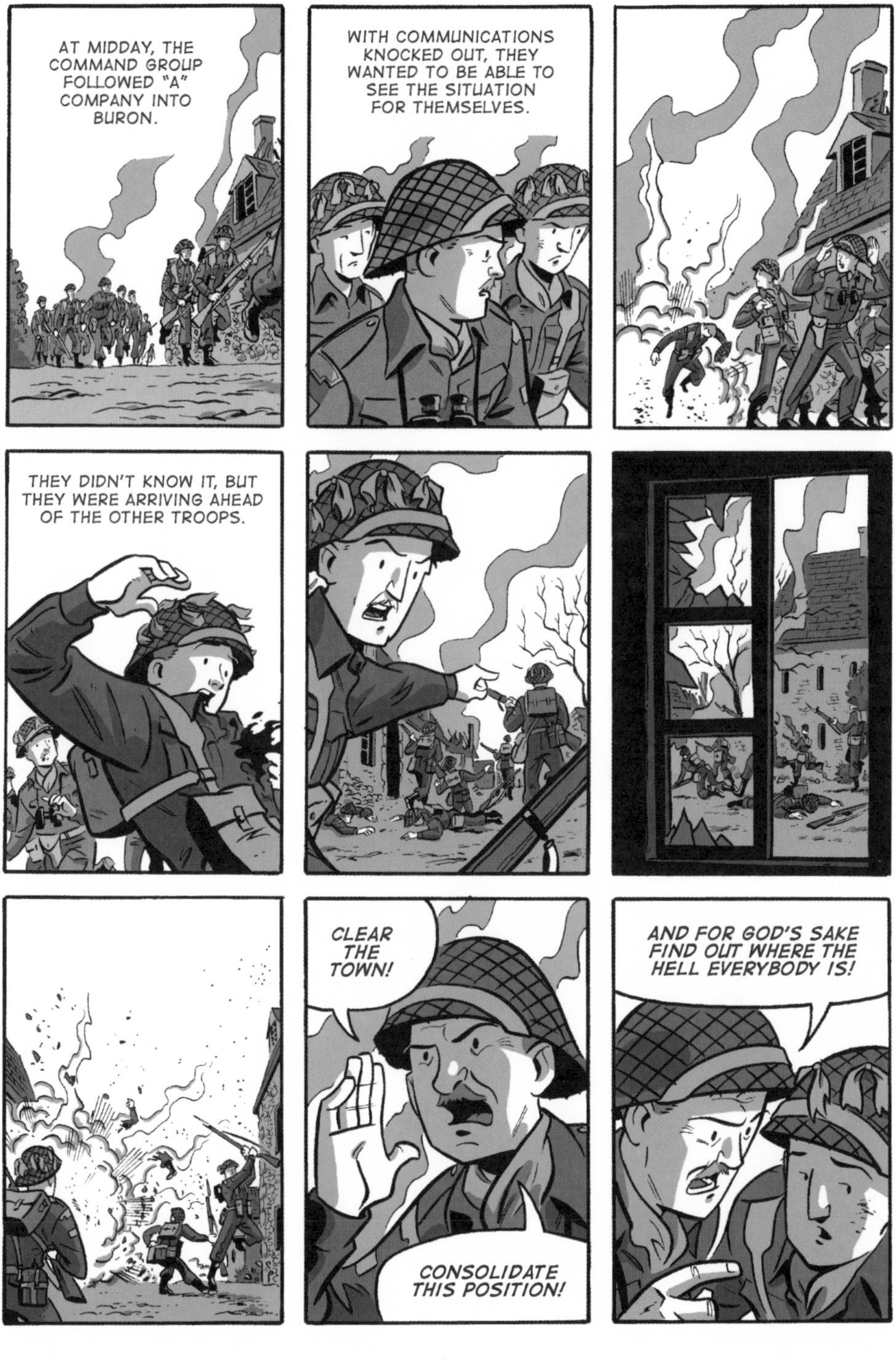
AT MIDDAY, THE COMMAND GROUP FOLLOWED "A" COMPANY INTO BURON.
WITH COMMUNICATIONS KNOCKED OUT, THEY WANTED TO BE ABLE TO SEE THE SITUATION FOR THEMSELVES.
THEY DIDN'T KNOW IT, BUT THEY WERE ARRIVING AHEAD OF THE OTHER TROOPS.
CLEAR THE TOWN!
CONSOLIDATE THIS POSITION!
AND FOR GOD'S SAKE FIND OUT WHERE THE HELL EVERYBODY IS!

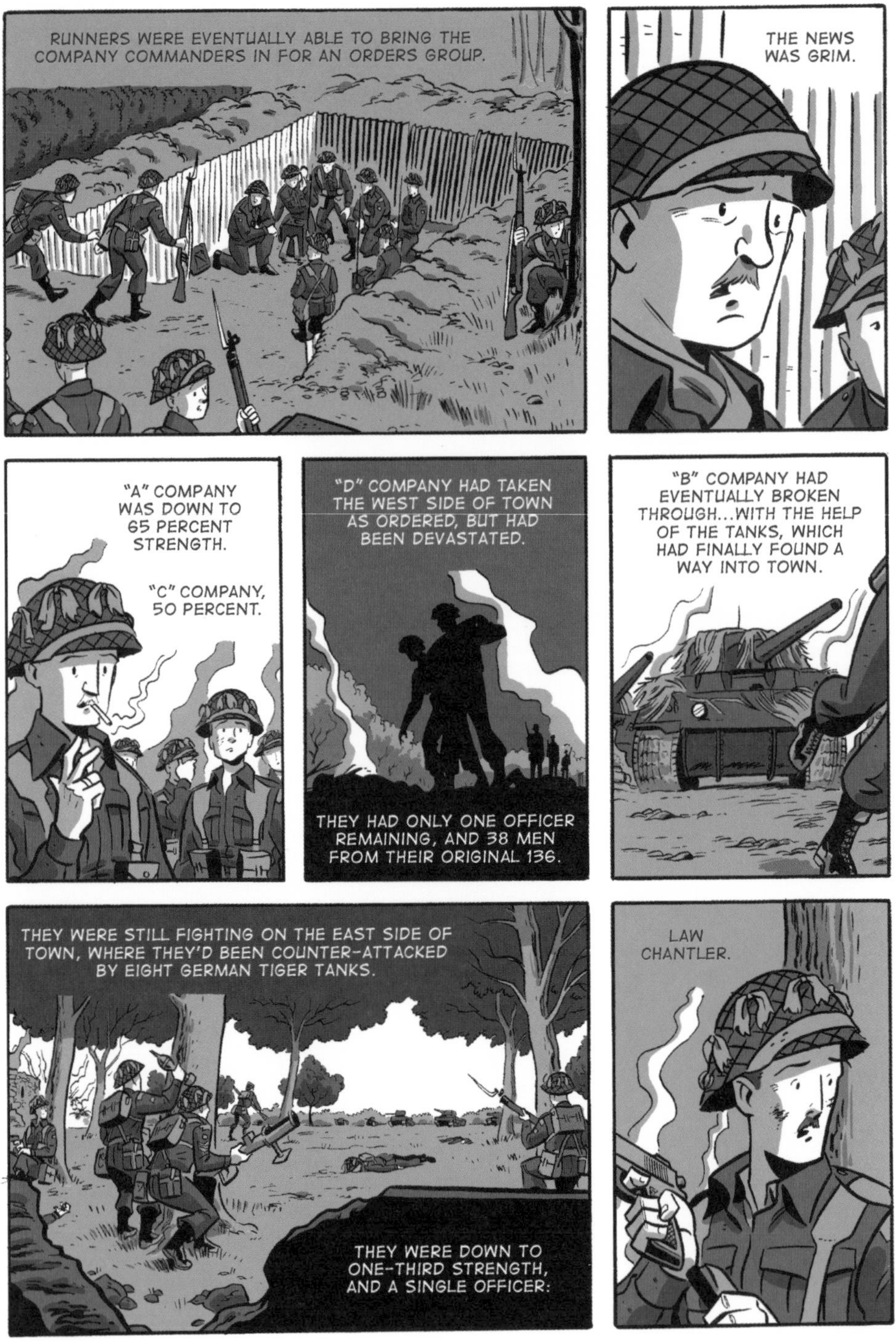
RUNNERS WERE EVENTUALLY ABLE TO BRING THE COMPANY COMMANDERS IN FOR AN ORDERS GROUP.
THE NEWS WAS GRIM.
"A" COMPANY WAS DOWN TO 65 PERCENT STRENGTH.
"C" COMPANY, 50 PERCENT.
"D" COMPANY HAD TAKEN THE WEST SIDE OF TOWN AS ORDERED, BUT HAD BEEN DEVASTATED.
THEY HAD ONLY ONE OFFICER REMAINING, AND 38 MEN FROM THEIR ORIGINAL 136.
"B" COMPANY HAD EVENTUALLY BROKEN THROUGH...WITH THE HELP OF THE TANKS, WHICH HAD FINALLY FOUND A WAY INTO TOWN.
THEY WERE STILL FIGHTING ON THE EAST SIDE OF TOWN, WHERE THEY'D BEEN COUNTER-ATTACKED BY EIGHT GERMAN TIGER TANKS.
THEY WERE DOWN TO ONE-THIRD STRENGTH, AND A SINGLE OFFICER:
LAW CHANTLER.

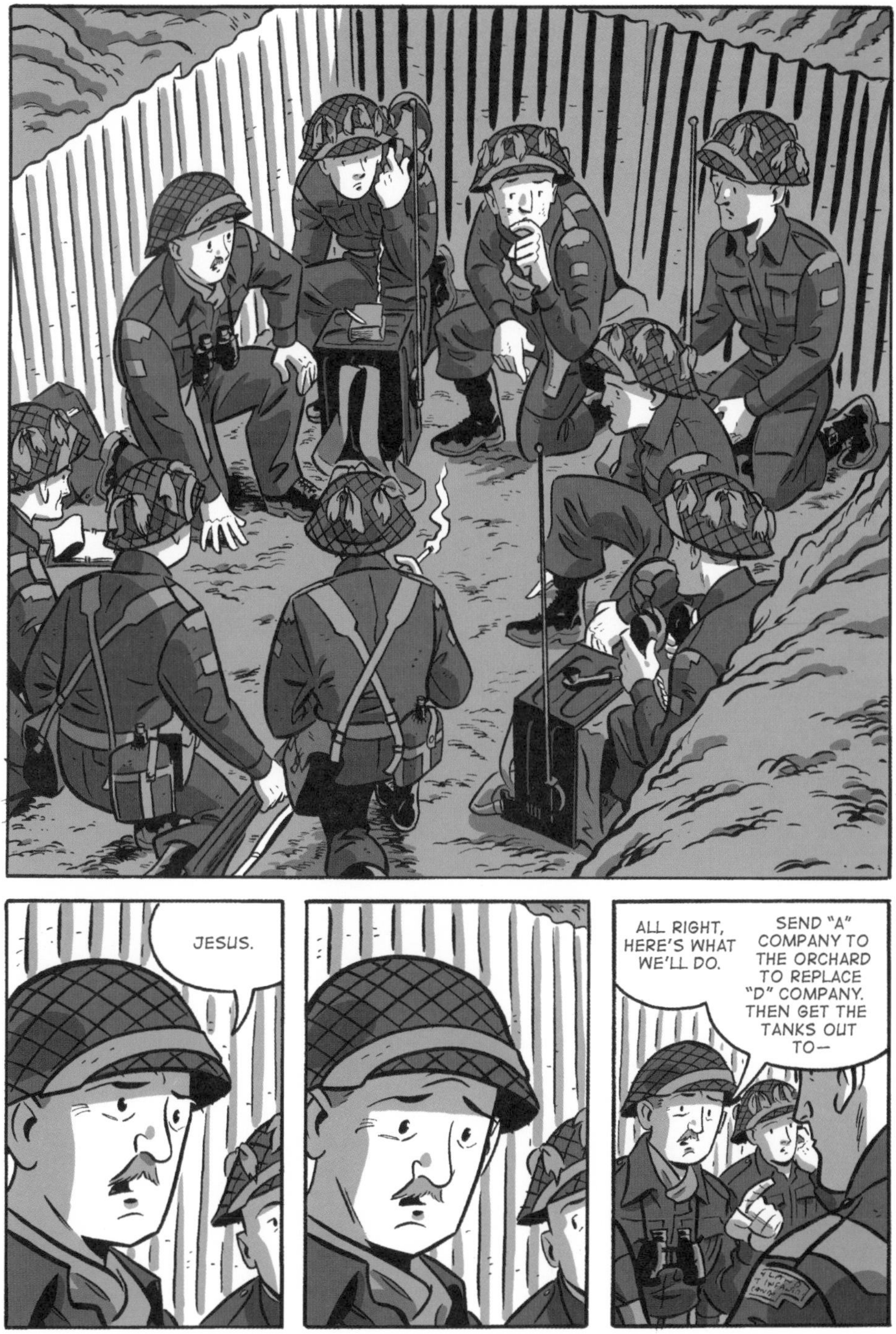
JESUS.
ALL RIGHT, HERE'S WHAT WE'LL DO.
SEND "A" COMPANY TO THE ORCHARD TO REPLACE "D" COMPANY. THEN GET THE TANKS OUT TO—

THAT'S WHEN
THE COMMAND
GROUP WAS HIT.

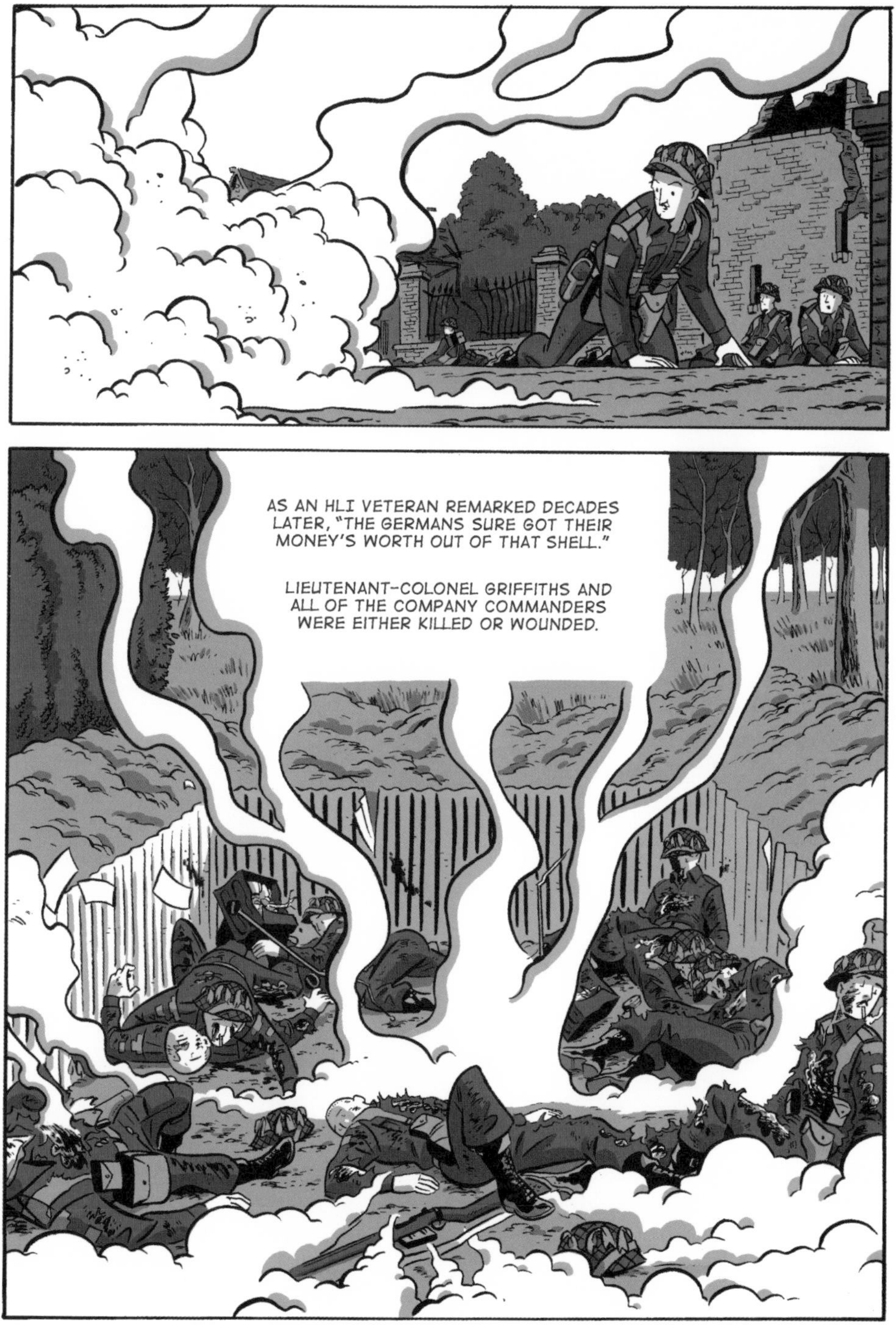
AS AN HLI VETERAN REMARKED DECADES LATER, "THE GERMANS SURE GOT THEIR MONEY'S WORTH OUT OF THAT SHELL."
LIEUTENANT-COLONEL GRIFFITHS AND ALL OF THE COMPANY COMMANDERS WERE EITHER KILLED OR WOUNDED.

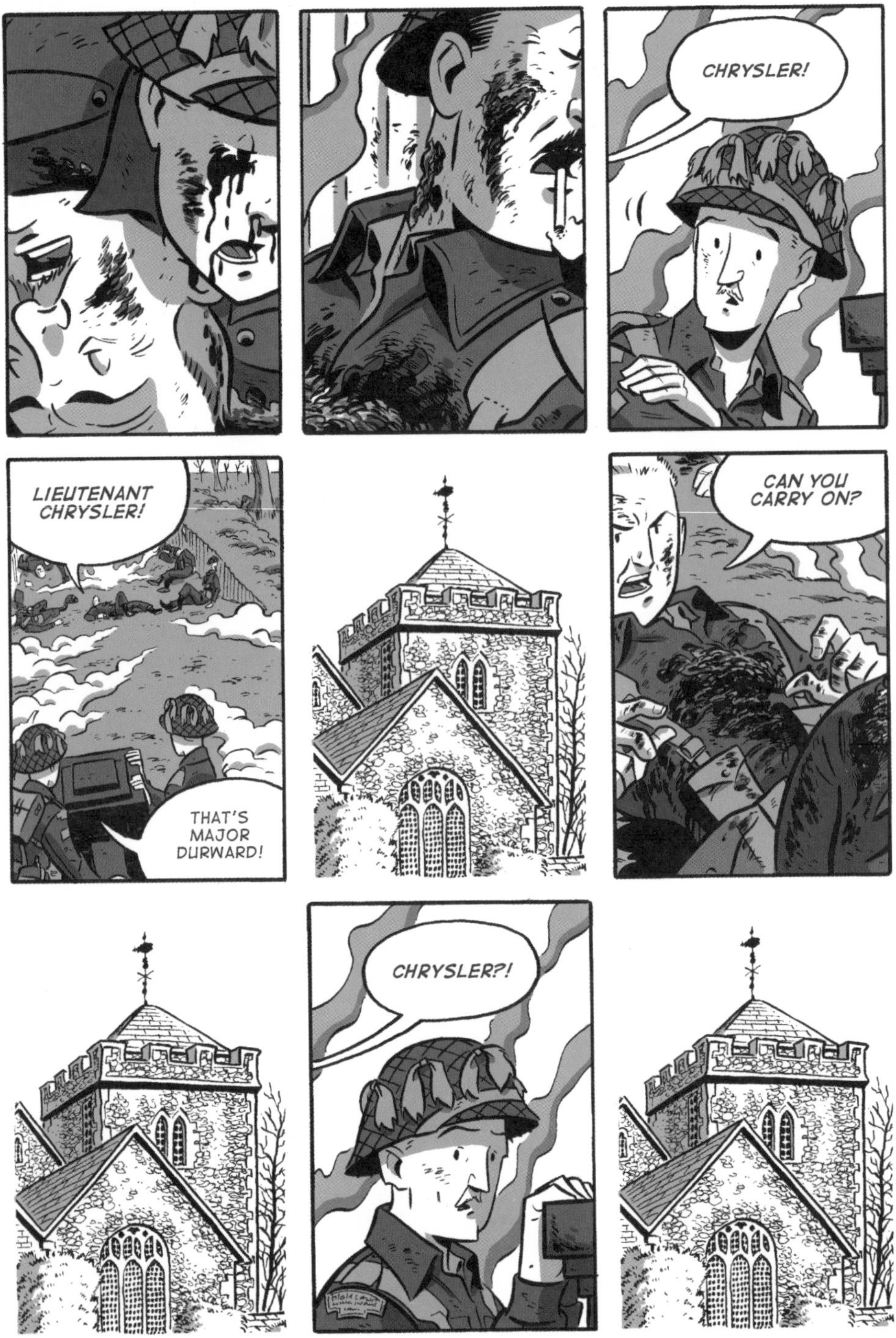
CHRYSLER!
LIEUTENANT CHRYSLER!
THAT'S MAJOR DURWARD!
CAN YOU CARRY ON?
CHRYSLER?!

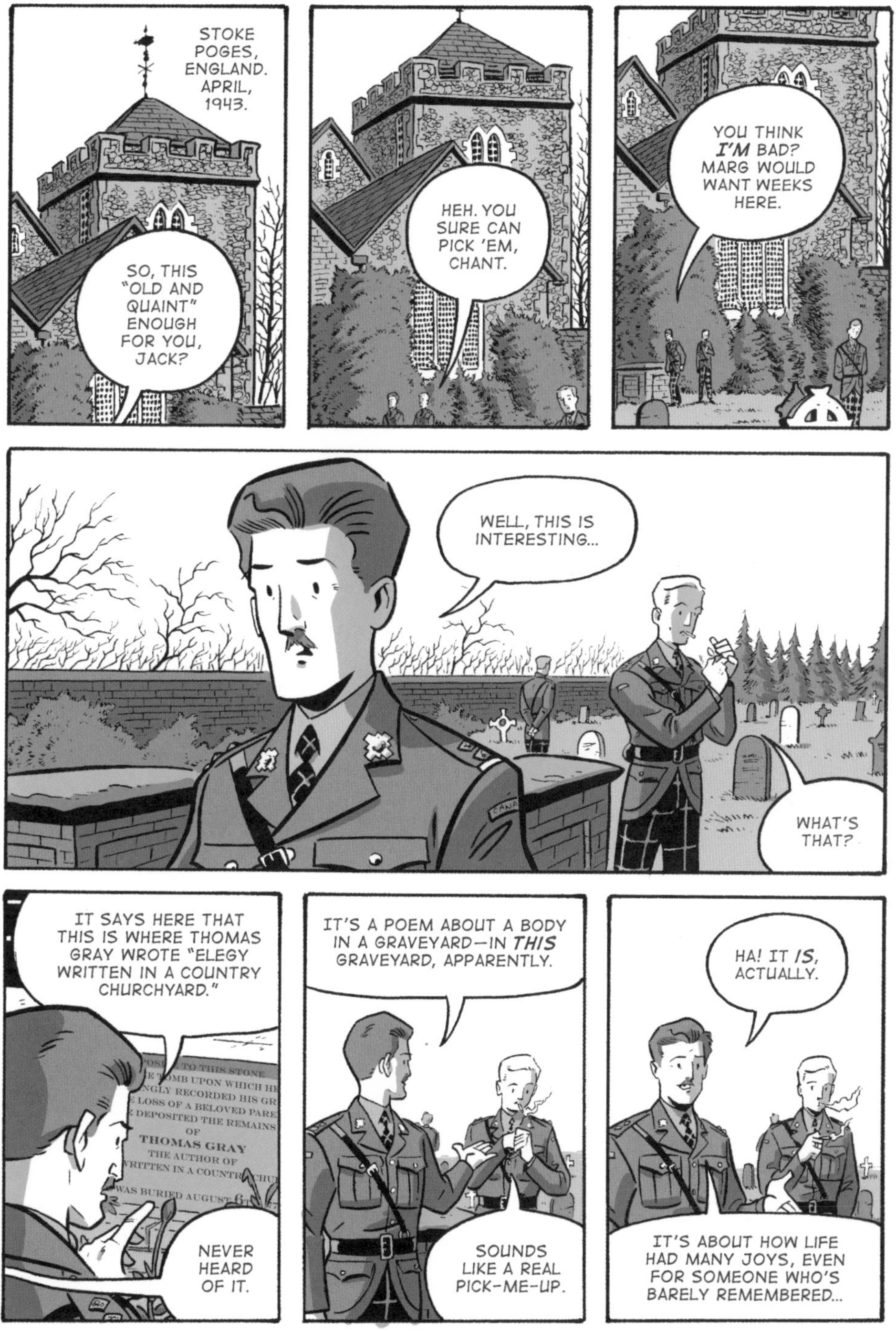

STOKE POGES, ENGLAND. APRIL, 1943.
SO, THIS "OLD AND QUAINT" ENOUGH FOR YOU, JACK?
HEH. YOU SURE CAN PICK 'EM, CHANT.
YOU THINK *I'M* BAD? MARG WOULD WANT WEEKS HERE.
WELL, THIS IS INTERESTING...
WHAT'S THAT?
IT SAYS HERE THAT THIS IS WHERE THOMAS GRAY WROTE "ELEGY WRITTEN IN A COUNTRY CHURCHYARD."
THOMAS GRAY
THE AUTHOR OF
NEVER HEARD OF IT.
IT'S A POEM ABOUT A BODY IN A GRAVEYARD—IN *THIS* GRAVEYARD, APPARENTLY.
SOUNDS LIKE A REAL PICK-ME-UP.
HA! IT *IS*, ACTUALLY.
IT'S ABOUT HOW LIFE HAD MANY JOYS, EVEN FOR SOMEONE WHO'S BARELY REMEMBERED...

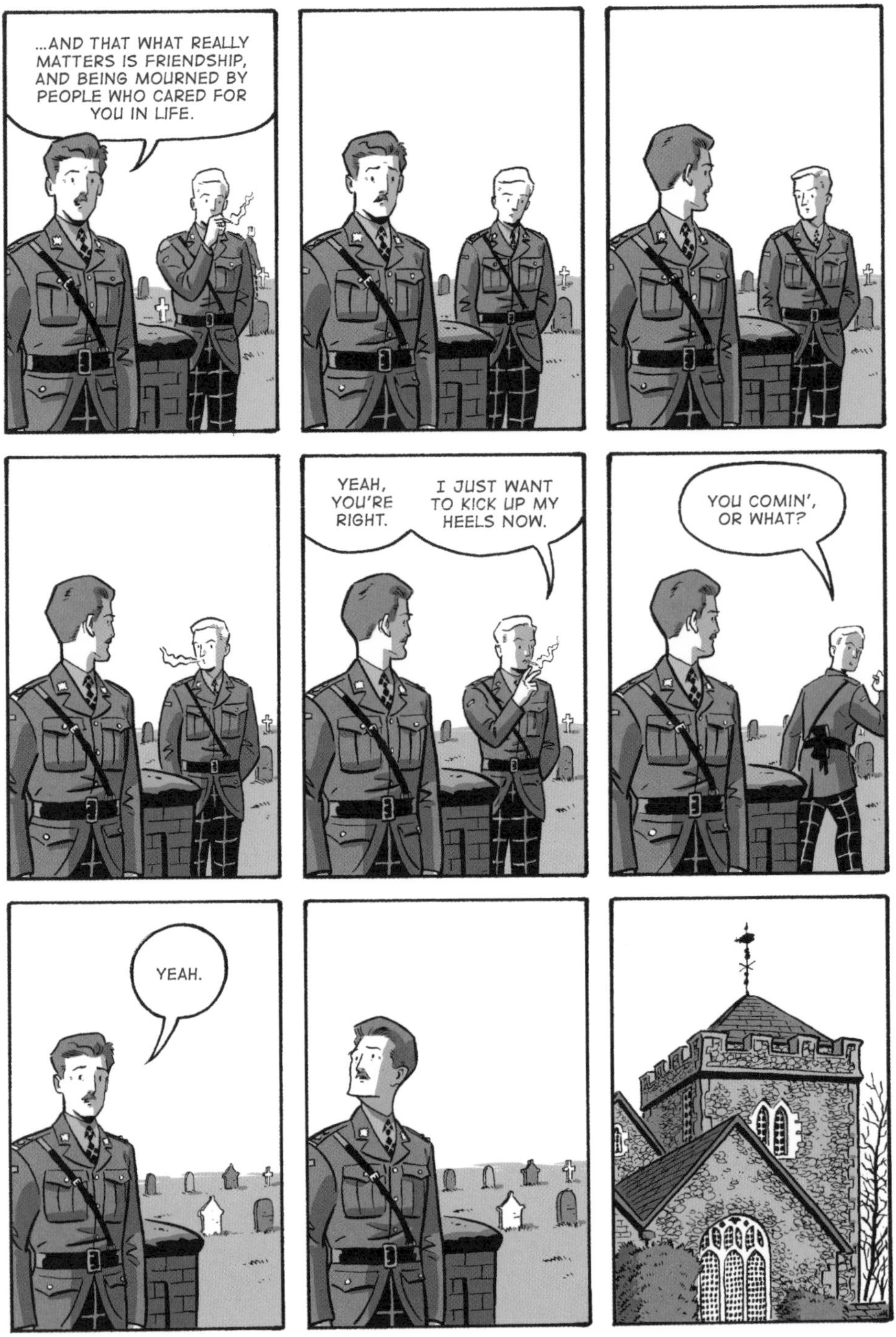
...AND THAT WHAT REALLY MATTERS IS FRIENDSHIP, AND BEING MOURNED BY PEOPLE WHO CARED FOR YOU IN LIFE.
YEAH, YOU'RE RIGHT.
I JUST WANT TO KICK UP MY HEELS NOW.
YOU COMIN', OR WHAT?
YEAH.

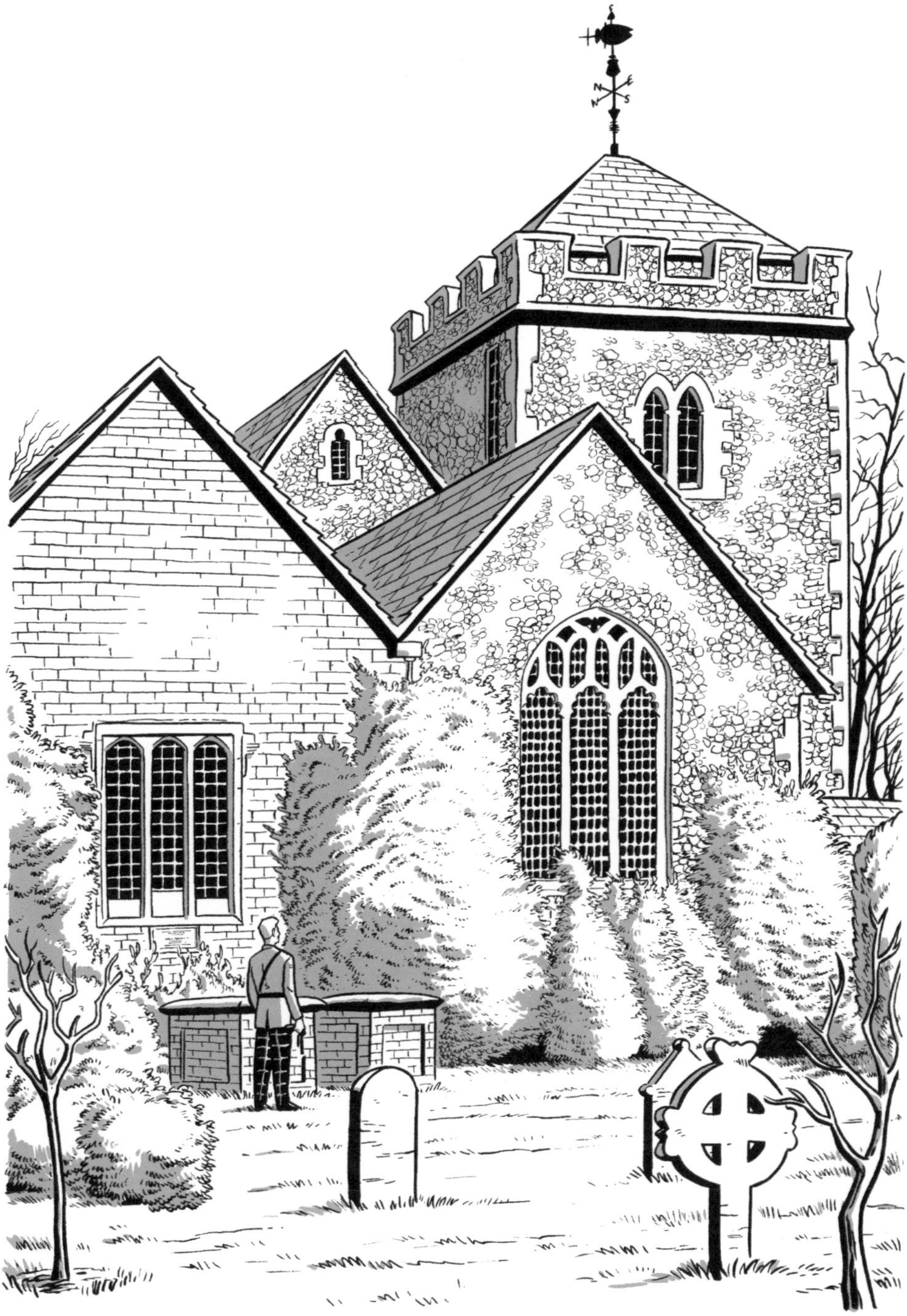

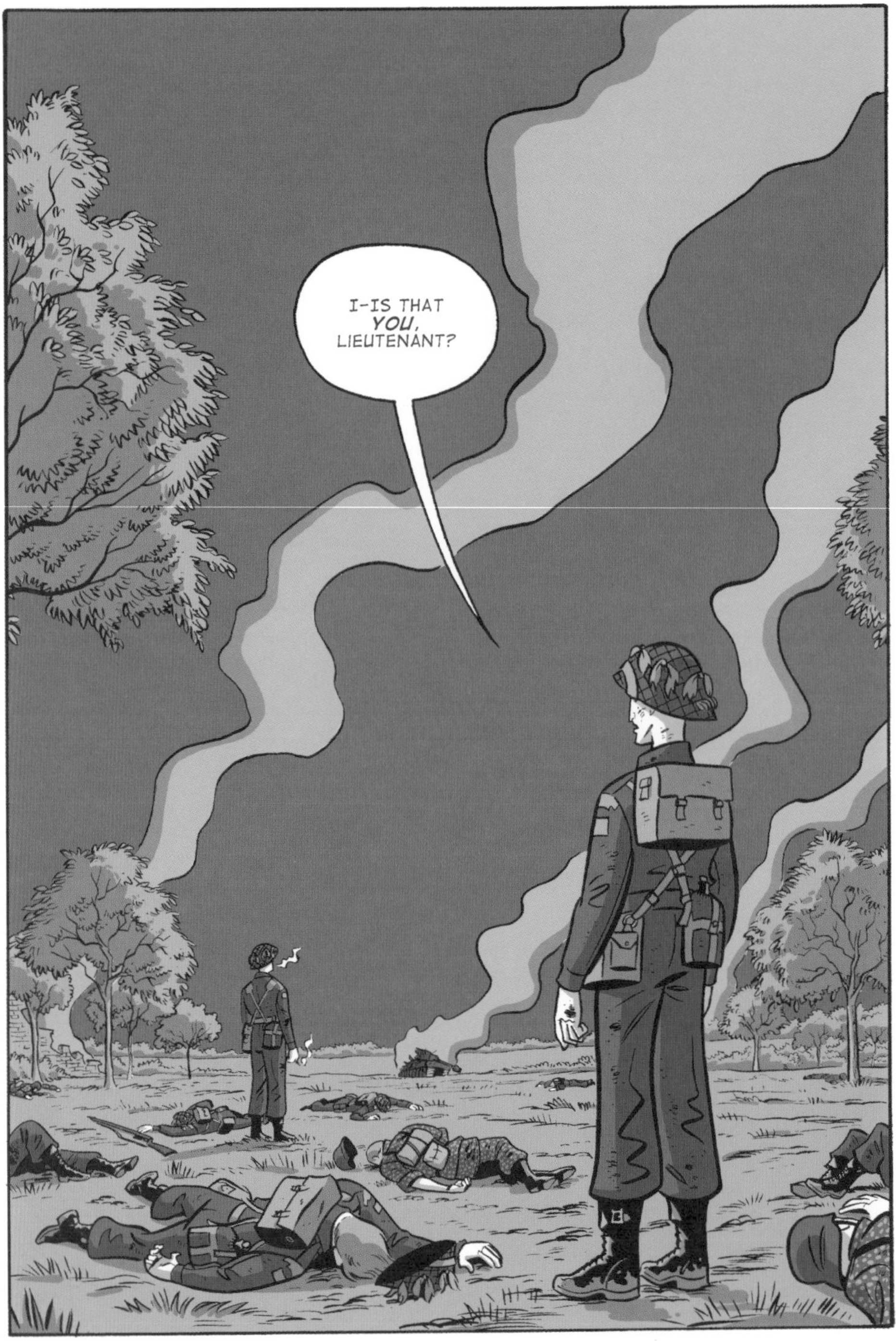
I-IS THAT *YOU*, LIEUTENANT?

DESPITE THE LOSS OF THE COMMAND GROUP, THE HLI WAS ABLE TO CONSOLIDATE AND TAKE THE TOWN.

I THINK IT'S OVER, SIR... I-I THINK WE'VE WON.

NOT A SINGLE BUILDING WAS LEFT STANDING.

BUT THE ROAD TO CAEN WAS NOW CLEAR AT LAST, AND WHEN CANADIAN TROOPS FINALLY MARCHED INTO THE ANCIENT MEDIEVAL CITY ON JULY 9TH, 1944, THE HLI WAS AMONG THEM.

CAEN HAD BEEN SO DEVASTATED BY THE MONTH-LONG BOMBING CAMPAIGN THAT EVEN TANKS COULDN'T GET THROUGH ITS STREETS.

DESPITE THAT, ITS CAPTURE WAS A TURNING POINT IN THE BATTLE OF NORMANDY.

BY TYING UP 80 PERCENT OF AVAILABLE GERMAN TANKS FOR WEEKS ON END, THE CANADIANS HAD ALLOWED AMERICAN FORCES IN THE WEST TIME TO BUILD STRENGTH.

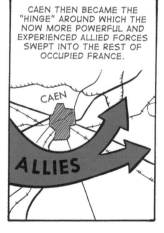

CAEN THEN BECAME THE "HINGE" AROUND WHICH THE NOW MORE POWERFUL AND EXPERIENCED ALLIED FORCES SWEPT INTO THE REST OF OCCUPIED FRANCE.

CAEN

ALLIES

GENERAL EISENHOWER WOULD LATER SAY THAT EVERY FOOT WON AT CAEN WAS WORTH TEN MILES ELSEWHERE.

THE HIGHLAND LIGHT INFANTRY OF CANADA REGROUPED AND SAW CONTINUOUS ACTION THROUGHOUT THE REST OF THE WAR IN EUROPE.

THE SAME METTLE THEY HAD SHOWN AT BURON WAS TESTED AGAIN BY CLOSING THE FALAISE GAP IN AUGUST...

...AND HELPING CAPTURE BOULOGNE IN SEPTEMBER, WHERE 9,000 NAZIS WERE CAPTURED BY CANADIAN TROOPS.

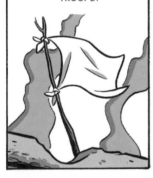

AFTER SILENCING THE GUNS AT CAP GRIS-NEZ, THEY SENT THE SWORD OF THE GERMAN GARRISON COMMANDER THERE TO THE LORD MAYOR OF DOVER.

IT ARRIVED ALONG WITH A MESSAGE.

"Via Imperial"

GREETINGS, ENJOY YOUR PINT OF BEER IN PEACE FROM NOW ON—WE HAVE ALL OF JERRY'S BIG BERTHAS.

IN OCTOBER THEY STORMED THE SCHELDT ESTUARY.

AND IN MARCH 1945 THEY BECAME THE FIRST CANADIAN REGIMENT TO CROSS THE RHINE RIVER INTO GERMANY.

RIVER

RHINE

GERMANY

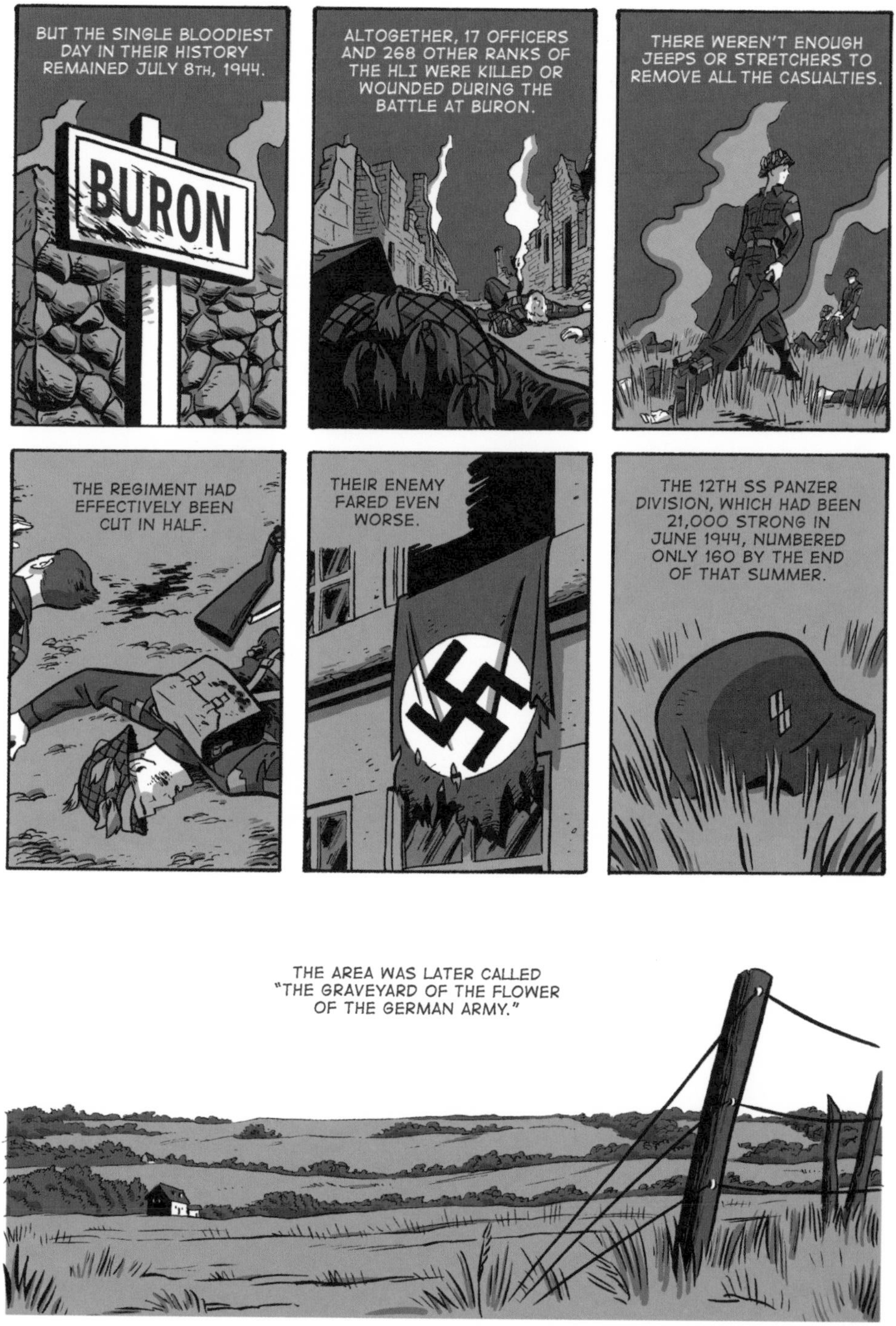
BUT THE SINGLE BLOODIEST DAY IN THEIR HISTORY REMAINED JULY 8TH, 1944.
BURON
ALTOGETHER, 17 OFFICERS AND 268 OTHER RANKS OF THE HLI WERE KILLED OR WOUNDED DURING THE BATTLE AT BURON.
THERE WEREN'T ENOUGH JEEPS OR STRETCHERS TO REMOVE ALL THE CASUALTIES.
THE REGIMENT HAD EFFECTIVELY BEEN CUT IN HALF.
THEIR ENEMY FARED EVEN WORSE.
THE 12TH SS PANZER DIVISION, WHICH HAD BEEN 21,000 STRONG IN JUNE 1944, NUMBERED ONLY 160 BY THE END OF THAT SUMMER.
THE AREA WAS LATER CALLED "THE GRAVEYARD OF THE FLOWER OF THE GERMAN ARMY."

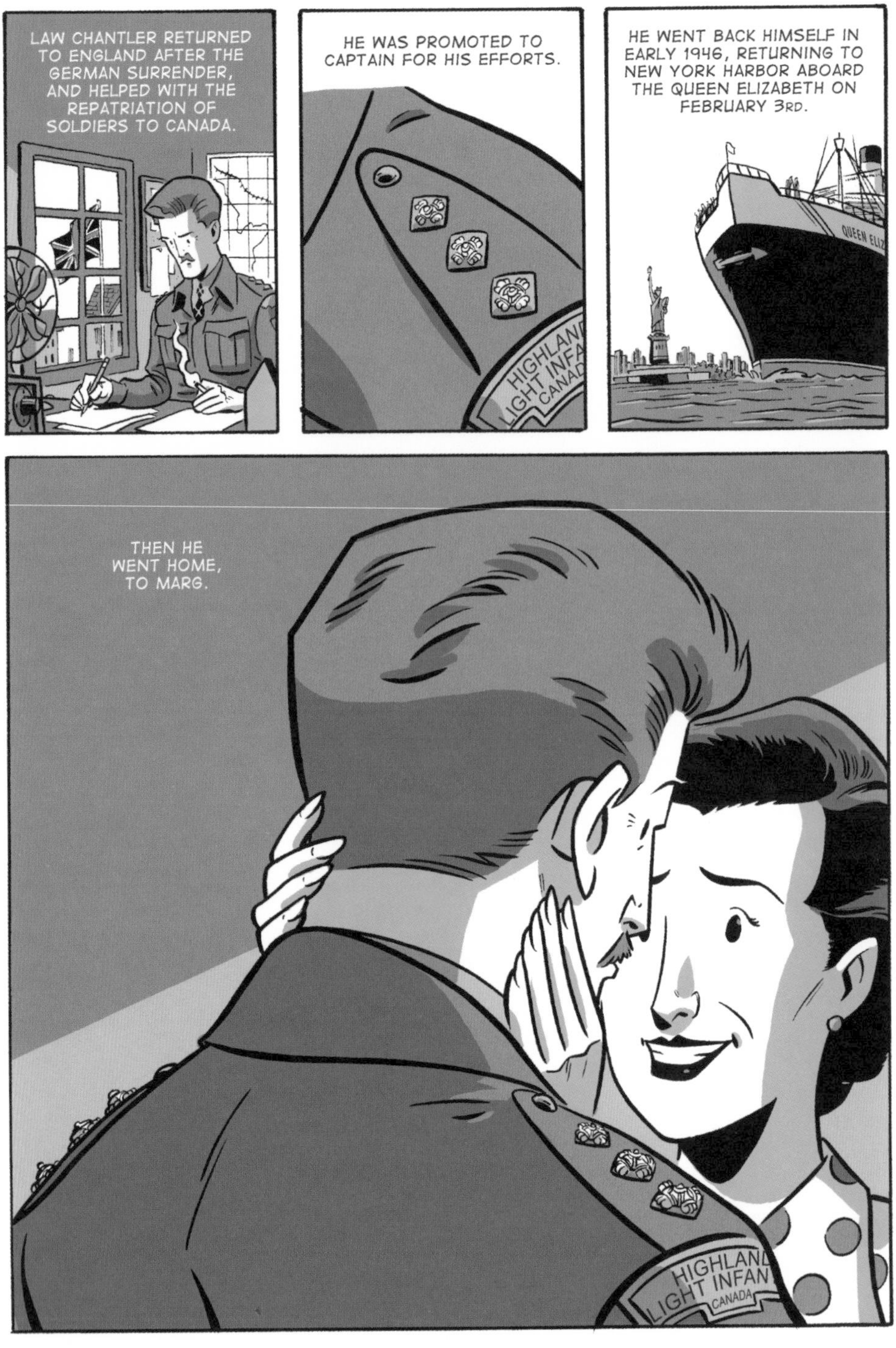
LAW CHANTLER RETURNED TO ENGLAND AFTER THE GERMAN SURRENDER, AND HELPED WITH THE REPATRIATION OF SOLDIERS TO CANADA.
HE WAS PROMOTED TO CAPTAIN FOR HIS EFFORTS.
HE WENT BACK HIMSELF IN EARLY 1946, RETURNING TO NEW YORK HARBOR ABOARD THE QUEEN ELIZABETH ON FEBRUARY 3RD.
THEN HE WENT HOME, TO MARG.

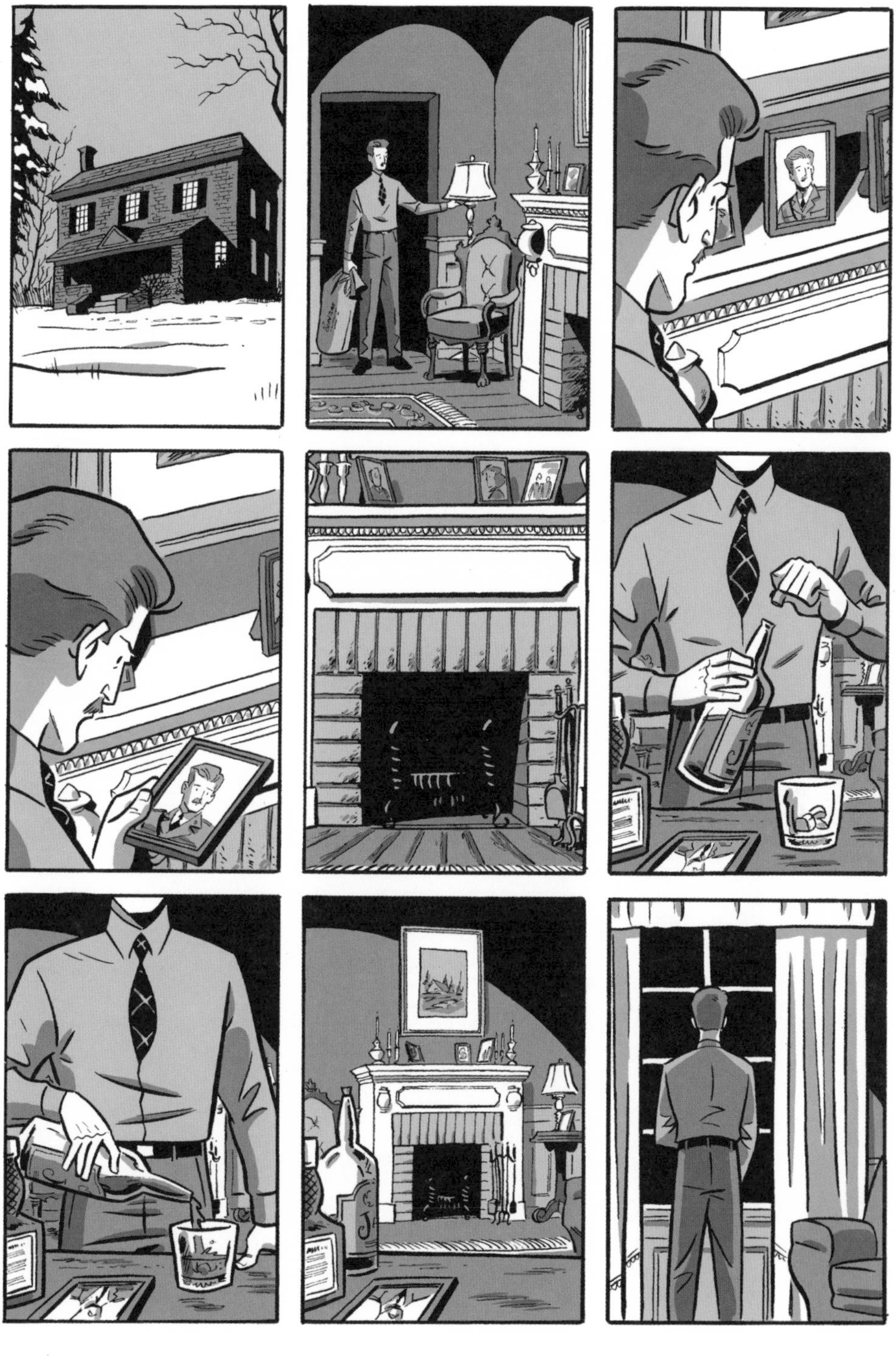

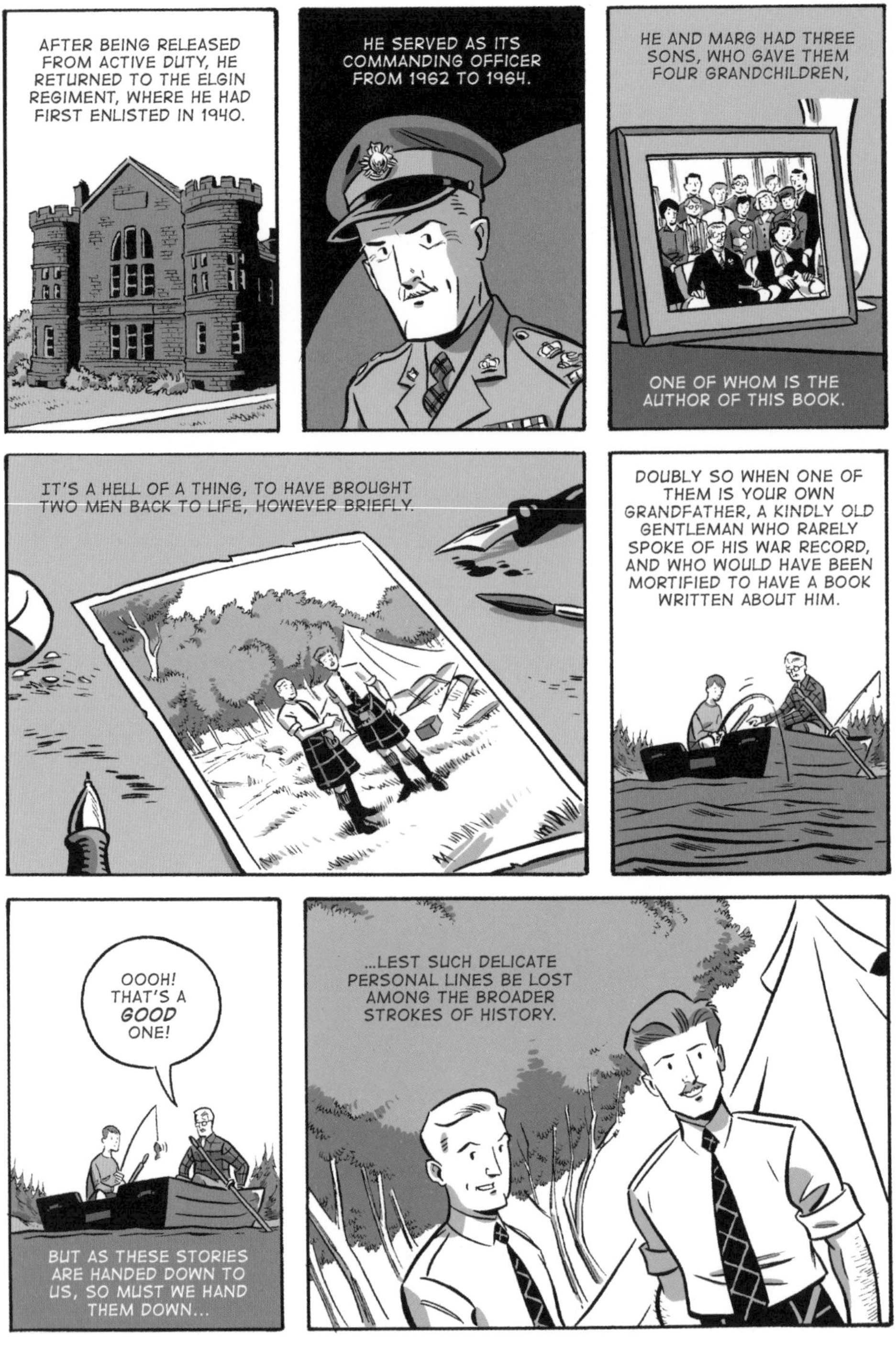
AFTER BEING RELEASED FROM ACTIVE DUTY, HE RETURNED TO THE ELGIN REGIMENT, WHERE HE HAD FIRST ENLISTED IN 1940.
HE SERVED AS ITS COMMANDING OFFICER FROM 1962 TO 1964.
HE AND MARG HAD THREE SONS, WHO GAVE THEM FOUR GRANDCHILDREN,
ONE OF WHOM IS THE AUTHOR OF THIS BOOK.
IT'S A HELL OF A THING, TO HAVE BROUGHT TWO MEN BACK TO LIFE, HOWEVER BRIEFLY.
DOUBLY SO WHEN ONE OF THEM IS YOUR OWN GRANDFATHER, A KINDLY OLD GENTLEMAN WHO RARELY SPOKE OF HIS WAR RECORD, AND WHO WOULD HAVE BEEN MORTIFIED TO HAVE A BOOK WRITTEN ABOUT HIM.
OOOH! THAT'S A *GOOD* ONE!
BUT AS THESE STORIES ARE HANDED DOWN TO US, SO MUST WE HAND THEM DOWN...
...LEST SUCH DELICATE PERSONAL LINES BE LOST AMONG THE BROADER STROKES OF HISTORY.

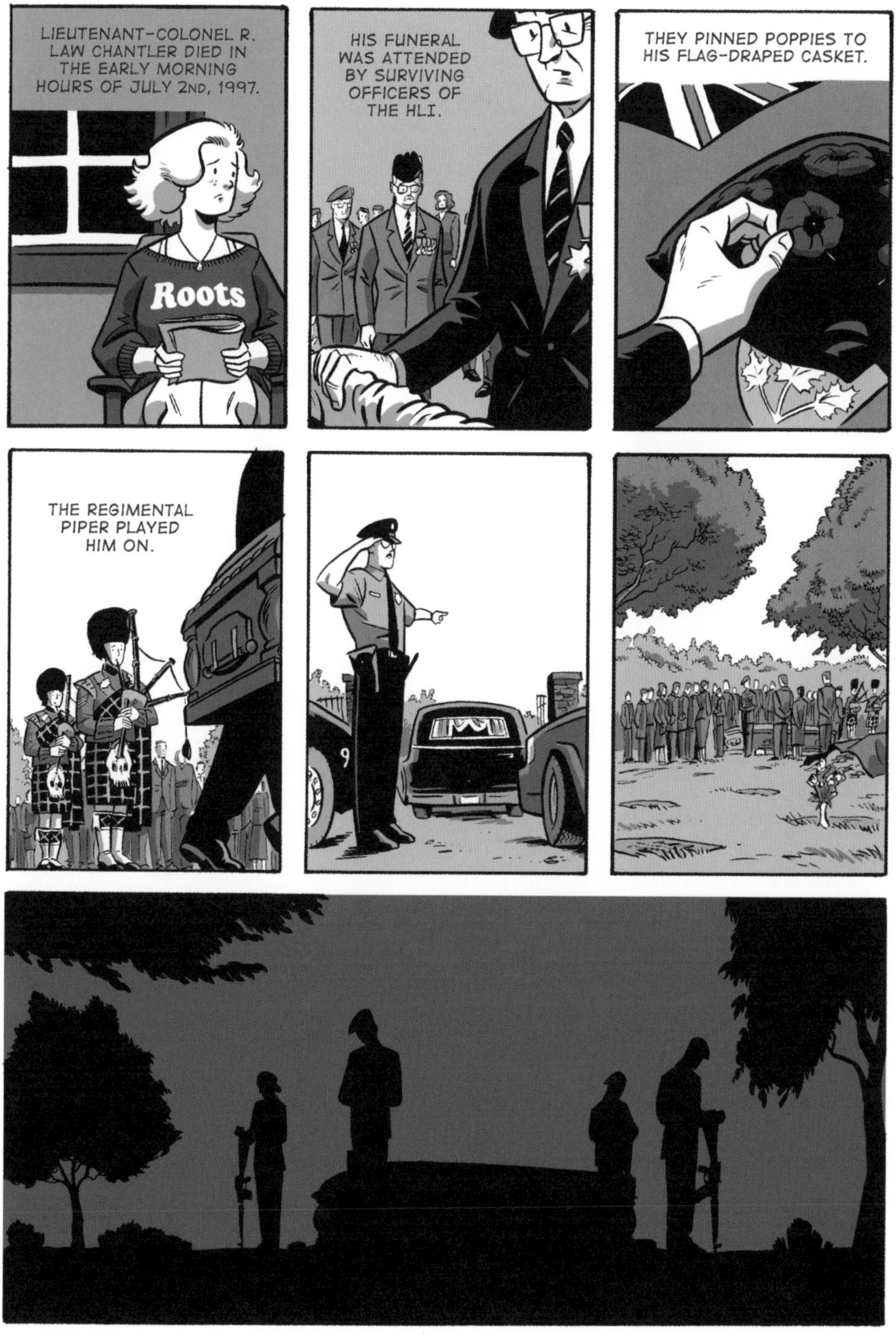
LIEUTENANT-COLONEL R. LAW CHANTLER DIED IN THE EARLY MORNING HOURS OF JULY 2ND, 1997.
Roots
HIS FUNERAL WAS ATTENDED BY SURVIVING OFFICERS OF THE HLI.
THEY PINNED POPPIES TO HIS FLAG-DRAPED CASKET.
THE REGIMENTAL PIPER PLAYED HIM ON.

LIEUTENANT JOHN HARTWELL CHRYSLER WAS KILLED IN ACTION ON JULY 8TH, 1944, CROSSING THE OPEN ROAD TO ASSIST MAJOR DURWARD.

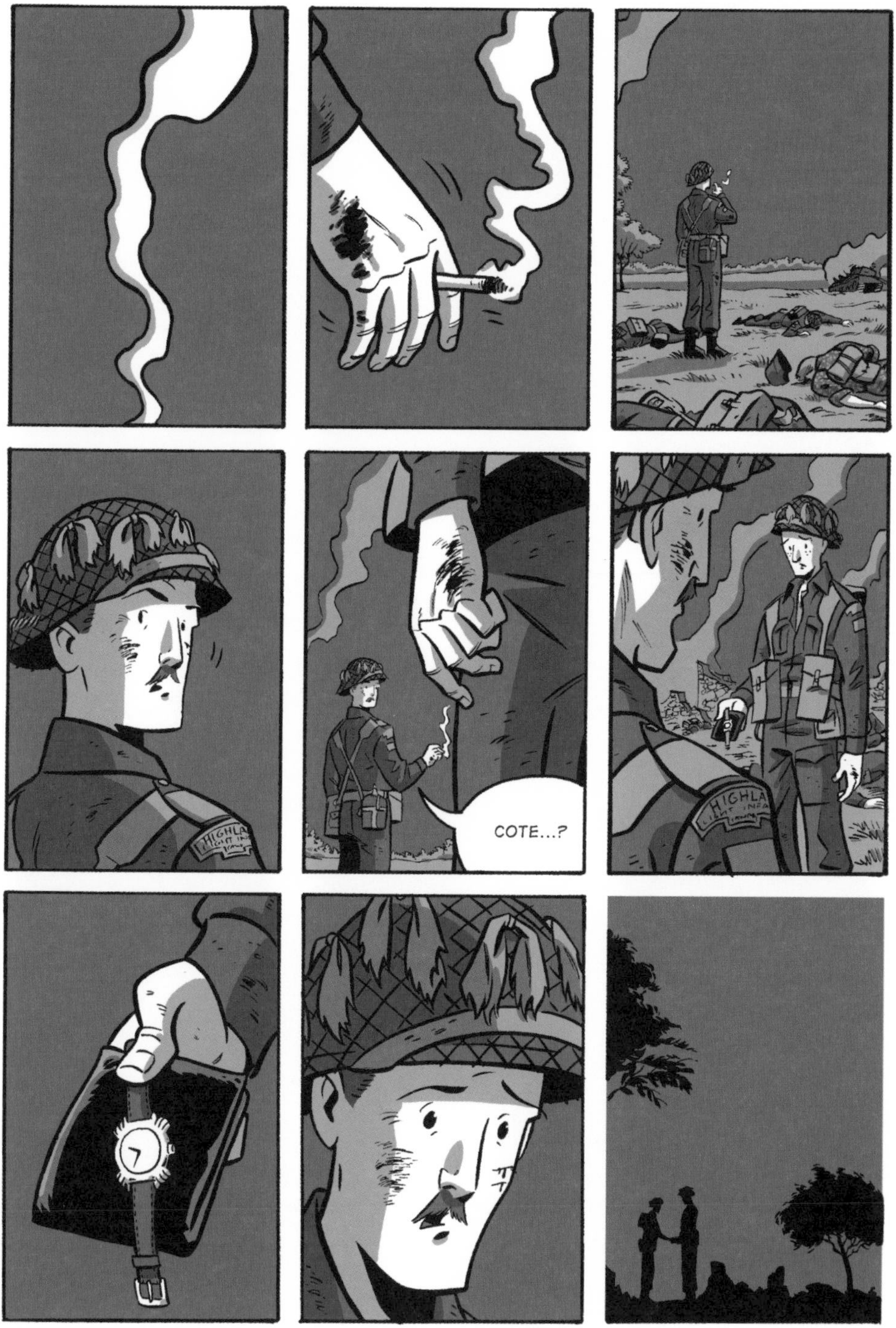
COTE...?

HE WAS 27
YEARS OLD.

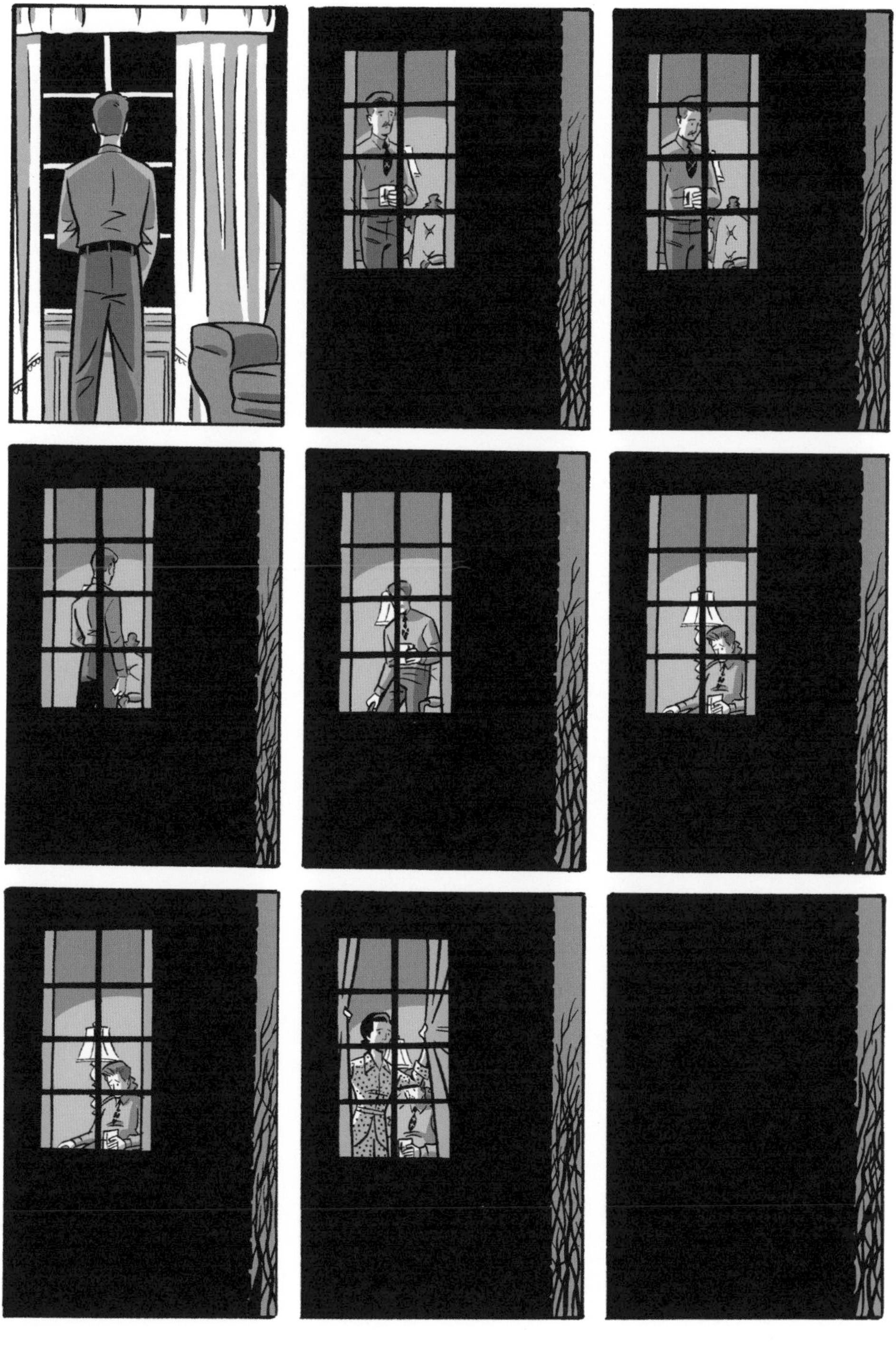

*Nae man is happy without a friend, or sure of him until he is unhappy.*

— OLD SCOTTISH SAYING

# ACKNOWLEDGEMENTS

The bulk of *Two Generals* is based on three primary sources: the 1943 diary of Law Chantler; Jack Chrysler's 1944 letters from France to his wife; and the War Diary of the Highland Light Infantry of Canada, the relevant portions of which were written by then-Intelligence Officer Lieutenant Charles Campbell. This book could not have existed without the records left behind by all three, and for that as well as their service and sacrifice I extend to their memory the highest possible amount of respect, gratitude, and love.

Two other primary sources greatly informed portions of the narrative. The personal recollections of Colonel Douglas Barrie, who passed away late last year, helped give me a feel for these events in a way that no written record ever could have. And the contributions of Winifred Walker of Southampton, England, through her daughter Jan Spiers and Jan's husband Robert, helped to flesh out the character of Jack Chrysler, about whom I knew so very little when the project began. To these fine people, who lived parts of this story, my profound thanks.

Very little has previously been written about the Highland Light Infantry of Canada or the battle of Buron. But two secondary sources proved quite valuable: Captain J. Allan Snowie's excellent *Bloody Buron*, and Zen Karp's self-published *War Diary: The Highland Light Infantry of Canada in Northwest Europe 1944–45*. I was both delighted by and envious of the amount of access that both of these authors had to living veterans of the HLI of C, having written their books earlier than I did mine. Captain Snowie's book in particular is as compelling and detailed a record of a single battle as you're likely to read. (Unfortunately, it seems to have gone out of print. Hopefully some historically-minded publisher will correct that soon.)

Where visual reference was concerned, my "bibles" were Jean Bouchery's *The Canadian Soldier in WWII* and Crescent Publishing's *Weapons and War Machines*, both of which sat open on my desk most of the time I was drawing.

A special thank you should go to The Royal Highland Fusiliers of Canada (which is what the Highland Light Infantry of Canada became when it merged with the Scots Fusiliers in the 1960s), both for their current service to our country and for the access they granted me while researching this project. Particularly Sergeant Lance Harrisson, who runs the regimental museum, and who allowed me to hold and photograph weapons and gear from the period. He was also happy to answer questions by email whenever I needed clarification on which headgear goes with which uniform, the peculiarities of filling out a wound tag, and other things that only a true military historian would know.

This project was blessed from the start by the enthusiasm of so many people who encouraged me to take it on, and who provided personal or professional support as it progressed. Family members Bob Chantler, my parents Russ and Doreen Chantler, Bill and Diane Chantler, Sarah and Mark Baughman, and Ian and Jennifer Chantler were all willing to share memories and stories, and their continued faith and interest in the project has meant a lot to me. My wife Shari also pitched in with some colouring help, not to mention her seemingly endless patience with having to live with a workaholic cartoonist who continually risks his livelihood on such increasingly demanding creative projects.

Thanks are also due to: Jennifer Lum, who has done an outstanding job with the design of this book, and who was responsible for bringing it to McClelland & Stewart in the first place; Nancy Morrey, who kept me company with good conversation on Thursday nights in the officer's mess as both of us pored over the War Diary; Shawn Richter, who lent a hand with some last-minute colouring assistance; Jane Naisbitt and the rest of the staff at the Canadian War Museum Research Centre; my good friend Chris Scholey, who is always the first to read my stuff and tell me what he thinks; writer Antony Johnston, who set me on the path that eventually led to me finding Jack Chrysler's widow; and my friend and *Northwest Passage* editor Randal C. Jarrell, who will be pleased to know that he appears as an American Air Force officer on page 32 of this book.

To any and all of the small army of people who bothered to ask me how the book was coming along, or who told me to keep going, thank you. Knowing how many people were looking forward to *Two Generals* is what kept me going during what turned out to be both the most difficult professional endeavour I've ever taken on as well as an enormous personal challenge. If I've risen to the occasion on either count, it's because of their support.


Scott Chantler
June 2, 2010

**SCOTT CHANTLER** is an acclaimed graphic novelist and illustrator who has been nominated for numerous awards, including the Eisner, Harvey, Russ Manning, Joe Shuster, and Doug Wright Awards. He is the author of *Northwest Passage*, and the artist of graphic novels including *Days Like This*, *Scandalous*, and *Stephen Colbert's Tek Jansen*.

Just an informal
shot of the two
Generals.

JACK CHRYSLER
LAW CHANTLER
1944